Death
and the Humanities

Death
and the Humanities

Sharon Scholl

Lewisburg
Bucknell University Press
London and Toronto: Associated University Presses

Associated University Presses, Inc.
440 Forsgate Drive
Cranbury, NJ 08512

Associated University Presses Ltd
25 Sicilian Avenue
London WC1A 2QH, England

Associated University Presses
2133 Royal Windsor Drive
Unit 1
Mississauga, Ontario
Canada L5J 1K5

Library of Congress Cataloging in Publication Data

Scholl, Sharon.
　Death and the humanities.

　Bibliography: p.
　Includes index.
　1. Death in art—Addresses, essays, lectures.
2. Arts—Addresses, essays, lectures.　I. Title.
NX650.D4S36　1983　　　700　　　81-72025
ISBN 0-8387-5047-8

Printed in the United States of America

097109

Contents

Illustrations

Acknowledgments

The author wishes to express appreciation to the following for permission to reprint copyrighted material:

"Dirge without Music," and "Lament," by Edna St. Vincent Millay, from *Collected Poems,* copyright 1921, 1928, 1948, and 1955, by permission of Harper and Row and Norma Millay Ellis.

"Irony," by Louis Untermeyer, from *Long Feud,* copyright 1914 and 1942, by permission of Harcourt Brace Jovanovich.

"Home Burial," by Robert Frost, from *The Poetry of Robert Frost,* edited by Edward Connery Latham, copyright 1930, 1939, and 1968. Copyright 1958 by Robert Frost and 1967 by Lesley Frost Ballantine, by permission of Holt, Rinehart and Winston.

"Musée des Beaux Arts," by W. H. Auden, from *W. H. Auden: Collected Poems,* edited by Edward Mendelson, copyright 1940 and renewed 1968, by permission of Random House.

"Remembrance," by Emily Brontë, from the *Complete Poems of Emily Jane Brontë,* edited by C. W. Hatfield, copyright 1941, by permission of Columbia University Press.

Selected lines from "Dulce et Decorum est pro patria mori," "Anthem for Doomed Youth," "Bugles Sang," "The Next War," "The Parable of the Old Man and the Young," and "The End," by Wilfred Owen, from *The Collected Poems,* copyright 1963 by Chatto and Windus, used by permission of New Directions Publishing Corporation.

"A Dead Statesman" and "Common Form," by Rudyard

Autumn, copyright 1976, 1977 by the estate of Loren Eiseley, by permission of Charles Scribner's Sons.

The author is grateful to the faculty research fund of Jacksonville University, which furnished partial funding for the creation of this book.

Acknowledgment is also due to Editorial Photocolor Archives, Inc. and its art sources, Scala Fine Arts and Alinari Photos, for many of the illustrations which appear in the book.

Introduction

This is not a book about medical technicalities, legal and economic importunities, historic or sectarian traditions about death. It deals sparingly with such situations as generate tabloid headlines and are often mistaken for the critical aspects of death and dying. Rather, this work is devoted to experiences and reflections upon death as transmitted by the expressive forms of art, music, and literature. Further, it is a study of the collective imagination created and reflected by these forms. Thus, in dealing with death and the humanities, we are at the generative center where the reality of death resides for all of us.

Viewing death through the humanities is not a vague form of well-wishing; nor is it some narcissistic libertarianism. It is not, in short, humanitarianism or humanism. The humanities are collectively free from special pleading and adept at dealing with diverse fundamental questions. From the perspective of the humanities the central issues are the meaning of death in human existence and the effect exerted upon our personal and collective lives by consciousness of death. The humanities do not aim for some ultimate physical or philosophical solution, for a cure for or postponement of death. Their aim is not the dissemination of accurate data and skill, laudable as that may be. The humanities invite individual participation in vicarious experiences with death so that we are able to appropriate such confrontations as our own.

This book has no theory that must be served, but rather two assumptions about the humanities, which are worked out

13

in concepts and examples. One is that the forms of experience collectively labeled "the humanities" are the most fundamental and revealing of our true relationships with death. The second is that those many aspects of death and dying assumed to be sociological, medical, or legal in nature are as suitably understood through the humanities. The book is primarily directed to a general readership and those professinals in medical, legal, and sociological disciplines who would like to extend their understanding of death and dying by reference to the humanities in ways that enhance their contextual relationships.

The forms (music, art, literature) through which the most memorable human experiences with death are transmitted are coexistent with mankind. The earliest myths and images of all societies focus upon the twin phenomena of birth and death, origin and extinction. No single book can hope to achieve control over such an abundance of mateials without some system of selectivity. This book uses forms created in Western culture predominantly from the past three centuries, grouped in terms of themes and viewpoints rather than in order of historic origin. The collection is hardly exhaustive; interpretation, rather than meticulous cataloguing, is emphasized. Individual works are selected for their richness of suggestion, significance to the mainstream of Western culture, contemporary validity, and contrast with other works. The four perspectives of realism, idealism, expressionism, and abstraction discussed in the first chapter are maintained throughout the book. The materials presented here should serve not as a substitute for, but as a stimulus to personal contact with and enjoyment of the concepts and examples discussed.

Death
and the Humanities

1
How the Humanities Speak about Death

*T*here are many forms of language available to speak about death. A physician would use the terminology of physical symptoms, citing such factors as a flat brain pattern, absence of heartbeat, or lack of pupil dilation. His account would be terse and descriptive, allowing an itemized verification by any qualified observer. A lawyer would speak in terms of material possessions, the distribution procedures of the state, and the recorded intentions of the deceased. In both cases the ultimate object is to reduce the unverifiable or unprecedented elements involved in decision-making. The funeral director appeals to custom and social expectation in making critical choices, conforming to preestablished patterns of action.

The humanities appear almost as weeds in such well-tended conceptual gardens. The object of a great novel is not to provide orderly solutions but to probe the limits of language and idea, leaving us with a wealth of possibilities. Its purpose is to confuse, to challenge obligatory patterns, forcing us to confront unverifiable and unprecedented elements of life. Poetry, paintings, and musical compositions work more suggestively. We may become caught up in such works emotionally before their literal content is revealed to our conscious consideration. These forms speak through the elements of

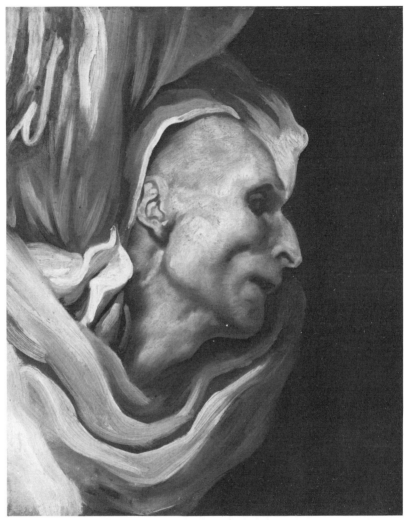

Fig. 1 Theodore Géricault. ***After Death.*** 1818–19. Oil on canvas, 17¾ × 22″.
Courtesy of the Art Institute of Chicago; A. A. Munger Collection.

color, rhythm, texture, line, and the principles of cohesion that hold these materials in a satisfying balance. Ultimately, it is out of an imaginative ground shaped by literary and artistic works that legal precedents, medical procedures, and social conventions evolve.

Despite the fact that works that exemplify the humanities range far beyond simple data or straightforward logic, there are a few general patterns of predictability that are universally observed. These patterns reflect viewpoints, identifiable perspectives. There are also certain recurrent symbols, particularly in connection with death, that embody identifiable associations. These latter can fill even a small canvas or a short poem with long extensions of meaning. A work replete with such associative elements is described as "rich," as something that can be encountered many times without being exhausted of possibility. Recurrent symbols may be such pedestrian items as skulls, scythes, or hourglasses, or such abstract items as dark colors and jagged lines. They are always influenced by the context of presentation and their position in relation to other elements within the composition. Thus a dictionary that matched a symbolic figure to its typical meaning would merely obscure its meaning in a new work that uses the symbol in a fresh way.

An individual work may involve more than one perspective or maintain more than one viewpoint, but these frames of reference are applicable to the whole range of human experience. They are eternal, alternating in influence throughout the course of history, and each can be understood better by reference to the others.

The point of view most people would identify as typifying life as it is experienced is called *realism* when describing an artistic or literary style. The aim of realism is to produce a work that closely resembles the world we daily encounter. The artistry consists of presenting this familiar world in a way far more complete, selective, or closely examined than most people are capable of sustaining. Géricault's painting of a corpse is an excellent example of the style. Despite its documentary nature, this study has much more artistic than biological interest because of the strong linear rhythms of the sheet, which enhance the depressions and protrusions of the face. It is a compelling presentation because of the strength of line and its controlled organization. The contrast of light and dark between the body and the background frames and isolates the image. The limited range of color strengthens the role of line and value contrast in our experience of the work. Its basic orientation to realism as the dominant point of view lies in the fact that the object is shown for what it is in the state in which it was encountered.

A poem by Edna St. Vincent Millay also presents death as a normal part of everyday experience:

> Listen, children:
> Your father is dead.
> From his old coats
> I'll make you little jackets;
> I'll make you little trousers
> From his old pants.
> There'll be in his pockets
> Things he used to put there,
> Keys and pennies
> Covered with tobacco;
> Dan shall have the pennies
> To save in his bank;
> Anne shall have the keys
> To make a pretty noise with.
> Life must go on,
> And the dead be forgotten;
> Life must go on,
> Though good men die;
> Anne, eat your breakfast;
> Dan, take your medicine;
> Life must go on;
> I forget just why.[1]

The poem could be accurately described as hardhearted; it is remarkably unemotional until the wistful hesitation of the last line. Yet, true to the viewpoint of realism, this is the way death is lived through after the eulogies and flowers have faded. Even here the details of artistry shine through in the imagery of "keys and pennies covered with tobacco." No work of art is exclusively realistic in the documentary sense, but uses commonly observed reality as the point of orientation.

Other categories of meaning may be understood as inflections within this commonly shared reality. Such shades of meaning are easily perceived in ordinary conversation. The statement "she went to the store" would be accepted merely as a point of information. If that statement included rhythmic emphases, as in "*she* went to the *store*," accompanied by raised

Fig. 2 Anne Louis Girodet. ***The Death of Atala.*** 1808. Oil on canvas, approximately 6'11" × 8' 9". The Louvre, Paris.

eyebrows from the speaker, such a rendition would give the hearer pause. In our culture this inflection suggests that going to the store was the occasion for some dispute or resentment.

Inflection cues are omnipresent in works of art, and understanding their point of view depends upon the perceiver's familiarity with such cues. The style called *idealism* is an exceedingly ancient arrangement of such cues that can be easily recognized today in the quasi-art of cemetery monuments. At a higher technical level, the masterpieces of Greek sculpture were conceived from this viewpoint. A painting by Girodet describing the burial of Atala contains many of the typical cues of idealism. In contrast to Géricault's corpse, this body is reclining in undiminished beauty. A mellow light falls across her flawless skin; every hair is perfectly in place. Instead of being ungainly and sacklike, her body curves gently across the middle area of the painting. The open grave is not made obvious;

there are no elements such as bones that might add a grisly touch. Her mourners lean inward over the light area of her clothing, which is illuminated from the reflection of a clear sky. The internal symbols of the cross and the monk's garb connote religious consolation and spiritual security. Idealism typically presents the world as more appealing or glamorous than we normally encounter it. This style is well suited to express aspirations, visions, or timeless concepts in an intellectually satisfying and emotionally convincing manner.

The familiar poem "Thanatopsis" exemplifies the literary style of idealism. At the beginning of the middle stanza Bryant pictures the state of the dead:

> Yet not to thine eternal resting place
> Shalt thou retire alone, nor couldst thou wish
> Couch more magnificent. Thou shalt lie down
> With patriarchs of the infant world—with kings, ·
> The powerful of the earth—the wise, the good,
> Fair forms, and hoary seers of ages past,
> All in one mighty sepulchre. The hills
> Rock-ribbed and ancient as the sun,—the vales
> Stretching in pensive quietness between;
> The venerable woods—rivers that move
> In majesty, and the complaining brooks
> That make the meadows green; and poured all round,
> Old Ocean's gray and melancholy waste,—
> Of the great tomb of man.

Here is no arena of excitement abounding with the challenge of great deeds; yet it is a place of dignity. The greater bulk of human beings lies within this bosom of nature in a state of vast equality. Present are the largeness of concept and nobility of expression that characterize idealism. In the final verse are found the image of the final journey toward the destination and the spirit in which it must be undertaken:

> So live, that when thy summons comes to join
> The innumerable caravan, which moves
> To that mysterious realm, where each shall take
> His chamber in the silent halls of death,
> Thou go not, like the quarry-slave at night,
> Scourged to his dungeon, but, sustained and soothed
> By an unfaltering trust, approach thy grave,
> Like one who wraps the drapery of his couch
> About him, and lies down to pleasant dreams.[2]

The description of death as a journey is one of the oldest and most universal of images. Ancient Romans were buried with coins between their teeth to pay the boatman on the mythical river Styx. Like all artistic images, this one has varying interpretations. Tennyson's poem "Crossing the Bar" sets the soul on its voyage accompanied by "sunset and evening star." But Wagner presents the most desperate and protracted of voyages in his overture to *The Flying Dutchman*. The object of every creator is to use vital images in fresh, powerful ways.

Idealism is an exaggeration of realism in the direction of glamorization; however, exaggeration can take another route. Irony, satire, or caricature depends upon a different kind of rupture between the ordinarily experienced world and that which a work of art creates. Unlike idealism, these forms of exaggeration can create a world that we hope is not true, or that we could not endure if it were. Sometimes this approach enables the perceiver to face almost unbearable aspects of the real world with a modicum of grace. Louis Untermeyer's poem "Irony" serves such a function:

> Why are the things that have no death
> The ones with neither sight nor breath!
> Eternity is thrust upon
> A bit of earth, a senseless stone.
> A grain of dust, a casual clod
> Receives the greatest gift of God.
> A pebble in the roadway lies—
> It never dies.
> The grass our fathers cut away
> Is growing on their graves today;
> The tiniest brooks that scarcely flow
> Eternally will come and go.
> There is no kind of death to kill
> The sands that lie so meek and still . . .
> But man is great and strong and wise—
> And so he dies.[3]

The contrast between the rationality and resourcefulness of man and his helplessness in the face of death creates the irony. The contrast between senseless globs of matter and their eternal persistence is calculated to make man's weakness even less bearable. The emotional impact of irony and satire may range from laughable to lamentable, and artists who employ this genre are as loath to explain their statements as are racon-

Fig. 3 Jack Levine. *Gangster Funeral.* 1952–53. Oil on canvas, 63 × 72″. Collection of Whitney Museum of American Art. Photograph by Geoffrey Clements.

teurs to explain their punch lines. Knowledge of the inflection cues is necessary to translate visual and verbal imagery into the skeptical vision of life.

In art the satiric point of view may be indicated by caricature. Simplification and exaggeration of size, shape, and proportions are standard approaches. Jack Levine's painting of the funeral of a gangster juxtaposes the solemn and ritualistic with the raucous and random. All the resources of the cartoonist's trade have been used to produce the jaded, pudgy men uncomfortably attired and architecturally constrained. The Irish priest, the veiled ladies, and the coffin itself are presented from a position that suggests a privileged vantage point. The probability is that these colleagues, so appropriately mournful, may well have been the instigators of the occasion.

Exaggeration may take the path of laughter, or of despair.

Such a great deal of art has sprung from this latter alternative in this century that it has acquired a specific style designation, *expressionism*. The Dylan Thomas poem "Do Not Go Gentle into That Good Night" is expressionistic in its emotional fervor, if not in actual technique. The poet pictures men of different temperaments facing death, and each of them he asks not to take the acquiescent path but to "rage against the dying of the light." The work was written as a response to the death of his father who, the poet believed, assented far too easily to life's outrages. Here at this last moment the poet desperately wants to see his father's spirit rebel. Verse after verse recites the failures of existence: wise men whose words failed to arouse others; good men whose deeds lacked power; wild men who sought to intensify life and merely hurried it along. Now that they are all there "on the sad height" from which, presumably, the truth about life can be glimpsed, they are urged to rage against this last failure. As a work that captures the anguish and unappeased emotions of life, the poem exemplifies the spirit of expressionism.

In music, this point of departure is easily detected by the use of extreme dissonance, extreme sound ranges, erratic melodies, and unpredictable rhythms. It can be emotionally exhausting to the perceiver, and has not yet become as popular as that same point of view in either visual arts or literature. In the visual realm, Willem de Kooning's series of paintings of women are clearly expressionistic works. In each the subject is so surrounded by erratic, slashing lines that it is difficult to determine immediately what it is. The emotional element emerges as dominant over the subject matter. The artist chose the woman motif because of historic associations and the powerful personal memories elicited by that subject. The formless violence with which the figure is perceived radiates at once psychological power, ferocious aggression, and sexual enticement. She is devoid of sentimental associations with beauty; she is woman, the devourer. The painter finds her to be a metaphor for the rootless violence of modern life. Half shattered, both alive and broken, she advances toward us with animal vitality radiating from the grinning mouth. As in expressionistic music, primary inflection cues are erratic lines, a dissonance of color, and unpredictable patterns across the surface. Practice in perceiving these cues is the only way to avoid mistaking humorous exaggeration for a deeply serious emotional statement.

Fig. 4 Willem de Kooning. *Woman I.* 1950–52. Oil on canvas, 6′ 3⅞″ × 58″.
Collection, The Museum of Modern Art, New York.

Finally, exaggeration beyond realism can extend to a treatment of form. At this point all recognizable subject matter often disappears and leaves *abstraction*. The absence of subject matter from the ordinary world does not render a work incomprehensible; music has no subject, but is enjoyed on the basis of its eloquence of form. A Beethoven symphony is no less impressive because it lacks a detailed story. Visual arts and literature have flirted with this musical sort of abstraction for at least a hundred years, beginning with the Symbolist poems written for sound alone. As far back as the Renaissance, painters have been able to think of art as assemblages of simple geometric forms. Abstract works avoid the specific example, referring rather to the essence of a person, place, or thing. They may include aspects of reality that are unseeable simultaneously. They may reduce an initial image to its minimal state. Even though they do not literally refer to death, Ad Reinhardt's subtly modulated monochromatic paintings sometimes offer a powerful analogue of death—lonely, stark, endless, and impenetrable. Static and contemplative, they reflect no particular time or place. The perceiver's response, in turn, must be more suggestive and universal than literal and particular. All those traditionally labeled figurations which can be perused like objects on a coffee table have been eliminated; we are left only with imagination and intuition for guides. Though death may be communicated eloquently through abstraction, our perceptions are not easily explainable or transferable to another viewer. Abstract art is fundamentally art as experience; life and death are presented as modes of participation.

When one is reading an unfamiliar work or viewing a new piece of art, the most helpful initial step is to determine how to interpret the item. Does the creator intend to be angry, funny, analytical, or simply observational? Is there, perhaps, some mixture of these intentions? An accurate decision on this issue will prevent the wasted time and misdirection exhibited by viewers who grow hilarious when confronted by a painting that does not reflect the ordinary world in every detail. When one is able to detect modes of thought besides realism, the basic imagery and details fall into meaningful place.

Creative works in the humanities speak about death in quite different ways from creations in science or business. Though less straightforward and not simply informative, the languages of art, literature, and music are as clearly under-

Fig. 5 Ad Reinhardt. **Red Painting.** 1952. Oil on canvas, 6½ × 12'. The Metropolitan Museum of Art; Arthur Hoppock Hearn Fund, 1968.

standable as any other language. In approaching the study of death through these languages, the perceiver is afforded a maximum of emotional and conceptual involvement for some initial effort. The chapters that follow will focus on aspects of death transmitted through these contexts of image and idea.

2

Death and the Survivor

*E*very living person shares one relationship to death—that of a survivor of the deaths of others. On some occasions we have been mourners, grieving over the loss of some dear person and desiring to perpetuate the memory of the deceased. The desire to commemorate has been responsible for some of the most remarkable architectural, literary, and musical works in human history. The record of our species is captured in temples, palaces, and tombs, the latter far outnumbering all the rest. The fact of death is responsible for a vast amount of what is meant by the general term *culture* in its broadest designation. This chapter will reflect upon the experiences of survivors as recorded in many symbolic modes and review the enormous contribution to Western culture of the urge to commemorate.

The Monument

Many buildings of all kinds exist as commemorations. College campuses are dotted with Smith Hall, Jones Library, Brown Auditorium. Malls, fountains, and even books are neatly labeled with the names of the dead. We live daily with evidences of grief and memory, for these states have elicited much of the physical accoutrements of our surroundings. Be-

Fig. 6 Augustus St.-Gaudens. Mrs. Henry Adams Memorial *(Grief).* 1891.
Bronze, Rock Creek Cemetery, Washington, D.C. *Photo courtesy of SANDAK,
Inc.*

fore the cemetery became a lackluster meadow strewn with uniform bronze markers, a common form of commemoration was the grave monument with suitable epitaph. These items captured something of the essence of the deceased and the special functions he served when alive. Occasionally grave monuments commissioned by families to assauge private grief attain the status of art, expressing some universal meaning of death. Such is the case with the memorial for Mrs. Henry Adams at the Rock Creek Cemetery in Washington, D.C. Created by Augustus St.-Gaudens in 1887, it is a poignant work that includes elements both of realism and of idealism. The proportions and detailing are faithful to our everyday experience; however, the togalike garment and bare feet dispel any air of modernity. It is somber without being despairing. No tears are present, nor is there any hint of dramatic force. There are, instead, the leaden solitude of loss and the protracted process of acceptance. The work is true to the inner life without denying actuality.

At another time under different circumstances images of the most grisly exaggeration were created to express an all-too-common experience of the physical symptoms of death. The tomb of Bishop Richard Fleming (d. 1431) in Lincoln Cathedral, England, shares the general preoccupation of that period with the macabre, resulting from the ravages of the Black Plague. Like many others, this monument features a sculpted figure clad in its appropriate ceremonial costume reposing above a matching figure of the deceased in a ghastly state of decay. The point of this juxtaposition is made clear by an inscription reading, "Such as I am you shall become." Other such figurational duos might include vermin, snakes, or faces covered with toads. Considering the mixture of horror and fascination these works exert, they are very nearly pornographic treatments of death. Such portrayals were popular for several centuries throughout much of Europe, forming an artistic legacy from the plague years. They were created to express the inevitability and universality of death along with the inference that immortality resides not in physical preservation but in a spiritual connection with the collective body of Christ.

As with all other offspring of the imagination, works of commemoration are important cultural statements in direct proportion to the skill of the creator. It is a great irony that a gifted artist who never knew the deceased can produce a more

Fig. 7 Michelangelo. ***Tomb of Giuliano de' Medici.*** 1524–34. Marble. Height of central figure: 71". New Sacristy, San Lorenzo, Florence. *Photo courtesy of Alinari-Scala and EPA.*

Fig. 8 Auguste Rodin. ***Naked Balzac.*** 1892–97. Plaster, 29¾". Philadelphia Museum of Art. Given by Mr. and Mrs. Sheldon M. Gordon, Mr. Gerson Bakar, and Mr. and Mrs. Norman Perlmutter. Photograph by the Philadelphia Museum of Art.

enduring memorial than a devoted but less-skilled relative. The aims of the artist and the public are not always in harmony, and their disagreement is usually over the choice of style. A famous instance is that of the Medici family tombs for which Michelangelo created sculptural decoration. Though the family probably expected a moderate resemblance to the deceased in their memorial figures, Michelangelo believed that future generations would find little interest in their actual appearance. There were, after all, many accurate portraits of these very people. The sculptor wished to create idealistic versions of the deceased as men of thought and accomplishment. Following the interest of his culture in the Classical past, he chose to clothe the fifteenth-century bankers in the garb of noble Romans. That he was able to create works that fulfilled more than a private urge to perpetuate memory was due to the respect for artistic ingenuity that was generally shared by society at that time. St. Gaudens also had the rare good fortune to execute his commission for Henry Adams, a man singularly free from the artistic provincialism of his time.

The nineteenth-century sculptor Rodin was not so fortunate in his dealings with the association that commissioned the Balzac monument. As one of the leading sculptors of the time, Rodin was asked to create a suitable memorial to the French novelist. The results so horrified the commission that they refused to have the work cast into bronze, and it remained for many years in its plaster state. Once more, the basic argument was over style. Like most committees, this one was expecting some reproduction of the life appearance of Balzac. Rodin was more interested in the essential spirit of the writer, his tumultuous moods and violent periods of inspiration. Rodin had the temerity to lean too far toward expressionism, producing in one version a nine-foot-ten-inch analogue of energy and defiance. The preliminary nude version particularly exhibits his pugnacity. Here is the Promethean man ready to do battle with the universe, and capable of seeing dispassionately the species whose behavior he documents in *The Human Comedy*. The committee might well have settled for idealism, but this was too much.

The Literary Memorial

Just as there are varying degrees of sculptural eloquence to be found among commemorative works, so there are works revealing many degrees of skill among the literary parallel—the epitaph. An example of one extreme is the cryptic statement W. C. Fields wrote for his own tombstone: "Better here than in Philadelphia." A more serious example is the epitaph that Benjamin Franklin made for himself and copied in varying forms for his friends:

> The Body of B. Franklin,
> Printer,
> Like the Cover of an Old Book,
> Its Contents Torn Out
> And
> Stripped of its Lettering and Gilding,
> Lies Here
> Food for Worms,
> But the Work shall not be Lost,
> For it Will as He Believed
> Appear Once More
> In a New and more Elegant Edition
> Revised and Corrected
> By the Author.[1]

Such statements may occur in conjunction with some physical marker located at the grave site; many others exist (as did Franklin's) as independent literary statements. Epitaphs are of extreme age in Western culture; one carved into the stone of an ancient Greek monument contains the earliest known musical notation. The stylistic choice among these items has always been extremely wide, and even humor is not uncommon. Some famous examples of this latter tendency can be found in Boot Hill Cemetery, Tombstone, Arizona.

> Here lies Butch;
> We planted him raw;
> He was quick on the trigger
> But slow on the draw.

Sentiments of the "parting shot" variety are occasionally found. One Georgia cemetery inscription (this one by a hypochondriac) reads "I *told* you I was sick." Another inscription, over the grave of a husband, reads "Gone but not forgiven." Probably too short to be justified as true epitaphs, these examples show none of the potential power of the form when essayed by a master. One of the most memorable examples of the genre occurs in Act 5, Scene 4, of Shakespeare's *Julius Caesar* in Antony's summary of the life of recently deceased Brutus:

> This was the noblest Roman of them all;
> All the conspirators save only he
> Did that they did in envy of great Caesar;
> He only, in a general honest thought
> And common good to all, made one of them.
> His life was gentle, and the elements
> So mix'd in him that Nature might stand up
> And say to all the world, "This was a man."

But what of the millions of obscure persons whose unremembered lives have long since moldered into dust? An equally obscure poet, Paulus Silentarius, created an epitaph for this numberless host in a remarkably sober and uncompromising realism:

> My name, my country—what are they to thee?
> What, whether base or proud, my pedigree?
> Perhaps I far surpassed all other men;
> Perhaps I fell below them all; what then?
> Suffice it, stranger, that thou seest a tomb;
> Thou know'st its use; it hides no matter whom.[2]

A step beyond the epitaph, in terms of length and complexity, is the elegy, a poem expressing sorrow for the dead. On the simplest level there is the "in memoriam" section of the daily newspaper where families express, under the name of the deceased, such typical sentiments as: "You left this earth a year ago today. Our hearts still ache for our dear father. You are in our thoughts always." Elegiac, certainly, though a true elegy is a longer work full of intense imagery and a mood of sorrow, regret, and spiritual vision. Probably the best-known work in this form is Thomas Gray's "Elegy Written in a Country Churchyard." A tribute to nature and the humble life, the poem describes in a pastoral manner the beauties of the country and the people who farm it. Decrying more pretentious styles of existence, Gray warns us in his memorable line that "The paths of glory lead but to the grave." He characterizes the dead who rest in this quiet place as people who,

> Far from the madding crowd's ignoble strife,
> Their sober wishes never learned to stray;
> Along the cool sequestered vale of life
> They kept the noiseless tenor of their way.[3]

In the same spirit of moral teaching as the medieval tomb sculptures, Gray's elegy warns its readers not to mock useful toil or disparage tombs that bear no evidence of worldly influence. All the half-realized potentials of these plain souls are laid to rest in this democracy of death.

One of the most famous elegies has no reference to that form in its title. In his poem "Lycidas," to the memory of Edward King, John Milton prefaces his work with the statement that he intends to "bewail a learned Friend, unfortunately drowned in his passage from Chester on the Irish Seas, 1637." In a highly idealistis style Milton creates a world of classical antiquity in which the gods themselves mourn the death of Lycidas, and all the flowers of the English countryside weep along the river banks. True to the spirit of the elegy, Lycidas is pictured as risen above the waters

> Through the dear might of Him that walked the waves,
> Where, other groves and other streams along,
> With nectar pure his oozy locks he laves,
> And hears the unexpressive nuptial song,
> In the blest kingdoms meek of joy and love.[4]

The urge to commemorate is one of the most significant stimuli to the production of artistic and literary works. Shakespeare realized that in an earthly sense he held the power of immortality for those whose lives he fixed forever in the form of words. In the concluding lines of Sonnet 81 he boasts:

> When all the breathers of this world are dead;
> You still shall live—such virtue hath my pen—
> Where breath most breathes, even in the mouths of men.

The Musical Memorial

The elegy, epitaph, and lament are also musical forms of mourning and commemoration. Unlike their literary counterparts, these musical works are neither widespread nor voluminous. The seventeenth and eighteenth centuries produced the most famous of the laments, many of them occurring within the context of operas. Monteverdi's opera *Arianna* is remembered from its one surviving fragment, a lament, which became a universally admired song. Purcell's opera *Dido and Aeneas* also contains a justly famous song of that genre. Howard Hanson's *Lament for Beowulf* and Norman Lockwood's *Epitaphs* represent major twentieth-century orchestral and choral works in this musical tradition.

Within Western culture there are significant musical works that serve to memorialize the dead. The most prominent musical form used for this purpose is the requiem. As a religious service for the dead, the requiem has, even without considering the music, the necessary symbolic connotations. Its texts and general form have been in continuous use since the thirteenth century. As the standard form of commemoration of the Roman Catholic Church, the musical setting attains by association the universal element necessary for great and lasting works. Indeed, such works as Vittoria's requiem for the funeral in 1603 of the Empress Maria of Spain are still performed today. Currently the most famous examples of this form are the requiems of Mozart, Verdi, Fauré, Berlioz, and Brahms, composed in the eighteenth and nineteenth centuries. Despite the fact that most of these works share a common literary source, each has a distinct aesthetic and commemorative function.

The earliest of the group is the Mozart *Requiem*, commissioned by a person later revealed to be Count Von Walsegg. In his debilitated state of health, Mozart imagined that the count's emissary had been death itself in disguise. The thought preyed upon his mind until he became convinced that he was writing his own memorial. Such forebodings occasionally become self-fulfilling, and in this case Mozart did not live to complete the work. It is performed today as finished by his pupil, Süssmayr.

As a structure, the *Requiem* is a composite of sections exemplifying a variety of emotional qualities. The initial section, from which the form takes its name, is a prayer for rest and for the light of God's presence to shine upon the dead. There follow prayers for mercy and deliverance from the darkness of death. The most fearful section, the *Dies Irae*, pictures the terrors of the Last Judgment, after which the *Lachrimosa* repeats the mood of sorrow in a less vigorous format. At the opposite pole is the radiant *Sanctus*, suggesting the heavens filled with the glory of God. The quiet, harmonious mood of the *Agnus Dei* returns to the image of rest and eternal light. Though this literary content remains stable, it may be set to musical styles of vastly different effect. Mozart chose to base his *Requiem* on older liturgical forms rather than the melodious lyricism characteristic of his operas. For example, the fugue form is used at the beginning in the *Kyrie* and again at the conclusion of the *Requiem.* Though formal and traditional, his fugues are much more than scholarly exercises. The wonderful fugue at the end of the *Sanctus* evokes the image of an infinite line of heaven-bound pilgrims mentioned in "Thanatopsis." With its evenly balanced phrasing and engaging lyricism, the Requiem shares the stylistic idealism of the poem.

The Verdi *Requiem*, written in 1874, was dedicated to the memory of Alessandro Manzoni, the most famous Italian novelist of the nineteenth century. In contrast to the Mozart *Requiem*, it is a work of utmost theatricality. The *Dies Irae* (day of wrath) is the expressive focal point of the entire work, producing a nonliturgical composition in which the wild and dramatic are the reigning spirit. In this expressionistic work the arias appeal primarily to the emotions, evoking pity, anguish, and the painful upward striving of the soul. Daring and colorful tonal effects mark the work, which one critic called "Verdi's finest opera." The vision of Christ coming in judgment is that of Michelangelo's altar painting for the Sistine Chapel, a Christ with arm raised ready to smite instead of bless. Choruses range from the vast and dramatic *Dies Irae* to the hushed and contemplative *Libera Me.* There are such memorable arias as the soprano *Requiem aeternam*, supported by and contrasted with the accompanying chorus. The *Lux aeternam* is set for the typical operatic trio with intricate interplay of individual voices and constantly changing tonal colorations in the orchestra.

Manzoni was a personal hero to Verdi, who called his novel *The Betrothed* "more than a book, it is the consolation for mankind." Verdi fervently believed that Manzoni had created some of the finest works to have sprung from the human brain. Shortly after the novelist's death Verdi wrote to city officials of his intention to produce a musical memorial for the occasion of the first anniversary of the death. The resulting *Requiem* was a gift from the composer and performers and was performed first in the San Marco Church and then at La Scala. Especially in the less restrained setting of the opera house, the enthusiastic response of the audience was overwhelming. Verdi's view of death in the work is both splendid and terrifying. It is as cosmic in vision and large in scope as the composer felt was appropriate to commemorate a novelist whose works had scaled those heights. Thus a man who spent his musical career in the opera theater produced a work suffused with spiritual longing and unkempt religious ecstasy.

The Brahms *Requiem* was the first work by this composer to win wide public acclaim. Unlike previous composers, Brahms approached death as an agnostic, whose *Requiem* was for all mankind rather than a specific individual or religious denomination. However, two personal experiences of death shaped the work and account for Brahms's attraction to the project. In 1865 Robert Schumann, his chief musical friend and inspiration, died. As a result of his subsequent meditations on death, Brahms created a choral setting of words from the First Epistle of St. Peter, "Behold, all flesh is as the grass." A four-movement chorus evolved around this central chorus. His mother's death intensified his preoccupation with this project, and another segment was created specifically in her memory:

> And ye now therefore have sorrow,
> But I will see you again
> and your heart shall rejoice,
> and your joy no man taketh from you.
> As one whom his mother comforteth,
> so will I comfort you.
> Behold with your eyes
> how I labored but little
> and found much rest.

The work is a clear departure from the standard form, its texts being derived from scriptures that were particularly appealing to the composer. It has little in common with the traditional requiem except the name. Ironically enough, the work is usually more suitable for liturgical use than the massive, theatrical works of Verdi and Berlioz, which use authorized texts. Much of the music is decidedly somber. There is no entreaty for salvation, no prayer for the souls of the dead. The emphasis is upon the consolation of the living and upon the survivor experience itself. Its predominant spirit is that of realism, lightened by the hope of happiness in such brief moments as the setting of Psalm 84:1–2,4 beginning "How lovely is Thy dwelling place, O Lord of Hosts." Though all the sections are rooted in this mortal condition of uncertainty and suffering, many end with statements of hope, such as "they shall have joy and gladness, and sorrow shall flee away."

There are a few significant musical memorial works in the twentieth century; few, however, follow the traditional requiem form. The *Lincoln Portrait*, by Aaron Copland, features a spoken narration with orchestral accompaniment. The texts are drawn from the speeches of Lincoln. Created during the years of the Second World War, the work was intended both to commemorate a great president and to contribute to the spiritual strength of the nation in a time of crisis.

In Memoriam, Dylan Thomas, by Igor Stravinsky, is one of the most unusual contemporary commemorative works. It begins with dirge-canons for trombones which, like solemn voices, call to each other through space. The main body of the work is a setting of "Do Not Go Gentle into That Good Night" for tenor soloist and string quartet. This section features highly angular melody, irregular meters, and disturbingly erratic tonality. The fierce and uneasy expression perfectly fits the combative mood of the poem. A postlude of dirge-canon concludes the brief work.

To summarize, music, as well as poetry and sculpture, often evolves from a desire to commemorate, to perpetuate the presence of a venerated person. This motive is responsible for the creation of some of the most significant works in the Western cultural tradition. The epitaph, memorial, elegy, monument, and requiem have similar roots and manners of manifestation in whatever guise each appears.

The Portrait

As a universal type of human art, the portrait owes its existence to two factors that characterize human life: change and death. Portraits of children and young adults typically record the process of change, while portrayals of older persons are often posited upon the fact of death and intended mainly for their descendents. The attempt to capture individual features with recognizable veracity is an exceedingly old artistic aim. As one might expect, the first efforts were expended upon persons of central position in the culture. There are extant likenesses of Gudea, a ruler of ancient Sumeria. The famous bust of the

Egyptian Queen Nefertiti ("the Beautiful One is come") has been traditionally regarded as an accurate representation of the lady.

Portraits of ordinary persons appear later in history, but they fully reveal the style preference and philosophical orientation prevalent in their respective cultures. Greeks of the Classical era did not indulge in recognizable portraiture, preferring instead an idealistic style that identified class types. Even humble tombstones carried the physical perfection and ideal facial configurations common to grander sculptural works of that period. However, under the hands of mere craftsmen the grand ideas were standardized into clichés. There is the seated lady choosing an ornament from a jewel box, or the family patriarch grasping the arm of a younger man as if in farewell. Even before the appearance of gravestones there were huge ceramic vases placed over graves to receive libations. These massive markers were decorated with geometric designs showing elaborate funeral corteges, but without identifying personal features.

The Romans had an entirely different philosophy of memorializing. They began as early as the Republican period to take wax impressions of the face after death, later having these perishable molds cast into bronze likenesses. The result was an intense realism, literally a topographical reading of the face. Indeed, ugliness was valued for its testimony that the bearer had lived a rugged life, wasted no time on frivolity, and sacrificed for the good of the state. The "pater familia" busts were displayed with pride in the central receiving room of the family home, forming a genealogical gallery that greatly enhanced their patrician lineage. Even after more idealized "pater patri" statues created to honor political figures became popular, the old realism remained standard for intimately shared works for many generations.

The uncounted millions of photographs that today adorn dressing tables, peep from lockets, or fatten wallets are descendants from this ancient tradition of portraiture. The preferred style in America is certainly idealism. Only photographers as famous as Karsch have the artistic authority to override the powerful urge in all of us to eliminate nature's imperfections. True artists create either more honest or more imaginative interpretations of their subjects than those offered in the standard photographic studio. As a contrast, Ingres's portrait of Louis Bertin is realistic to a high degree. Yet it ex-

Fig. 9 Jean-Auguste Dominique Ingres. ***Portrait of Louis Bertin.*** 1832. Oil on canvas, 46 × 37½". The Louvre, Paris. *Photo courtesy of Alinari-Scala and EPA.*

presses more than the topographical rendering of Roman sculpture. Bertin possessed a formidable personality, and it is this stolid intensity that is the real subject of Ingres's work. The quietly composed, almost arrogant face regarding the viewer assumes a position of power. The very largeness of the man is complemented by the bulk of his chair, its solid arm emphasizing the turn of the body. The position of the man's hand, posed as though grabbing his knee, is vividly suggestive. It provides a hint of action, as though the figure were about to rise; and it conveys a sense of energy and determination. The plain background provides no distraction from the evenly lit face with its frame of white collar. Louis Bertin is an analogue for permanence, solidity, and power.

In quite another mood, the artist Degas portrays his own father in a quiet moment totally absorbed in the music being played by the guitarist Pagans. The old gentleman is not the major focus of this painting; the guitar may well be the most interesting object. The fragility and sensitivity of the elder Degas is the real subject of the portrait. The rapidly executed brush strokes and some unblended patches of color add to the sense of transitoriness, capturing the fleeting nature of our most treasured moments. The painting is much less about the exterior appearance of the father than about his inner satisfactions. It is neither realistic nor sentimental, but achieves a balance that is simply touching.

In a highly contrasting mode of portrayal, the likeness of Daniel-Henry Kahnweiler is captured in an abstract manner by Picasso. The artist is not, in this case, interested in either the sitter's façade or character. The face is a point of departure for a structural analysis of the geometric relationships it contains. It has dissolved into a mosaic of interlacing segments. The neutral and almost unvaried color eliminates all distractions from the formal complexity, which is the real subject of the work. Thus the style of abstraction offers still another alternative to the urge to commemorate by portrayal. As in the case of the Medici tombs, the appearance of the subject will be long forgotten, while his evocation lives in this newly created form.

The Survivor Experience

Creative works motivated by the fact of death reveal much of the distinctive hallmarks of a collective life-style. On an indi-

Fig. 10 Edgar Dégas. ***Dégas' Father Listening to Pagans Playing the Guitar.***
1870. Oil on canvas, 81 × 65 cm. *Courtesy, Museum of Fine Arts, Boston;*
bequest of John T. Spaulding.

Fig. 11 Pablo Picasso. **Daniel-Henry Kahnweiler.** 1910. Oil on canvas, 9⅝ ×
28⅝″. *Courtesy of The Art Institute of Chicago;* gift of Mrs. Gilbert W. Chapman.

vidual scale creative works can reveal the crosscurrents of human emotions as experienced by survivors. One powerful reaction is that of resistence or resentment. Often submerged because it is socially unacceptable, such an attitude lingers under the more obvious reaction patterns. In her biographical novel, *A Very Easy Death,* Simone de Beauvoir concludes her account of the protracted death of her mother with the observation that death is always an affront to mankind. It is never truly natural, no matter how old a person may be; we always die of something. Death itself, she concludes, is an outrage.

Edna St. Vincent Millay expresses resentment about the very nature of mortality:

> I am not resigned to the shutting away of loving hearts
>   in the hard ground.
> So it is, and so it will be, for so it has been, time
>   out of mind:
> Into the darkness they go, the wise and the lovely.
> Crowned with lilies and with laurel they go; but I am
>   not resigned.
>
> Lovers and thinkers, into the earth with you.
> Be one with the dull, the indiscriminate dust.
> A fragment of what you felt, of what you knew,
> A formula, a phrase remains,—but the best is lost.
>
> The answers quick and keen, the honest look, the
>   laughter, the love,—
> They are gone. They are gone to feed the roses.
>   Elegant and curled
> Is the blossom. Fragrant is the blossom. I know
>   But I do not approve.
> More precious was the light in your eyes than
>   all the roses of the world.
>
> Down, down, down into the darkness of the grave
> Gently they go, the beautiful, the tender, the kind:
> Quietly they go, the intelligent, the witty, the brave.
> I know. But I do not approve. And I am not resigned.[5]

The refusal of death is couched in the mythology of all lands in the universal prototype of the standoff. In one version death is stranded up a tree, and the people will not let him come down. In another, death is as yet uncreated and people live forever. Inevitably the suffering find no release; the world becomes crowded and quarrelsome. Eventually death must be released or created in response to simple human need.

Two famous art songs are based upon the refusal of death. Both are sung as dramatic personifications, and both involve children, to whom death seems most unwelcome.

One of Schubert's most famous songs is the "Erlking," the very term standing metaphorically for death. The piano accompaniment begins with a drumming pattern of rapid rhythm followed by an upward scale and a foreboding drop down a minor triad. The singer enters with the description of a dark forest and three figures on horseback racing through the night. The main body of the song is a dialogue between a father and his son, whom he holds in his arms as they flee on the first horse. The father tries to comfort the son, but the boy hears behind them the ingratiating voice of death and is frightened. Out of the woods they burst in the last verse. But when the father looks down, he finds the son dead in his arms.

Among his collected works called *Songs and Dances of Death,* the Russian composer Moussorgsky features a similar instance of the survivor in a tragic battle against death. "Cradle Song" is written as a dialogue between death and a mother whose child is mortally ill. The mother begins each verse with a rapid, angular melody, pleading with death to leave her child alone. Death sings the second half of each verse in a slow, dramatic style and lower register, wheedling the child to come with him. In the last verse the music slows, an ominous drum roll is heard, and death snatches the child away.

Resistance to death by survivors can become almost pathological in its force and effect. Such a case is presented in Robert Frost's poem "Home Burial." The pretext is simple and familiar; a farm couple has experienced the death of their only child. The boy has been buried in the family plot near the house; the couple must deal with this grief and continue their life together. But this process has come upon an insurmountable barrier. Neither understands the other's way of mourning. The husband complains:

> I do think, though, you overdo it a little.
> What was it brought you up to think it the thing
> To take your mother-loss of a first child
> So inconsolably—in the face of love.
> You'd think his memory might be satisfied—

This mild remonstrance unexpectedly unleashes all her hidden anger at the way her husband behaved at the simple funeral. He dug the grave himself, probably regarding the act as the last devotion owed to one he loved. But the wife saw it in quite a different light:

> If you had any feeling, you that dug
> With your own hand—how could you—his little grave.

To the wife his behavior had been that of a stranger. To acquiesce to death, to abet its grim activity, was an admission of defeat she was not willing to make. To compound this, in her eyes—treason, he returned with the grave dirt clinging to his shoes and remarked to the neighbors gathered in the kitchen: "Three foggy mornings and one rainy day will rot the best birch fence a man can build." How utterly unfeeling, the woman thought.

The bereaved mother has her own grim philosophy about death:

> No, from the time that one is sick to death,
> One is alone, and he dies more alone.
> Friends make pretense of following to the grave,
> But before one is in it, their minds are turned
> And making the best of their way back to life
> And living people, and things they understand.
> But the world's evil. I won't have grief so
> If I can change it. Oh, I won't, I won't.[6]

She is willing to risk her marriage, friendships built over a lifetime, even her emotional stability to protest the injustice of death and the insensitivity of humankind. There will be no normalcy for her; each day will be a reenactment of her loss. She will be an affront to the callous indifference of the world.

In their attempts to deal with death, survivors sometimes slip into a helpless nihilism, a desperate feeling that life is worth very little if it escapes so easily. Such an attitude can become an emotional crutch that enables one to deal with life in a noncommittal fashion. A painting by Pieter Brueghel takes just this point of view. The poet W. H. Auden explains his philosophy of death in a poem about the painting:

> About suffering they were never wrong,
> The Old Masters: how well they understood

Fig. 12 Pieter Brueghel. ***Landscape with the Fall of Icarus.*** ca. 1558. Oil on canvas, 73.5 × 112 cm. Musées Royaux des Beaux-Arts de Belgique, Brussels.

Its human position; how it takes place
While someone else is eating or opening a window
   or just walking dully along;
Now, when the aged are reverently, passionately waiting
For the miraculous birth, there always must be
Children who did not specially want it to happen, skating
On a pond at the edge of the wood:
They never forgot
That even the dreadful martyrdom must run its course
Anyhow in a corner, some untidy spot
Where the dogs go on with their doggy life and
   the torturer's horse
Scratches its innocent behind on a tree.
In Brueghel's "Icarus," for instance: how everything
   turns away
Quite leisurely from the disaster; the ploughman may
Have heard the splash, the forsaken cry,
But for him it was not an important failure; the sun shone
As it had to on the white legs disappearing into the green
Water; and the expensive, delicate ship that must have seen
Something amazing, a boy falling out of the sky,
Had somewhere to go and sailed calmly on.[7]

Fig. 13 James Smillie. Engraving after Thomas Cole's *Voyage of Life: Old Age.*
1839. Print collection, Art Prints, and Photographs Division of The New York
Public Library; Astor, Lenox and Tilden Foundations.

There are other survivor attitudes besides fear, resistence,
or a kind of grudging stoicism. There is an acceptance of death
based on a belief that it is part of some grand metaphysical
scheme. One of the most memorable works expressing this
philosophy is Thomas Cole's "Old Age," commissioned by a
New York lawyer, Samuel Ward, as part of a cycle called the
Voyage of Life. The four works of the series, which were intended for each of the four walls of Ward's drawing room, trace
man's existence from childhood to death. In his first stage, a
child is seen emerging in a small boat from a mysterious cavern
into the dawn of day. His head is still surrounded with the
sparks of eternity and his hourglass on the boat prow is full.
Youth shows the youngster seeking his destiny in the vision
that trembles in the clear air of heaven. *Manhood* brings the
storms and currents of life, fearful to the rider in the little boat.
At last, in *Old Age*, the man arrives, his hourglass now gone
and surrounded by darkness, at a place of calm and light. The
same angel who beckoned him out of the cavern is indicating

the way to his next destination; the man folds his hands prayer-fully in assent.

Among the musical works with the most graciously accept-ing attitude toward death are the funeral cantatas by J. S. Bach. Cantata 106 is titled *God's Time is the Best*. It is a mixture of two clear but combinable ideas. The first is the universality and inescapability of death. The second is the promise of immortal-ity. These two ideas meet in the middle of the work in a chorus of great beauty. Using low registers and rather mournful melody, the voices begin with a loosely polyphonic setting of the words, "This is the condition of man from the beginning; he must die." After numerous repetitions of this idea a high, lyric, and joyous melody is taken by the sopranos to the words: "Yes, yes, come, Lord Jesus." Here is the ultimate assent, a full recognition of the fact and even the gloominess of death, but in addition a glad and faithful trust in the ultimacy of life. Those two ideas then combine in the final section until the chorus reaches a place of rest. Instead of closing on some firm, cumulative resonance, Bach trails the soprano voices off quietly as though they were indeed departing for other spheres. This chorus leaves no room for doubt of the soul's destiny, with its vigorous setting of a text expressing praise to God and confidence in divine strength even in the face of death.

There is the still optimistic, but somewhat varied view-point, expressed in the cycle-of-life concept. Here is not the spiritual cycle as found in the works by Cole and Bach, but the physical cycle as represented in the *Four Last Songs*, by Richard Strauss. Written in his old age, these songs express the com-poser's intuitions about death in musical settings of poems he loved. They contain imagery of sleep, rest, and longing for renewal. The setting of the poem "September," by Herman Hesse, begins with an orchestral sound of great intricacy and color. The voice emerges from this glittering spectrum to sing of a garden in the fall, with the slow rain seeping into the flowers. The leaves falling from the yellow acacia trees are sug-gested by fluttering melodies in the flutes. The shifting to-nalities and tangled melodies of the orchestra evoke the lingering summer and the last roses sleeping on their folding branches. The soloist's endless lines on a single vowel sound give the impression of sleep, and yet also of ecstatic joy. The work radiates optimism, not for spiritual redemption, but for the human participation in the seasonal process, our secure place in the unending cycle of physical death and renewal. It falls far short of theism, while projecting a powerful sense of the meaning and purpose of human existence.

Finally, among the varied images of survivorship is the reminder—here by Emily Brontë—that death may be suffered and healed, but never forgotten;

> Cold in the earth—and fifteen wild Decembers
>   From these brown hills have melted into spring:
> Faithful, indeed, is the spirit that remembers
>   After such years of change and suffering!
> . . . .
> No later light has lightened up my heaven,
>   No second morn has ever shone for me;
> All my life's bliss from thy dear life was given,
>   All my life's bliss is in the grave with thee.
> But when the days of golden dreams had perished,
>   And even despair was powerless to destroy;
> Then did I learn how existence could be cherished
>   Strengthen'd, and fed without the aid of joy.
>
> Then did I check the tears of useless passion—
>   Weaned my young soul from yearning after thine;
> Sternly denied its burning wish to hasten
>   Down to that tomb already more than thine.
> And, even yet, I dare not let it languish,
>   Dare not indulge in memory's rapturous pain;
> Once drinking deep of that divinest anguish,
>   How could I seek the empty world again?[8]

Two Novels of Survivorship

Clearly the masterpiece of the survivor experience in American literature is *A Death in the Family*, by James Agee. As a boy, the author was a witness to the events he reports in a style so exhaustively penetrating that it might be best described a psychological realism. Yet, although this label aptly designates the bulk of the novel, the poetic reflections included by the editors in this posthumous publication are in the highest tradition of idealism, expressing as they do the universal significance of life and death.

The characters in the novel are all based upon real persons caught up in the events surrounding an actual death. In the variety of their reactions to this situation, they constitute a microcosm of all human attitudes, from serene acceptance to bitter cynicism. There are touches of humor as the author discovers his momentary advantage of knowledge over the older boys, who usually torment him. The attempts of his little sister, Catherine, to comprehend the fact of death are in turn funny, pathetic, and macabre. Having no understanding of permanence, she listens to all the explanations and then asks when her father will be home. Several cruel instances of the deaths of pets constitute her sole contact with death; thus Catherine's references to the brutality of death sharply contradict her mother's attempt to use more spiritual imagery.

It is, of course, the mother who bears most grievously the anguish of the death of her husband, Jay Follet. Mary is sustained by the immediate work of running a household, and diverted from collapse by the demands of her children. She is sustained economically, no small item for a widow in 1917, by her father's assumption of the role of provider. Most significantly, from Mary's point of view, she is sustained by a strong religious faith. Aunt Hannah is the only other member of the family to share this particular religious tradition. Yet she has experienced death before, is wary of the use of religious faith as a crutch, and knows that only time and events hold the power of healing. The novel traces the survivors through the funeral and shortly thereafter; the future is left uncertain. The interrelationships and conflicts among characters with personal beliefs and ways of mourning form the major interest of the novel.

Mary expresses her belief about death in her explanation to the children the morning after the accident that killed their father. "Daddy was on his way home last night—and he was—he—got hurt and—so God let him go to sleep and took him straight away with him to heaven." Mary experiences the presence of the spirit of her husband in a scene shared by others in the family, which further supports her interpretation of the meaning of death.

The diametrically opposed attitude is held by Mary's father, Joel. He sees no evidence of divine providence in the situation. "As flies to wanton boys are we to the gods; they kill us for their sport," he laments, quoting Shakespeare's *King Lear* (Act 4, Scene 1, Gloucester's speech). Joel has found nothing dependable in life except his common sense, and to him death is simply a bare fact that one must deal with practically. The only possible response is to grit one's teeth and suffer it through. To his credit, he is careful to cause as little friction as he can with Mary's own faith in some cosmic meaning to death.

Somewhere at the fringe of every death lurks the bumbling incompetent who wishes to do well but succeeds only in trying everyone's patience. Jay's brother, Ralph, assumes this role. Suffering from guilt because his hasty phone call brought Jay to take the trip that led to his death, Ralph tries to become an officiant and comforter. As a funeral director, he should be able to carry it off, but he fails because of inherent personal inadequacies and gets drunk to hide his anguish. In Ralph one finds demonstrated the primacy of character over physical resources or social connections, and the desperate result of the lack of character.

Serving as a balance between these clearly delineated modes of survivorship, Andrew, Mary's brother, is unsure of anything connected with this death. At first he feels guilty that he did not die instead of Jay. His role as bringer of the news to Mary further complicates his anguish, as does his pivotal position as funeral arranger. He gravitates between Joel's outrage at the universe and Mary's belief in the necessity of things. But even Andrew comes to some resolution in the last pages of the novel, one that has special appeal to him as an artist. A butterfly rises from Jay's coffin into the sunlight, and Andrew receives this sight as a pledge that all is well in ways beyond verbalization.

Finally, the author himself, through the poetic reflections inserted before main narrative sections, sets the incidents of this death against a cosmic background. The simplest acts of making cocoa or watering the lawn are transformed into acts of ritual significance. With the penetrating insistence of a Zen devotee, Agee presents this series of discrete moments as portions of an ultimate mystery. He ends the first long soliloquy about a typical summer evening in Knoxville, Tennessee, with

> After a little I am taken in and put to bed. Sleep, soft, smiling, draws me unto her; and those receive me, who quietly treat me, as one familiar and well-beloved in that home: but will not, oh, will not, not now, not ever; but will not ever tell me who I am.[9]

In high contrast to the eloquent realism of Agee's novel is the brilliant satire *The Loved One*, by Evelyn Waugh. A horrified

British observer of the America funeral industry, Waugh delivers an outrageous attack on the various ploys used to console, divert, and occasionally fleece the survivor. His protagonist, Dennis Barlow, falls heir to the somber task of burying his old friend Sir Francis Hinsley. Whispering Glades, a plush Southern California funeral establishment, is the focus of Waugh's irreverent opus on the techniques of consolation. The purpose of that establishment is to disguise the fact of death and create the appearance of a spiritualized sleep. This attitude extends even to the Happier Hunting Ground animal mortuary and cemetery where Dennis is employed.

The various elements that implement this philosophy of death are the subjects of occasionally gruesome satire. Mr. Joyboy, the chief embalmer, is a master at creating (via cotton balls, folded paper, and clips) a range of expressions, from a childlike smile to a state vaguely referred to as "soul." The cosmetician, Miss Thanatogenos, adds a rosy complexion with faintly blue stippled eyelids that enhance the effect of the corpse under the stained glass light of the Slumber Room. The Loved One, as the corpse is called, is then placed as though resting on a couch to receive the Waiting Ones, as the survivors are termed.

As a British expatriate, Dennis is not used to this peculiarly American version of death. His first view of the remains of Sir Francis strike him as "entirely horrible; as ageless as a tortoise and as inhuman." Though Sir Francis, a suicide, was ghastly in appearance when Dennis discovered him hanging from a noose, that guise now seems "a festive adornment, a thing an uncle might don at a Christmas party" in comparison to his present "beautified" state.

The funeral service reflects Waugh's disdain for pretentiousness and falseness to reality. Dennis is assigned to write an ode for Sir Francis that should include all the appropriate and utterly untruthful sentiments valued on such occasions. The only honest, and therefore useless, words that spring to poor Dennis's mind form this satiric elegy:

> They told me, Francis Hinsley, they told me you were hung
> With red protruding eyeballs and a black protruding tongue.
> I wept as I remembered how often you and I
> Had laughed about Los Angeles and now 'tis here you'll lie;
> Here pickled in formaldehyde and painted like a whore,
> Shrimp-pink incorruptible, not lost or gone before.[10]

The cemetary, with its detailed reconstruction of a Norman church, takes its share of disdain. Lake Island, Poet's Corner, and the apiary are some of the attractions of this Disneyworld of the dead. And as with that establishment, it is considered wise to make prior reservations! Dennis is urged to "choose now, in leisure and in health, the form of final preparation which you require, pay for it while you are best able to, shed all anxiety. Pass the buck, Mr. Barlow; Whispering Glades can take it."

Thus is death commemorated, mocked, resisted, and celebrated in all the products of the humanities. Written, carved, sung, or painted, these works are part of an enduring focus. They are guidebooks through the survivor experience, providing a truth to reality beyond the statistical superficialities of our time.

3
Death and War

"*H*e had, of course, dreamed of battles all his life—of vague and bloody conflicts that had thrilled him with their sweep and fire. . . . But awake he had regarded battles as crimson blotches on the pages of the past."[1] In these confessional terms Henry Wilson, hero of *The Red Badge of Courage*, expresses the schizophrenic attitude toward war that characterizes most historic cultures. War unites a people, inspiring them to the highest pinnacle of the communal ideal. The experience of war, in turn, pervades the social fabric. National anthems serve remarkably often as the ideological repositories of past military conflicts. Religious observances couch the imagery of spiritual conflict in such mortal terms as "Onward, Christian Soldiers." Team sports are metaphoric enactments of armed aggression in which "hitting the line" and "mounting a defense" assure the most powerful opponent the "victory." Even sexual activity shares with military tactics such terms as "assault," "thrust," and "penetration," and, at least on the spider level, the sacrifice of male life.

War also separates nations internally in ways that are lightly considered by historians caught up in the strategies of generals and politicians. Soldiers regard conflict from an entirely different perspective from that of families and friends safely removed from the battle lines. The population at home is seldom unanimous in support of the war effort. There has been dissension, demonstration, and even riot by Americans, who have objected to every war in the country's history. Draftees and officers have a remarkably different view of war, sometimes sharing an enmity more vociferous than that bestowed upon the opposing army. The cruelty and despair of war is most painfully experienced by noncombatant civilians who are less concerned with which side wins than with what may be left to them after the conflict ceases.

Smoldering suspicion or outright anger is often expressed between these contending groups. The young German soldiers in *All Quiet on the Western Front* believed that German industrialists were profiting handsomely by selling rotten food and antiquated arms to the military. D. H. Lawrence cynically declared: "At home stayed all the jackals, middle-aged, male and female jackals. And they bit us all. And blood poisoning and mortification set in."[2]

Walt Whitman, who spent months as a volunteer nurse among the wounded during the Civil War, expressed similar feelings of estrangement from the viewpoint of civilians not involved in the struggle. They obviously expected a lofty, idealistic presentation of the events of the war. To their complaints about his realistic descriptions of events, Whitman replied poetically:

> Did you ask dulcet rhymes from me?
> Did you seek the civilian's peaceful and languishing rhymes?
> Did you find what I sang erewhile so hard to follow?
> Why I was not singing erewhile for you to follow, to
>   understand—nor am I now;
> (I have been born of the same as the war was born,
> The drum-corps' rattle is ever to me sweet music, I love well
>   the martial dirge,
> With a slow wail and convulsive throb leading the officer's
>   funeral;)
> What to such as you anyhow such a poet as I? therefore leave
>   my works,
> And go lull yourselves with what you can understand, and
>   with piano tunes,
> For I lull nobody, and you will never understand me.[3]

In one of the most famous poetic warnings of this century Wilfred Owen, a British poet killed in World War I, tells his readers:

If in some smothering dreams, you too could pace
Behind the wagon that we flung him in,
And watch the white eyes wilting in his face,
His hanging face, like a devil's sick of sin,
If you could hear, at every jolt, the blood
Come gargling from the froth-corrupted lungs
Bitten as the cud
Of vile, incurable sores on innocent tongues,—
My friend, you would not tell with such high zest
To children ardent for some desperate glory,
The old Lie: *Dulce et decorum est*
Pro patria mori.[4]

Rudyard Kipling's *Epitaphs* exposes the scar tissue that temporarily hides the bitter feelings between soldiers and politicians. His epitaph for the common soldier reads:

If any question why we died,
Say, "because our fathers lied."

His epitaph for the statesman reads:

I could dig. I dared not rob.
So I lied to please the mob.
Now all my lies are proved untrue.
And I must face the men I slew.
What tale shall serve me here among
These angry and defrauded young?[5]

Yet just as valid an experience of war is the ecstasy of victory, the parades and pageantry in such varied forms as the medieval tournament and the military exercise. Rupert Brooke, an English poet who lived during World War I, created this minor masterpiece in the heroic tonality:

Blow out, you bugles, over the rich dead!
There's none of these so lonely and poor of old,
But, dying, has made us rarer gifts than gold.
These laid the world away; poured out the red
Sweet wine of youth; gave up the years to be
Of work and joy, and that unhoped serene,
That men call age; and those who would have been,
Their sons, they gave, their immortality.

Blow, bugles, blow! They brought us, for our dearth,

> Holiness, lacked so long, and love, and pain.
> Honor has come back, as king, to earth,
>   And paid his subjects with a royal wage;
>   And nobleness walks in our ways again;
>   And we have come into our heritage.[6]

Brooke's poem is the equivalent of innumerable public park statues and such sites as the Tomb of the Unknown Soldier. With its eternal flame, the unflagging watchfulness of its soldier guardians, and the mystery of its identity, the American tomb is a nexus of man, God, and history. Its very plainness conveys the stark monumentality of life lost in defense of national pride. The spacious setting is testimony to the importance of this place as a focus for meditation. It is, indeed, "holy ground."

The contention between Kipling and Brooke is largely philosophical. One regards death in war as an indefensible loss perpetrated by persons in power, whose own self-interest causes them to squander the young and lie about their motives. The other celebrates the sacrifice of life as a ritual cleansing of the social body, restoring the ideals of holiness, nobility, and honor. These gifts are imperishable regardless of circumstance. One sees the oft-repeated history of carnage, while the other sees only the singular impulse of individual self-sacrifice. These attitudes have been in conflict at least since the beginning of modern warfare.

In addition to war as waste and war as sanctification, there is the theme of war as pure adventure. The major exponent of this viewpoint during this century has been the movie industry, and its major protagonist, John Wayne. *Back to Bataan, Sands of Iwo Jima, Flying Leathernecks,* and *The Green Berets* represent more than a twenty-year span of military heroics. In the classic war film, battle sequences in an endless array of settings are the center of attention. Before the advent of television, public visualization of combat was largely dependent upon Hollywood's combination of on-site footage with recreations on location. Though some films were pointedly propagandistic and others merely posings of utterly forgettable actors running through completely predictable plots, many of the class and viewpoint clashes cited previously found their way into the more memorable of the genre.

*Merrill's Marauders,*produced in 1961, centered on the separation of viewpoint between soldiers and officers. Merrill is ordered to lead his regiment on a series of raids, even though the group is depleted by death and stricken with hunger and disease. His second-in-command, at the end of his patience, complains that the regiment is seen as nothing more than legs for walking, shoulders for carrying packs, and arms for shooting rifles. The men eventually refuse to go on, and only the death of Merrill shows them a pattern of sacrifice they feel compelled to emulate.

Pork Chop Hill, produced in 1959, was drawn from the Korean episode, exploring the conflict in values between soldiers and politicians. In a lengthy series of crosscuts from battle sequences to peace talks, the grim determination of the soldiers is contrasted to the intricate posings of the peace delegates. The soldiers hold their assigned position against massive human odds and endless broadcast propaganda. To the negotiators at Panmunjom this small piece of earth is a negligible pawn in a game of pride.

Though the various rituals of the uniform were consistently romanticized, impatience with regulations and intractable circumstance occasinally broke into the comic mode. Charlie Chaplin's *Shoulder Arms* was the pioneer film in the irreverent treatment of war. The ex-tramp character finds himself unable to fit into the neat column of marching men and appears peculiarly equipped with an eggbeater, grater, and mouse trap. Through sheer bumbling he captures the Kaiser and ends the war, only to awaken and find that the whole episode was a dream. This alternative divests the film of direct social criticism, while permitting a satisfying level of mockery. Such later comic films as *Mister Roberts, Hogan's Heroes,* and *What Did you Do In the War, Daddy* railed against intractable officers and superfluous paper work to the extent of faked battles and flourishing private enterprise schemes.

It remained for *Tora, Tora, Tora,* produced in 1970, to tell both the Japanese and American side of the war in the Pacific. It is a film without heroes, and with disastrous miscalculations on both sides. Finally, the top film of 1946, *The Best Years of Our Lives,* explored the strain between soldiers and the people at home, who knew much of the heroics but little of the reality of war. The ex-fighters returned, crippled or transformed, to a world without a sense of place. They were permanently marked by an experience that had no ready justification, and each faced the collision of conflicting contexts in his own way.

To turn to the celebrational aspect of war, surely no Fourth of July festivity is complete without a rendition of the *1812 Overture,* that tonal apex of the heroic perspective. Based upon the successful Russian campaign against the army of Napoleon, Tchaikovsky's orchestral fantasy embodies the most vivid symbolic gestures of communal struggle and victory. Whatever there is about war that makes it the pinnacle of a man's lifetime memories solidifies into colorful detail in this popular work.

Planned for an outdoor performance (which subsequently failed to materialize), the composition was to have marked the dedication of the Cathedral of the Redeemer, itself a memorial to the liberation of Russia from the French armies. Thus the use of actual cannon and bells in modern performances is not a distortion of the composer's intention, though his premiere occurred under conventional concert hall conditions. Following the example of Beethoven in his *Wellington's Victory, the Battle of Vittoria,* Tchaikovsky delineates the fate of the opposing armies in terms of familiar folk or patriotic tunes. The music begins in a solemn mood with the hymn "God Preserve Thy People," which culminates in a rather different style. A sudden drumbeat initiates a dramatic, energetic section concluding with overlapping brass choirs. This suggestion of skirmish ends with snare drumrolls and a military march, which in turn lapses into folk-song material. The long mid-section of the overture contains extensive repetition of two motifs, the first of which introduces the *Marseillaise,* serving as symbol of the aggressor. It alternates with a sweetly lyrical Russian folk tune evoking nostalgic associations with peaceful life before Napoleon's conquests. The concluding section features the famous sonic display. It begins with a slow increase in tempo and volume, culminates with a burst of cannon, and subsides with a long descending pattern of repeated tones suggestive of pushing back massive force. The initial tune of "God Preserve Thy People" recurs in full, dramatic chords in a mood of dignified jubilation. "God Preserve the Czar" follows in combination with a jolly march tune and rhythmic accents of cannon, melding into an extended peal of bells and trumpetings of brasses. War as a means to freedom from oppression and as a dramatic triumph over darkness and pain is expressed with something of the ebullience of the original experience. It remains a believable philosophy, amply testifying to the persistence of this idea in story and song from the beginnings of human history.

Music expresses not only the triumphant aspect of war, but the irreparable loss of life as well. One of the most memorable modern compositions in this latter vein is Paul Hindemith's *Requiem for Those We Love,* based upon the Walt Whitman poem "When Lilacs Last in the Dooryard Bloom'd." In one respect it was a requiem for the composer's own past. He had fled Germany during a wave of expulsions during the Hitler regime. When the war ended in 1945, he received many invitations to return. However, he decided to make America his permanent home, because it had given him shelter and offered scope for the development of his talent. The requiem marked this decision and was his personal expression of condolence for the death and destruction endured by both the nations he loved.

A massive structure featuring two soloists, orchestra, and choir, the work was dedicated to the recently deceased Franklin Delano Roosevelt and the American dead in World War II. Appropriately enough, the Whitman text commemorated the death of another president, Abraham Lincoln. Hindemith found in the Whitman poem a full expression of the grandeur of sorrow and hope for peace among men. The music was equally personal, remaining throughout the composer's life closest to his heart.

The initial impression of the music is that of intense gloom, the trombone announcing the solemn bugle call so beloved by the poet. In fact, the entire score is a careful translation into sound of the major symbols of the literary work. This introductory section is elegiac in spirit, pulled forward not by rhythm but by interconnected lines of strings. A roll of drums announces the theme in brasses and the sound surges forward to a cymbal-topped climax. At a lower level of sound the reeds repeat the bugle call.

The poem begins, sung in a almost ritual manner by the baritone soloist. This voice generally represents Whitman's own personal feelings about America, his vision for its future, and his sorrow at the death of his president. The image of the lilac recurs throughout the poem, representing rekindling of life and a delicate purity of exaltation. The star is most often a reference to Lincoln.

When lilacs last in the dooryard bloom'd,
And the great star early droop'd in the western sky in the night,
I mourn'd, and yet shall mourn with ever-returning spring.

Ever-returning spring, trinity sure to me you bring,
Lilac blooming perennial and drooping star in the west,
And thought of him I love.

The choir responds with an outburst of disorderly rhythmic sound, lamenting the death and crying out against the
helplessness that Americans felt at the time. This section leads
into the verse that introduces the thrush, warbling deep in the
wilderness a song of grief and death. The soprano sings the
verses that portray the bird, and the accompaniment is as son-
ically spare as an oriental painting. There is just the suggestion
of a bird in the solo flute passages. The bird's song becomes
death's song in a transition that occurs throughout the poem:

> In the swamp in secluded recesses,
> A shy and hidden bird is warbling a song.
>
> Solitary the thrush,
> The hermit withdrawn to himself, avoiding the settlements,
> Sings by himself a song.
>
> Song of the bleeding throat,
> Death's outlet song of life (for well dear brother I know
> If thou wast not granted to sing thou would'st surely die).

Another practice of the musical score is using the chorus,
Greek fashion, as the voice of the people. These sections are
often highly energetic, contrasting with the more lyric, elegiac
solo verses. The chorus becomes the crowd of Americans waiting for Lincoln's funeral train "With all the mournful voices of
the dirges pour'd around the coffin." Or they enliven Whitman's vision of Manhattan and the cities of the nation. In a
section of almost unparalleled sadness the baritone soloist, as
the voice of Whitman, confronts death as a companion of life:

> Then with the knowledge of death as walking one side of me,
> And the thought of death close-walking the other side of me,
> And I in the middle as with companions, and as holding the
>   hands of companions,
> I fled forth to the hiding receiving night that talks not,
> Down to the shores of the water, the path by the swamp in the
>   dimness,
> To the solemn shadowy cedars and ghostly pines so still.

In that place of ultimate despair he hears the death carol of
the thrush, and Hindemith has chosen to make this section the

most expansive and intricate of the entire work. Both soloists join to portray the spiritual conversation between Whitman and the bird:

> Come lovely and soothing death,
> Undulate round the world, serenely arriving, arriving,
> In the day, in the night, to all, to each,
> Sooner or later delicate death.
> . . . .
> Over the tree-tops I float thee a song,
> Over the rising and sinking waves, over the myriad fields and
>   prairies wide,
> over the dense pack'd cities all and the teaming wharves and
>   ways,
> I float this carol with joy to thee O death.

The chorus responds with resonant and often dissonant moving chords to Whitman's portrayal of the carnage of the Civil War:

> I saw battle corpses, myriads of them,
> And the white skeletons of young men, I saw them,
> I saw the debris and debris of all the slain soldiers of the war.

An animated orchestral interlude presents snatches of military marches and a sombre rendition of "taps." It is a scene both of glory and of desolation. The requiem ends as it began, with a pensive duet between baritone and flute (as the thrush). The soprano and chorus join, and the imagery returns to the single focal death about which the poem gravitates:

> For the sweetest, wisest soul of all my days and lands—
>   and this for his dear sake,
> Lilac and star and bird twined with the chant of my soul,
> There in the fragrant pines and the cedars dusk and dim.[7]

The Combatants

At the very center of war, Karl Shapiro reminds us, is the single experience of the individual soldier:

> We ask for no statistics of the killed,
> For nothing political impinges on
> This single casualty, or all those gone,

> Missing or healing, sinking or dispersed,
> Hundreds of thousands counted, millions lost,
> More than an accident and less than willed
> In every fall, and this one like the rest.
> However others calculate the cost,
> To us the final aggregate is *one*,
> One with a name, one transferred to the blest;
> And though another stoops and takes the gun,
> We cannot add the second to the first.[8]

War becomes at last simply an element of individual experience. The Greeks at the beginning of Western history understood war as a means to personal immortality through collective memory. Achilles, the Achaian hero of the *Iliad*, had the choice of living a full life and dying unremembered or living a brief life and being immortalized in story and song. Without much reflection, he chose the latter. At the time of the *Iliad* war was waged by the individual hero and his retainers and, as in the case of Achilles and Menelaus, there might be as much jealousy and enmity between warriors on the same side as were displayed to a worthy hero of the opposing side. The *Iliad* has retained its position as a foundation of Western literature precisely because it renders vast, impersonal events in terms of individual lives. To these fighting men everything of importance centers upon the battlefield. Their social status, reputation, and wealth all rest upon courage and skill in battle. We are told that Achilles left to join the soldiers before his coming-of-age ceremony; he has literally grown up over eight years in the midst of war. He is there for personal glory and because this is all he has ever known of life.

On the Trojan side the leading warrior is Hector, who is given a larger frame of reference. He has a wife and a young child; his mother is terrified of losing this, her last son, to the seemingly endless war. But Hector is the last hope of that beleaguered city. In a moving farewell scene he goes to meet Achilles in combat, knowing it will mark his own death.

Although Homer does not hesistate to show the pettiness and cowardice of political leaders, he presents quite a different rationale for war from that of modern commentators. Parallel to the earthly panorama is a heavenly one, where individual gods directly affect human events. Beyond even this realm is the dark obscurity of fate, which even the gods cannot control, though they may delay or accelerate it. In the final analysis,

Achilles, Hector, and their comrades are suffering and triumphing according to some vast cosmic scheme. Nor is it entirely impersonal, for gods speak and appear among men, helping or hindering in remarkable ways. These dealings between mortals and immortals are sometimes anguishing but always seem appropriate and eventually reasonable to the warriors.

The war is between groups from the same cultural tradition, speaking the same language, and holding the same values. Typically, warriors in single combat will pause to find out what relationships they might have in common. Only when large, unmanageable groups join in battle are there the animalistic descriptions Homer reserves for such occasions. Death itself is never glamorized. In addition to vivid physical descriptions of mortal wounds, each death is marked by the phrase, "and his soul went down mourning and lamenting into hades." There is no paradise for battle heroes, nor are false promises held out on religious grounds. This present life accounts for everything, and making war is one of the most significant ways in which a man may live.

Several thousand years later W. B. Yeats portrays a fighter similarly smitten with the fatal attraction of war:

> I know that I shall meet my fate
> Somewhere among the clouds above;
> Those that I fight I do not hate,
> Those that I guard I do not love;
> My country is Kiltartan Cross,
> My countrymen Kiltartan's poor,
> No likely end could bring them loss
> Or leave them happier than before.
> Nor law, nor duty bade me fight,
> Nor public men, nor cheering crowds,
> A lonely impulse of delight
> Drove to this tumult in the clouds;
> I balanced all, brought all to mind,
> The years to come seemed waste of breath,
> A waste of breath the years behind
> In balance with this life, this death.[9]

This fighter, like his Greek forebear, has considered what he is doing with his life. Dying an old man seems a "waste of breath." His childhood and youth are equally unmemorable.

Fig. 14 Archaic Greek. ***Dying Warrior.*** ca. 490 B.C. Marble, 72" long. From East pediment of the Temple of Aphaia at Aegina. *Courtesy of Staatliche Antikensammlungen und Glyptothek, Munich.*

He has no personal grudge to settle with the enemy; moreover, he feels no particular duty toward his countrymen. Unlike Achilles, he has no goddess for a mother and no illusions about gaining social status through military heroism. But he is gripped by the same "impulse of delight" with the wild adventure of battle, with the speed and danger of events.

Though hardly an object of desire, death in war was as vivid an alternative to the Greeks as to the Irish airman. But its portrayal in the art of the Classic Period maintained an idealistic dignity absent in Wilfred Owen's vision of gurgling bodies heaped on wagons. The *Dying Warrior* from the east pediment of the Temple of Aphaia, Aegina, eloquently represents the Greek perspective. He signifies no specific Greek dying in a particular historic conflict, but the idealized spirit of sacrifice stated in universal terms. His bodily position is true not only to his condition, but to the architectural demands of the platform that housed him. His death has communal and religious significance, being displayed on a temple in public view. It has moral significance in indicating the appropriate death for those who defend national ideals.

Formally, the lack of physical detail suggests youthful innocence. The "archaic smile" conveys noble acquiescence to the decision of fate. Though weakness has caused one hand to slip from its grip on the shield, the other circles a weapon until the last possible moment. Here is no blood, agony, or despair. There is, on the other hand, no overly romanticized spirituality—no hint of the warrior's coming translation into paradise. We are shown a prototype warrior, having done all he could, experiencing the universal destiny of all things with quiet resignation. Though hundreds of years separate this work from the era of the *Iliad*, something of the same view of war suffuses them both.

Tides of change eventually swept through ancient Greek culture and were immediately reflected in the arts. Rhys Carpenter comments on the modifications to be found in Greek sculpture in the era of Alexander the Great:

> Truth to Nature, fidelity to the actual shapes and appearances, is the lodestar that leads sculptors on. It is also the song of the sirens, a Lorelei to bring their ships upon the rocks; for in the very moment of attainment the true art of sculpture goes to wreck and vanishes from sight, broken on the reefs of a mere imitative realism.[10]

Thus the aesthetic of the third century B.C. was realism, practiced most brilliantly in the city of Pergamon. King Attalus commissioned vast numbers of sculptural works to perpetuate the various wars of Greek history and especially his own victory over the Gauls. One of the most memorable to survive is the *Dying Gaul*, which provides a remarkable contrast with the *Dying Warrior*. To be sure, this Gaul is a barbarian and not strictly representative of the Greek ethos; however, realism of style was used to portray Greeks during this period.

Formally, the inclusion of a mass of detail gives the *Dying Gaul* the appearance of suffering life. The figure is actively fighting against death, reluctant to accept his fate. We can almost feel the strain of muscles and imagine the blood pumping

Fig. 15 Hellenistic Greek. *Dying Gaul.* ca. 230–220 B.C. Roman marble copy after a bronze original from Pergamum. Lifesized. Capitoline Museum, Rome. *Photograph courtesy of Alinari-Scala and EPA.*

through the carefully delineated veins. Battlefield accoutrements surrounding the expiring Gaul indicate a particular time, far from the more universal reference of Classic art. The gaping wound in the side, the flared nostrils, and the shocks of hair hung in knots over the head give this death violent, animalistic qualities unacceptable several hundred years before.

Several thousand years later the *Portrait of a German Officer,* by Marsden Hartley, delineates the individual soldier using a third alternative, the sardonic. An abstraction containing no personal physiognomy, the portrait is a composite of symbols. The person, if he ever existed, has become entirely hidden by the trappings of his office. He is an anonymous accretion of flags, military decorations, insignias, and various "perquisites." Among the latter are containers suggestive of liquor bottles, and a numbered keyhole suggestive of a hotel room. The man is a collection of cognitive signs to be recognized and

Fig. 16 Marsden Hartley. ***Portrait of a German Officer.*** 1914. Oil on canvas, 68¼ × 41⅜″. The Metropolitan Museum of Art; Alfred Stieglitz collection, 1949.

reacted to by those with lesser displays of power symbols. The result is both pathetic and terrifying. We are left laughing about the foolishness of such a man, but wondering if armies are merely collections of such impervious assemblages.

What turns a healthy young Greek into an egocentric slayer, an Irish boy into a fighter pilot, or a German citizen into a heap of patriotic emblems? Sometimes it is the sense of personal challenge found in Henry Wilson, hero of *The Red Badge of Courage*. Sometimes it is a sense of duty to a social group, as exemplified by Hector in the *Iliad*. But sometimes the answer lies in the machinations of political structures beyond the control of the individual, or so thought Thomas Hardy:

> Had he and I but met
> By some old ancient inn,
> We should have set us down to wet
> Right many a nipperkin!
>
> But ranged as infantry,
> And staring face to face,
> I shot at him as he at me,
> And killed him in his place.
>
> I shot him dead because—
> Because he was my foe,
> Just so: my foe of course he was
> That's clear enough; although
>
> He thought he'd 'list, perhaps,
> Off-hand-like—just as I—
> Was out of work—had sold his traps—
> No other reason why.
>
> Yes, quaint and curious war is!
> You shoot a fellow down
> You'd treat if met where any bar is,
> Or help to half-a-crown.[11]

This utterly arbitrary quality led Wilfred Owen to use his poetry as a weapon against the monstrous futility of the war that took his life. And it was the outspoken pacifism of Benjamin Britten a quarter of a century later that led him to create one of the most memorial musical compositions of our time based upon these poems. The *War Requiem* was commissioned for the reconsecration of Conventry Cathedral (St. Michael's), which had been nearly demolished in the air raids of World

War II. Some of the ruins are preserved as a permanent memorial to the dead. Britten wanted his music to serve this purpose—to warn about the destructive futility of war, but to offer a new structure of healing and hope.

Part of the effectiveness of the work lies in the conflict between the idealism of the cultural tradition and the realism of direct personal experience. The requiem as a liturgical form dates from the thirteenth century and, except for the *Dies Irae* section, expresses consolation and trust in the goodness of God. In direct opposition to this timeless contemplation of death are the Owen poems, which deny, accuse, and reject all the conventional condolences that justify death in war. These viewpoints remain unreconciled throughout the composition.

The sonic resources consist of two male soloists who sing the Owen poems as personifications of an English and German soldier. They express their bitterness at their wasteful deaths, offering no meaningful spiritual context for their experience. On a second level of meaning, the soprano soloist, chorus, and orchestra carry the liturgical framework, celebrating an inherent spiritual meaning to life's passage. The boys' choir and organ participate in some exalted level of innocence, far removed from mortal torment. Each of these levels creates contrast and sometimes abrasion with the others; their final combination during the last moments of the requiem is an uneasy truce at best.

The *War Requiem* begins quite traditionally with a prayer for rest and peace for the souls of the dead. Ethereal voices of the choirboys praise God as though from some heavenly distance. Abruptly, the first soldier breaks this calm ritual, asking in the lines of the Owen poem:

> What passing bells for these who die as cattle?
> Only the monstrous anger of the guns,
> Only the stuttering rifles' rapid rattle
> Can patter out their hasty orisons.[12]

How dare we, this juxtaposition implies, go comfortably on with such traditional formulae when these deaths are unforgivable? And as though in response to this accusation, the chorus replies with the Latin *Kyrie* ("Lord, have mercy upon us").

The *Dies Irae* contains the darker imagery of judgment within the Christian scheme of eschatology. In contrast to the tumult and terror of this spiritual vision of resurrection, the second soldier sings the Owen poem describing the sleep of tired, despondent men:

> Voices of boys were by the riverside.
> Sleep mothers them; and left the twilight sad.
> The shadows of the morrow weighed on men.
> Bugles sang.
> Voices of old despondency resigned,
> Bowed by the shadow of the morrow, slept.[13]

The ritual element continues, the soprano alluding to the justice of God. Mankind stands alone in the fear of death, asking the merciful intercession of God. The Owen poem again breaks in rudely upon this train of ideas, as both soldiers assert that death holds no fear for them anymore:

> Out there, we've walked quite friendly up to death;
> Sat down and eaten with him, cool and bland,—
> Pardoned his spilling mess-tins in our hand.
> We've sniff'd the green thick odor of his breath,—
> Our eyes wept, but our courage didn't writhe.[14]

War is truly a matter of life, not of flags, they assert. The chorus responds with the traditional prayer for forgiveness and blessing. The soldier rejoins with an image of the powerful artillery guns, asking that God curse them and "cut them from our souls." Was it for this, his companion joins in, that humans are on this earth?

The centerpiece of the *Offertory* is a parable based upon the story of Abraham and his sacrificial offering of Isaac. In the Old Testament version of the story the father's hand is stayed by an angel and a lamb provided instead of the child. In Owen's poem the angel offers the animal substitute and urges Abraham to

> Offer the Ram of Pride instead of him.
> But the old man would not do so, but slew his son,—
> And half the seed of Europe, one by one.[15]

The boys' choir, those voices of innocence beyond this scene of bloodshed, offer to God, instead, sacrifices of prayer and praise.

The *Sanctus* calls to mind God as the spiritual radiance infusing the natural world, giving it beauty and majesty. In ghastly opposition to this traditional vision of God in nature, Owen recalls the destruction of war and its effect upon the land:

> And when I hearken to the Earth, she saith:
> "My fiery heart shrinks, aching. It is death.
> Mine ancient scars shall not be glorified,
> Nor my titanic tears, the sea, be dried."[16]

The message of this juxtaposition is clear. We have by monstrous sacrifice and unforgivable pride desanctified the very earth we inhabit.

The *Libera me* is the final prayer for deliverance from the culmination of human history and a plea for resurrection. In response, the two soldiers appear as ghosts who, after death, relive their last ordeal. They mourn the lost years and together sing of the pity and futility of war. Standing beyond the arbitrary divisions of political circumstance, they join as comrades, singing simply "Let us sleep now." In the final measures the stark contrast is dissolved, and the choruses join the soldiers in a prayer for eternal rest.

The Victims

As pitiable as the lives and deaths of Owen's soldiers were, there is another group of people whose inevitable presence in every conflict is even more to be decried. They are the noncombatant civilians caught between opposing forces, pillaged and killed by both sides, and without weapons or training to defend themselves. A combination of the elderly, women, and children, they lack even the political and economic power necessary to rectify their situation. They are the anonymous unwanted: the displaced persons of World War II; the starving tribesmen of Biafra; of Japanese-Americans forcibly removed to "security camps." The politicians find them easy to forget; artists find them of singular significance. The nineteenth-century cartoonist-painter Daumier pictured them just as we see them on the evening television news. A faceless horde of ragged bodies moves away from the viewer, going nowhere and having come from no place. They move through a featureless land devoid of all save mottled brown earth, which coats even the sky with a dull pallor. Hopeless and helpless, their lives have dwindled to a series of futile movements without destination.

Euripides, fifth-century B.C. Greek dramatist, in his play *The Trojan Women*, gives a heartrending account of the desolation of the female inhabitants of that legendary city of Troy after its capture by the Greeks. Hecuba, once the Trojan Queen, waits amid the smoking ruins to learn what her fate will be:

> Alas! Alas! Whose wretched slave shall I be? Where, where on earth shall this old woman toil, useless as a drone, poor counterpart of a corpse, a feeble, ghastly ornament? To be posted to watch at the door, to become a children's nurse—I who in Troy was paid the honor of a queen!

At the end of the play, when they are being taken into exile to be made slaves by the conquering army, Hecuba and the chorus of women bid their last farewells to their homeland:

> Hecuba: And the dust, like smoke, with wing outspread to heaven, will rob me of the sight of my home.
> Chorus: The name of the land will pass into oblivion. One thing after another, everything disappears. Hapless Troy is finished.[17]

Aside from merely political or economic conflicts, millions of deaths have been caused by religious persecution. John Milton, who lived during a period of deep religious unrest, remembered these innocents:

> Avenge, O Lord, thy slaughtered saints, whose bones
> Lie scattered on the Alpine mountains cold;
> Even them who kept thy truth so pure of old,
> When all our fathers worshiped stocks and stones,
> Forget not; in thy book record their groans
> Who were thy sheep, and in their ancient fold
> Slain by the bloody Piedmontese, that rolled
> Mother with infant down the rocks. Their moans
> The vales redoubled to the hills, and they
> To heaven. Their martyred blood and ashes sow
> O'er all the Italian fields, where still doth sway
> The triple tyrant; that from these may grow

A hundredfold, who, having learnt thy way,
May early fly the Babylonian woe.[18]

Even people generally described as "safe at home" are not immune to death, which changes their lives forever. There are millions in every war—the "gold star" mothers with the emblems of loss worn as permanent scars upon their hearts. Walt Whitman pictured the scene in his poem "Come Up from the Fields, Father," as the family gathers to read the letter that has come from the battlefield bearing the name of the son:

Open the envelope quickly,
O this is not our son's writing, yet his name is sign'd,
O a strange hand writes for our dear son, O stricken mother's
    soul!
All swims before her eyes, flashes with black, she catches the
    main words only,
Sentences broken, "gunshot wound in the breast, cavalry
    skirmish, taken to hospital,
At present low, but will soon be better."
. . . .
"Grieve not so, dear mother," (the just-grown daughter speaks
    through her sobs,
The little sisters huddle around, speechless and dismay'd,)
"See, dearest mother, the letter says Pete will soon be better."

Alas, poor boy, he will never be better, (nor may-be needs to be
    better, that brave and simple soul,)
While they stand at home at the door he is dead already,
The only son is dead.

But the mother needs to be better,
She with thin form presently drest in black,
By day her meals untouch'd, then at night fitfully sleeping,
    often waking
In the midnight waking, weeping, longing with one deep
    longing,
O that she might withdraw unnoticed, silent from life, escape
    and withdraw,
To follow, to seek, to be with her dead son.[19]

But most unforgettable of all is the death of a child, whether it be Hector's infant son whom the Greeks hurled down a cliff, or a child who has bombs dropped on it in a modern city. Dylan Thomas pictures such a death and funeral after an air raid in 1946:

Myselves
The grievers
Grieve
Among the street burned to tireless death
A child of a few hours
With its kneading mouth
Charred on the black breast of the grave
The mother dug, and its arms full of fires.

Begin
With singing
Sing
Darkness kindled back into beginning
When the caught tongue nodded blind,
A star was broken
Into the centuries of the child
Myselves grieve now, and miracles cannot atone.

Forgive
Us forgive
Us your death that myselves the believers
May hold it in a great flood
Till the blood shall spurt,
And the dust shall sing like a bird
As the grains blow, as your death grows, through our heart.

Crying
Your dying
Cry,
Child beyond cockcrow, by the fire-dwarfed
Street we chant the flying sea
In the body bereft.
Love is the last light spoken. Oh
Seed of sons in the loin of the black husk left.[20]

One of the most powerful social critics in the Western art tradition was Francisco Goya, whose *Disasters of War* etchings documented the anguish left in the wake of Napoleon's invasion of Spain. His choice of medium enabled these works to be produced in quantity, much like dissident newspapers. The style is beyond realism, using exaggeration for emotional effect. Not merely the subject matter—garrotings, hangings, shootings, and beatings—but also the violence of line and value contrast speak of outrage at the treatment of innocent people. Like every good propagandist, Goya shows the enemy as impersonal and unfeeling. Sometimes they are represented

Fig. 17 Francisco Goya. ***The Disasters of War, No. 36: Nor This Tampoco.*** ca. 1814. Etching. The National Gallery of Art, Washington; Rosenwald Collection.

merely by weaponry thrust into the pictorial space. The Spanish citizens, on the other hand, seem delicately drawn with expressions of stunned surprise. They often cling together like children.

A painting that expresses equal sympathy in a different manner for such victims is Peter Paul Rubens's *The Consequences of War*. His style is decidedly idealistic, perhaps even Romantic, and meaning is communicated symbolically. Rubens himself provided a detailed explanation of the painting in a letter to a friend. Because it is the lightest, the figure that first catches the eye is that of Venus surrounded by cupids. Exerting all her powers of persuasion, she is grasping the arm of the dark figure of Mars, trying to restrain him. He has thrust open the temple of war and, brandishing his sword, is threatening the world with disaster. He is urged forward by the figures of Fury, Pestilence, and Famine. All about him lie symbols of the destruction of human culture. Harmony, with a broken lute, sits

Fig. 18 Peter Paul Rubens. *The Consequences of War.* 1637–38. Oil on canvas. Pitti Gallery, Florence. *Photograph courtesy of EPA.*

on the ground with her back to the viewer. The mother and child, symbols of the helpless, attempt to escape. A figure representing an architect for enterprises of peace lies upon his back, his instruments scattered. Books are trampled under the foot of Mars; the olive branch lies wilting on the ground. The wailing woman next to Venus is, allegorically, Europe, victim of plunder, outrage, and misery.

In the twentieth century the most powerful protest painting to date is Picasso's *Guernica*, which was displayed in a World's Fair pavilion to protest the Nazi bombing of a Spanish village. The style is a combination of distortion and abstraction, carrying an emotional as well as rational impact. Like the Rubens work, it communicates through timeless symbols, which the artist has resisted interpreting in the detailed manner of Rubens. The large design resembles a triptych, the traditional three-unit church altar painting. There are some significant internal religious allusions; the screaming mother with the dead child recalls the reverse imagery of the Madonna and child. The naked bulb shedding its light is a metaphor for the all-seeing eye of God, identifiable as far back in history as ancient Egypt. The screaming bird caught between horse and bull is reminiscent of the dove of the Holy Spirit or its near relation, the dove of peace.

There are references that deal with the Spanish heritage, for example, the bull as a metaphor for physical violence. His tail curls like smoke from a ruined city, and his horns thrust menacingly forward. The horse, in a bullfight the matador's helper, is screaming with pain from the spear that has been thrust into its side (perhaps a reference to the crucifixion). The broken statue of the warrior suggests the destruction of beauty and the arts that nourish life. The woman with the lamp (liberty, perhaps), leans out, surprised at this catastrophe. On the far side of the triptych a burning body falls from a burning building, calling pathetically up into the night. It is the power of these composite images that gives this huge canvas its memorable quality. None of it is "real" in the photographic sense; it is far more powerful than life at any one moment can be comprehended.

Another catastrophic event of World War II was the inspiration for a composition for narrator and orchestra by Arnold Schönberg called *A Survivor from Warsaw*. The incident it memorializes was precipitated by a classic siege situation in which Warsaw's entire Jewish population was packed into a few blocks under appalling conditions. The Nazis were slowly reducing their numbers through shipments to extermination camps. On April 19, 1943, the half-starved remnant of the population rebelled, managing to fend off Nazi tanks and machine guns with only the most rudimentary equipment. It took a month for the Nazis to storm the ghetto walls and subdue the assorted civilians who constituted the resistance force.

Schönberg, an Austrian who fled Europe at the onset of the war, felt particular sympathy for those caught in the suffering he escaped. His life had been spent developing a highly abstract individual style not well suited to expressing immediate reality. However, in *A Survivor from Warsaw*, written close to the end of his life, Schönberg adapted the intellectual demands of the twelve-tone system to an extremely affective musical format. He meant the work as a commemoration and a celebration of the spiritual richness of the human soul.

The narrator tells the story from the viewpoint of one survivor, relating his experiences on the day the Nazis broke through the walls. The story is not finished; we do not know what happened to the narrator or his companions after this series of events. The orchestra sets the emotional framework through eerie sounds, nervous plucked rhythms, and extremes of tonal ranges. The tempo becomes faster as the narrator comes to consciousness, lying on the ground and hearing the Germans rounding up his comrades. He believes that they are about to be killed, and the orchestra underscores their fear and pain with expressive effects that directly support the text. There are panic, shouting, and people falling dazed beside him. Then, as the narrator lies in a half-stupor, he hears the first tentative remnant of the Hebrew hymn *Shema Yisroel* ("Hear, O Israel, The Lord Our God, the Lord is One"). The sound of the male chorus representing the last defenders grows louder in a climax of affirmation. Here is a spirit that will not be defeated even in death.

A work of only five minutes' duration, *A Survivor from Warsaw* is a vivid combination of dramatic realism in the narration and atonal abstraction in the orchestral music. Perhaps this peculiar combination accounts for the vivid impression the work gives of experiencing a nightmare. Yet the majestic conclusion leaves us with a sense of the beauty of moral courage and confidence in the value of human life. The innocent victims have become heroes instead of Goya's remnants of civilization.

A remarkable work dealing with the deaths of innocent victims is the completely abstract composition by Krzysztof Penderecki, *Threnody to the Victims of Hiroshima*. Its sound resources are fifty-two stringed instruments; except for the title, it describes nothing. The reference is entirely to the emotional and imaginative level. Beginning with an eerie squeal in the high string registers, the sounds subside into a furtive scratching that conveys a sense of panic. Knowing the event of the title, we picture an early morning suffused with the element of doom. After a long pause, the music resumes with great sighing sounds at increasingly higher sound levels, finally joining in a steady, penetrating unison. The vague memory of air-raid sirens is aroused. Then a sustained chordal section of great dissonance subsides into a high wail, thrusting in again and tapering to a low hum. Scattered sounds of totally disparate character (much like morning traffic) slowly congeal into a quivering mass of sound, which unexpectedly lapses into total silence. Without warning, the loudest sonic burst of all billows from the strings with enormous density, slowly dissipating into nothingness.

The composer subtitles his work a threnody, that is, a lamentation or dirge. It is a highly expressive work in which emotion and memory are the subjects. Each separate segment forms a framework of feeling that symbolizes the spectrum of human reactions from terror to despair. There is no obvious sequence; the listener is attending to a selection of events happening all at once, as they might be remembered in an actual situation. The composer dissects the terrible moment when the atomic bomb fell just as a filmmaker might with stop-motion photography. At last, when the full range of anguish has been explored, the consummating sound of the bomb wipes out all consciousness.

Seemingly helpless people caught between marauding armies do not always accept their role without a struggle. In the case of the inhabitants of Guernica and Hiroshima, no defense was possible. With the Jews of Warsaw, their retaliation was magnificent, but doomed to failure. In the case of the Russians of Leningrad, however, the resistance movement was a resounding success. Aided by the coming of winter and the overextension of Nazi supply lines, a motley army of Russian civilians and a few military units stopped the Nazi drive and saved the city. This unexpected and terribly costly victory was one of the truly magnificent events of the whole sad Second World War. Dimitri Shostakovich, even then a well-known composer, was actually in the city during a great part of the siege and wrote his Seventh Symphony as a memorial to the heroism he witnessed. The subsequent performances of the work throughout Russia (sometimes in theaters during bombing raids) and its being smuggled into America added a touch of high adventure. Thus, like the Sibelius composition *Finlandia*, Shostakovich's *Leningrad Symphony* became a valued part of the Allied war effort.

It is a work of vast length and complexity, though it is not descriptive to any extent. The composer disavowed realistic portrayal, stating that he wished to represent the spirit and essence of events. The first movement suggests the peaceful, pleasant way of Russian life being broken by the threat of war. It begins with an assertive, marchlike melody. There follows a long section of high lyricism, as leisurely as a landscape painting. The solo flute lends a sweet, fragile effect, and many of the tunes are reminiscent of folk songs. The rattle of snare drums introduces the theme of war, couched in a rather powerful march tune. After a long swell of volume and intensity, the French horn passages and the sliding string chords evoke the wail of air raid sirens. This aggressive section runs into a rhapsodic melody that compresses all sense of grief into one huge outcry. The energy collapses into a hauntingly sad retrospection of the quiet introductory theme.

In the second movement the composer stated that he was trying to express the memory of happy times and the present melancholy. True to the dance origin of one of the symphonic movements, it contains a series of ingratiating tunes and rhythms from folk sources. Toward the middle of the movement the variety of mixtures resembles a lively, colorful folk festival. The movement proceeds as the composer indicated, however, reverting to a wistful, pensive tune and slow tempo. The melancholy of the present sweeps over the joyous past.

The third movement was intended to express love of life and the beauty of the Russian countryside. It begins with high string tones in a free lyricism with little sense of rhythmic pulse. One flute takes up a soliloquy and is joined by a second. The connotations are sweet and joyous, quickening to a dance-like section reminiscent of the second movement. Into this happy mixture drops the snare drum, recalling the war theme of the first movement. The orchestra responds with rich, rhapsodic melody and sorrowful chordal blocks of sound. The flute soliloquy returns, now grown both dissonant and forlorn.

The last movement the composer intended as the emotional culmination of the tragic first movement. He describes its content as the anguish of struggle and approaching victory. The movement begins in a manner even more bleak than the end of the third movement. Soon a stirring, jagged rhythm begins to work its way through various sections of the orchestra. Its energy increases to a bombastic level, melting into an expansive hymn. Unlike all the other movements, this one ends with rousing brass chords, pulsations of drums, and a tremendous surge of energy. Little wonder the Russians, knowing the events referred to, received the music as a personal challenge to sacrifice with high hopes of victory.

The War Machine

During the Revolutionary War twelve hundred American soldiers launched an assault on the fortress at Stony Point on the Hudson. Arthur Guiterman perpetuates the memory of the ensuing events:

> Little they tarried for British might!
> Lightly they recked of the Tory jeers!
> Laughing, they swarmed to the craggy height,
> Steel to the steel of the Grenadiers!
>
> Storm King and Dunderberg! wake once more
> Sentinel giants of freedom's throne,
> Massive and proud! to the Eastern shore
> Bellow the watchword: "The fort's our own!"
> Echo our cheers for the men of old!
> Shout for the hero who led his band
> Braving the death that his heart foretold
> Over the parapet, "spear in hand!"[21]

In 1939 Stephen Spender considered the collective mass of fighting men from quite a different perspective:

> Deep in the winter plain, two armies
> Dig their machinery, to destroy each other.
> Men freeze and hunger. No one is given leave
> On either side, except the dead, and wounded.
> These have their leave; while new battalions wait
> On time at last to bring them violent peace.
> . . . .
> From their dumb harvest all would flee, except
> For discipline drilled once in an iron school
> Which holds them at the point of the revolver.
> Yet when they sleep, the images of home
> Ride wishing horses of escape
> Which herd the plain in a mass unspoken poem.
>
> Finally, they cease to hate: for although hate
> Bursts from the air and whips the earth with hail
> Or shoots it up in fountains to marvel at,
> And although hundreds fall, who can connect
> The inexhaustible anger of the guns
> With the dumb patience of these tormented animals?[22]

Why is there such a dichotomous vision about the same phenomenon? Is one poet a participant and one a bystander? Is one poem written from the heat of battle, while the other has the perspective of time? Is one the commemoration of a successful campaign, and the other a poetic reflection on a failure?

The answers to such questions, even when known, are hardly conclusive. The differences are to some extent enduring alternatives inherent in the nature of Romantic idealism and exaggerated realism. The first poem centers upon panoramic action in the manner of the film battle epic. The mood is jovial and energetic. There is a clearly defined goal and a relatively swift culmination to the battle. The commander is mortally wounded, but the poem is allusive about this fact. Emphasis falls upon mass activity and high spirits. The second poem shows the other side of war; it could well be a description of Valley Forge. The collective mentality and the oppressive weather are the focal points. Thre is no stated goal, no action, and no purpose to the unrelenting oppression they endure. Which is the true picture of the war machine? Probably both perspectives would be needed to approximate the truth.

Old wars are not always remembered glamorously and recent wars disparagingly. Some images, in fact, recur through the centuries as though they were permanently engraved upon the human brain. In the *Iliad* Homer describes the vast army of the Achaians encamped on the plain before Troy:

> Proud and hearty they spent that night on the battlefield, with watchfires burning all around: fires as many between the ships and the river Scamandros, as the stars in heaven that shine conspicuous round the shining moon, when no wind blows, and all the peaks and headlands and mountain glades are clear to view; a strip is peeled away down through the mists of the infinite heaven, and all stars are seen, so that the shepherd is glad at heart. So ten thousand fires burnt upon the plain, and beside each sat fifty men in the light of the blazing fire. The horses stood by their cars, champing white barley and gram, and waiting for Dawn upon her glorious throne.[23]

Several thousand years later Walt Whitman beheld a similar moment in the life of the army in his poem "Bivouac on a Mountain Side:"

> I see before me now a traveling army halting,
> Below a fertile valley spread, with barns and the orchards of
>   summer,
> Behind, the terraced sides of a mountain, abrupt, in places
>   rising high,
> Broken, with rocks, with clinging cedars, with tall shapes
>   dingily seen,
> The numerous camp-fires scatter'd near and far, some away up
>   on the mountain,

The shadowy forms of men and horses, looming, largesized,
   flickering,
And over all the sky—the sky! far, far out of reach, studded,
   breaking out, the eternal stars.[24]

The war machine accumulates a remarkably similar core of
human situations throughout time. There are extremes of emotion, from exultation to dejection. Always there are the elemental rhythms of sleeping, eating, moving, and resting. The
clothing and weaponry change; human needs and feelings endure.

One of the earliest complex and meticulously detailed records of the deployment of armed forces is found on the long,
winding frieze of the *Column of Trajan* in Rome. The bottom
section is Trajan's tomb and the top his commemorative statue.
In between is the lengthy carved scroll that details his military
exploits against the Dacians; he appears seventy times in various directorial roles. Details of tactics, transportation, military
machines, building techniques, and even food acquisition and
distribution are meticulously portrayed. In this massive frieze
the oranism that is this fighting unit lives and moves in large
multiples. The design is in terms of collectives, with individuals sometimes only raised dots of stone among many other
such dots. Yet in some sections individuals are delineated in
minute detail down to their very musculature. The work is a
composite exposition of all that has been written about the
Roman military establishment. We see it as a privileged observer poised outside the drama of its internal dynamics and
historical accomplishments.

Yet another panoramic view of armies in conflict is the
grandiose sixteenth-century painting by Albrecht Altdorfer,
The Battle of Alexander. Commissioned by William IV, duke of
Bavaria, the work portrays the climactic battle in which Alexander the Great vanquished Darius of Persia. Disregarding the
actual, known physical details of the battle as told by the Roman historian Quintus Curtius, Altdorfer chose to emphasize
the grandeur and glory of this confrontation. As liberators of
the world, the Greek soldiers are poised, figuratively speaking,
at the threshold of the mysterious East. Altdorfer suggests a
cosmic significance to this event. With uncompromising realism of style the painter has spread the battle between the sea
and mountains, the setting sun (of the East) on the right, and
the rising moon (of the West) on the left. Color and movement
are the central emphasis; pain and suffering are all but unmen-

Fig. 19 Roman. ***Column of Trajan.*** A.D. 106–113. Marble. Height of relief band ca. 50″. *Photograph courtesy of EPA.*

Fig. 20 Albrecht Altdorfer. ***The Battle of Alexander.*** 1529. Oil on panel, 62 ×
47". Altepinakothek, Munich. *Photograph courtesy of Scala / EPA.*

tionable. Clothed in the military garb of the painter's own era, the armies of East and West clash on the outskirts of a Medieval town. The scene rises clean and shining, the horses and their riders resembling entrants in a Medieval pageant. During these last moments of daylight the sun touches banners and rooftops, plunging other parts of the scene into dramatic gloom. The great lakes and the blue mountains lean outward toward the ends of the earth. In the antlike activities of the human scale the turn of fortune on that day is destined, as the suspended sign indicates, to change even the history of the land. To be part of this, the viewer feels, is to participate in something more memorable than a single life; it is to belong to the course of fate. Should Homer have painted rather than written, this would have been his vision.

Many views of military confrontation are less glamorous. A downright cynical one is *The Eternal City*, by Peter Blume. Stylistically, it is a combination of realism and satire. The large green object is a caricature of Mussolini, dictator of Italy under the Fascist regime. The other major image in the painting is that of ruins. Beneath the bobbying head of Mussolini in the catacomblike basement, Italian citizens hover fearfully. Broken statues, remnants of the collapsed Roman Empire, lie strewn about. In the background black-shirted Nazi soldiers busily round up helpless people in the ruins of the forum. Religion, represented by the emaciated saintly image in its lighted cavern, is helplessly bound to its place. In this grim vision the military machine is turned upon the people of its own land in one of the many purges so tragically common to this century.

The large, conglomerated fighting force is a composite of intricate subrelationships, rivalries, and dependencies. Such successful productions as the television series *M.A.S.H.* are based upon these more comprehensible asides to the grand design. The opera *Wozzeck*, by Alban Berg, adopts just such a framework, and the lives revealed are gloomy indeed. During the period of World War I when he worked for the War Ministry in Austria, Berg came across a play written by George Buchner in 1879. Besides being true to military life, the play was in an expressionist style only then coming into popularity. Its highly subjective frame of reference was well suited to the musical mannerisms Berg had been developing, especially his instrumental writing devoid of tonal center and vocal writing that included approximation of speech tones. Berg spent the war

Fig. 21 Peter Blume. *The Eternal City.* 1937. Oil on composition board, 34 × 47⅞". Collection, The Museum of Modern Art, New York; Mrs. Simon Guggenheim Fund.

years completing a suitable libretto, and wrote the music once the war ended.

The mood of the resulting opera is that of a nightmare endured by one helpless individual caught inside a destructive military system. The agony of the hero, Wozzeck, and the means he chooses to free himself from it lead to tragedy. The opera was not to the taste of the public of that era. Performances between 1925 and 1930 caused such an uproar that in some cases the work was withdrawn from the repertoire. Not until after World War II had the reality of the situation and the innovations of Berg's musical style become familiar enough for audiences to participate in this tale of the lonely individual trapped in the oppressive system.

Wozzeck is a common soldier whose life is pulled apart by conflict between his personal life and the military establishment. Act 1, Scene 4, provides the clues to his peculiar behavior. He is becoming irrational and delusionary because of food deprivation experiments performed by the military doctor.

Wozzeck feels compelled to submit to the regimen in order to earn enough money to feed his child and his common-law wife, Marie. Wozzeck's increasing debilitation is proving the doctor's theories, and he is ecstatic at the thought of the fame he will gain by this experiment. To this scene, an extended duet between Wozzeck and the doctor, the orchestra adds infinite ranges of coloration from cymbal rolls to the merest wisps of melody. Tiny details punctuate the text, such as the xylophone tones to the doctor's emphatic "Wozzeck," or the sliding string chords that portray Wozzeck's mental state.

In the ensuing scenes Marie succumbs to the colorful, adventurous aspect of military life in the person of the Drum Major. Wozzeck comes to bring her money and sees the gold earrings the Drum Major has given her. Their poverty is the significant fact of their existence. The military maintains Wozzeck at the level of a serf; his economic need forces him to undertake secondary employment for the personal benefit of officers. Thus the military system is shown to have the same inescapable inequities, in a more concentrated manner, as society at large.

Wozzeck's continued physical deterioration, along with several incidents involving Marie and the Drum Major, drive him to the point of desperation. In Act 3, Scene 2, Marie is walking home through the woods, and Wozzeck follows to speak with her. The orchestra underscores the painful scene with a kaleidescope of groans, whispers, and shudders. Wozzeck sings nostalgically of the past until the moonrise, ascending tonally through the orchestra, stimulates him to a vision of blood. He stabs Marie, to the dramatic pulse of a kettledrum and the swelling volume of a single unison pitch.

After a scene in a tavern, Wozzeck returns to the woods to search for the murder weapon, and drowns trying to wash away the blood. The captain and doctor overhear the death struggle and hurry away without investigating. An array of slithering string melodies covers Wozzeck's body with the lake water. Such is the fate of the individual in the gigantic system beyond public scrutiny. The whole panorama, as Altdorfer presents it, is generally more appealing than the small unit of the specific participant.

Prokofiev's *War and Peace*, like the famous Tolstoy novel upon which it is based, gives some perspective on both the war machine as a whole and the vivid individuals of which it is composed. In his diary Prokofiev reports being enthralled by his first reading of the Tolstoy work in 1905. It was not until thirty-six years later, in 1941, that the Second World War turned his thoughts again to such serious topics. Because he was not acceptable for military service, the composer was determined to create the opera as a patriotic contribution. The struggle against Napoleon in the novel did, indeed, have a parallel in the more contemporary struggle against the Nazis. The Committee on the Arts especially encouraged him to include patriotic songs and scenes of mass cooperation. His final version has three musical elements: the symphonic sound, which carries the emotional understructure and continuity; tuneful choral and solo singing; and speechlike narrative based entirely on Tolstoy's prose. Polonaises, mazurkas, and military marches give a distinctive flavor of the era.

The love story of Natasha and Andrei rests uneasily amid all the patriotism; it is delegated almost entirely to the first act, recurring toward the end in Andrei's highly effective death scene. Marshall Koutouzov, the Russian militarist, and his counterpart, Napoleon, are the heroes of the second part of the opera. Scene 7 opens on the Battle of Borodino, which in actuality was the beginning of Napoleon's eclipse. While there is much attention to the movement of mass events, there is an effective balance of individual relationships. Andrei enters, full of enthusiastic plans for a new strategy and asking for only a few hundred men to lead. In contrast, survivors from Smolensk shamble in, lamenting the destruction they have witnessed. In a vigorous choral finale the assembled defenders of Borodino assert their fearlessness, vowing to drive the French from their land.

While the rank and file work optimistically at the battlements, the sung conversations between the officers reveal much skepticism. Even Andrei, overcome with apprehension, sings pensively that there are no rules to guide them except killing or being killed. Koutouzov, the realist, shrewdly surmises that Napoleon's supply lines are strained to the breaking. He counsels in a slowly paced bass aria that restraint is the only recourse until time takes its toll.

Though a discussion of strategy seems like the least possible basis for operatic writing, the music makes it live. Magnificent Russian male choruses create the sense of cumulative energy and assertion. There are melodies of intense dramatic sweep and a colorful parade of military units in review, complete with brass bands. A sudden, dramatic surprise ends the scene as several shots are heard offstage. The music grows solemn, and Andrei declares pensively, "Here it is."

Scene 8 opens with Napoleon watching the battle from a hillside and envisioning his coming conquest of Moscow. The orchestra carries the clamor of war as an undercurrent throughout most of the scene. Over this sonic ground Napoleon and his aides consult in dramatic entrances and exits. There are decision, recall, and indecision. The unsettled state of Napoleon's mind is noticed by his commanders and lieutenants. He wavers from visions of the future to the obvious difficulties of the present conflict. There are not enough people or resources, and this troublesome fact finally dominates the anguished discussions. In a symbolic conclusion a cannon ball falls at Napoleon's feet; an aide shouts in horror as it rolls aside.

In Scene 9 Koutouzov is holding a parallel council with his aides to the tune of a deep, heavy march. They must decide whether to hold on regardless of casualties or abandon their hopes to save Moscow and surrender Borodino. In a highly emotional melodic section Koutouzov imagines the great capital city he loves. As the melody soars to a climax, the commander decides that he must defend it regardless of the cost.

The concluding scene of the opera is the finale of the war. From a noisy introduction with sliding strings and rolling drums the music subsides to a deathly calm, transiting from the battle to its aftermath. Koutouzov and his soldiers enter, slowly making their way toward the ruins of Smolensk. In a somber aria, Koutouzov thanks them for their faith and courage. The concluding chorus rises like a hymn with rich, resonant solemnity: "We have shed our blood that the land may live. Hail to all who serve her well."

Four Novels of War and Death

One of the first, and some critics believe still the best, American war novel is Steven Crane's *The Red Badge of Courage*. Its setting is the Civil War, and its theme is the coming of age of Henry Wilson, known to the reader as "the youth." Despite the author's insistence upon the reality of experience as the only basis for literary endeavor, the novel is suffused with many idealistic qualities. For the youth the war has no philosophical or strategic dimension and is not identified in his mind with political principles or historic movements. He does identify strongly with symbols of the bond between himself and his comrades, things which serve as omens of life in the presence of death. "Within him, as he hurled himself forward, was born a love, a despairing fondness for this flag which was near him. It was a creation of beauty and invulnerability. It was a goddess, radiant, that bended its form with an imperious gesture to him."[25]

The youth has a highly emotional view of war as "the crash and swing of the great drama," and pictures the conflict as a "state of frenzy," a "sublime recklessness." In this exalted frame of mind he sees soldiers advancing to meet the enemy as a "procession of chosen beings moving as if they marched with weapons of flame and banners of sunlight." War is a pageant of events in which men become capable of profound sacrifices, in which the alternatives are survival or "a tremendous death." In a moment of illusory introspection the youth even considers "the magnificent pathos of his dead body." War is "the red animal, the blood-swollen god."[26]

For Henry Wilson the meaning of war is not tangled with societal implications, but rather involves his personal attainment of manhood. A youth becomes something more in battle, and from this dangerous rite of passage evolves the meaning of his existence. Thus his life is tormented by terrible fears of cowardice on one hand and the uncertainty of death on the other. To know yourself—to know what you will do when confronted by the trauma of conflict—this is the real object of the experience called war. In reflecting upon the infantry action that lies ahead, the youth thinks that he is about to be measured. He conceives of war as "the great trial." He tries to estimate his resolve by comparison with that of his companions, hoping to pry open their fears without revealing too many of his own.

When the intolerable waiting ends and the youth comes under fire, he finds that he can endure as well as his fellow soldiers until he mistakenly retreats and finds himself with the wounded moving back toward Union lines. To his humiliation, he finds himself neither dead nor the possessor of the "red badge of courage," the wound that signifies the combat ritual. He is envious of those who wear their signs of attainment openly, and is strangely cheered when the blow from a rifle butt gashes his head.

The sight of death becomes part of the essential mystery of these painful events, and the youth struggles to read in the eyes of the dead an answer to the question. Death is this question to which the whole vast tapestry of war is a response. Facing death without flinching is the final demonstration of the conquest of the inner life. The youth finds evidence of this truth in the behavior of a once loud and abusive soldier. "There was about him now a fine reliance. He showed a quiet belief in his purposes and his abilities." Henry himself emerges utterly changed because "he had been to touch the great death, and found that, after all, it was but the great death. He was a man."[27]

In the classic of the First World War, *All Quiet on the Western Front,* by Erich Maria Remarque, death in war is neither fulfilling nor justifiable. Henry Wilson never questions the existence of or the reasons for war; the German soldier Paul Baumer skeptically reflects on both issues. Emperors and generals become famous through war, and "there are other people back there that profit by the war, that's certain." The wrong people always seem to end up fighting each other. The French are told to protect their fatherland; the Germans are told to protect theirs. Who is right? muse Paul and his companions. They face endless days of bombardment devoid of the ideal of self-realization, suspecting that they are merely animate stuff to be thrown in the maw of a futile cause.

Like Henry Wilson, Paul and his fellow students joined the army after graduation, inspired by the patriotic fervor of family and teachers, "The iron youth," one teacher calls them, as he plays upon their guilt and the expectations of society. Unlike Henry, the young Germans come from basic training "hard, suspicious, pitiless, vicious, tough—and that was good; for these attributes had been entirely lacking in us." Out of this period of painful harassment arose the fierce comradship that is the only positive factor in the long agony of war.

Death takes on variety and subtle depth in the novel. Strangely enough, the death that proves to be most intolerable is that of wounded horses. "It's unendurable. It is the moaning of the world, it is the martyred creation, wild with anguish, filled with terror, and groaning. We are pale. Detering (a fellow recruit) stands up: "God! For God's sake! Shoot them."[28]

Henry Wilson never confronted the enemy in guises other than gray moving lines or scatterings of helpless dead. Paul shares a foxhole with a French soldier he stabbed by reflex when the latter fell into the pit during a bombardment. Guilt, the fear of discovery and revenge by the French army, and plain curiosity plague his sanity. Looking through the Frenchman's wallet after his lingering death, Paul finds the usual familial mementos and is overcome by a sense of personal responsibility. The young Germans have difficulty thinking of the French or the haggard Russian prisoners as enemies. "A word of command has made these silent figures our enemies; a word of command might transform them into our friends."[28] The only moment of joy and tenderness the comrades share is with a group of French girls. Yet they will return to the trenches and kill whoever is on the opposing side because it is the only way to survive.

The real enemies are not the French but the machines of war. Death comes not in a human shape but in the guise of bombs, bayonets, and gas. Survival consists of taking shelter in every slight depression the earth offers, or even, in one grisly case, the exposed coffins of a graveyard. The enemy is the corpse rat with its dreadful swollen body, making a feast at the table of death. The enemy is that whole class of beings called officers, who seem to conduct the grim charade of war for the sake of their own advancement. This appraisal includes the medical officers who, it is suspected, use the bodies of recruits for surgical experiments.

War is the scene of terror and death, not the arena for some personal rite of passage. One does not become a man, but merely a live, dead, or hopelessly mangled thing. Paul does not experience Henry Wilson's acquisition of calm purposiveness. He discovers that combat "fills us with ferocity, turning us into thugs, into murderers, into God only knows what devils." It is a sudden transformation. "We march up, moody or goodtempered soldiers—we reach the zone where the front begins and become on the instant human animals."[29]

So massive is the toll among the German soldiers that by the middle of the novel only 32 of the original 150 members of Second Company remain alive. Kemmerich is the first to die, slowly expiring in the makeshift front-line hospital. His comrades are torn between denying his impending death and coveting his good boots. Paul dreads visiting Kemmerich's mother, because there is no consolation for such a death, and one is forced to lie about its nature. Inexplicably, Kat dies from an errant shot as Paul is carrying him to the hospital tent. And finally, Paul suffers the most ironic death of all at the very end of the war when no military action is underway.

What determines who shall live and who shall die? It is a question that troubles the young soldiers, and to their horror, there is no reasonable basis for prediction. "In a bomb-proof dugout I may be smashed to atoms and in the open may survive ten hours' bombardment unscathed." When they hear a shot, all they can do is duck; they cannot know where it will land. It is this antic sense of chance that eventually makes them indifferent. If Kemmerich's legs had been six inches to the right, everything would be changed. They come to view war as a cause of death much the same as cancer or tuberculosis, except that on the battlefield death is more frequent and more terrible. Otherwise some vast, utterly neutral web of circumstance weaves its irreversible pattern of torment without selectivity, without design.

In the largest sense *All Quiet on the Western Front* is a memorial to an entire generation. "We stood on the threshold of life," Paul muses. "We had as yet taken no root. The war swept us away." Their knowledge of life has been limited to death. They wonder what might become of them afterward. In his foreword to the novel Remarque comments upon this larger death. The book, he asserts, "will try simply to tell of a generation of men who, even though they may have escaped its shells, were destroyed by the war."[30]

The Naked and the Dead, by Norman Mailer, is a composite portrait of World War II, using as a metaphor the invasion of Anopopei, a fictitious Japanese-held island. It is about the adventures of the 460th Infantry Regiment and characters as different as Julio Martinez, reared on Mexican beans and discrimination, and Sam Croft, reared on hunting, horsebreaking, and whoring. It exudes the same waiting, carping, doubting, and dark premonition as all war novels. However, it also portrays the resistence of the earth itself—dense jungle, oppressive heat, unfamiliar sound, torrential rains—and the first brutal contact of Americans with an utterly alien terrain and enemy.

The novel essays the endless jockeying for position among officers, their egotistical demands, and their petty forms of revenge. The work coldly assesses the strong class divisions among soldiers. The General believes war is won by adequate men and materials. However, the important thing is to have fighting soldiers derived from poor standards of living who turn their hatred of more privileged officers into action against the targeted enemy. Without apology he asserts that the army runs on injustice and fear. Goldstein discovers another class division, an anti-Jewish bias as pervasive as among the German enemy. The dozens of characters that populate this sprawling novel are present in the full context of their lives. We learn not only what they are now, but what they were before the war and how they became as we find them. The novel wanders over past and present, existence and memory, the whole configuration of persons sharing the shapeless tangle of war.

In the beginning death is casually accepted by these soldiers as something large and meaningless. Dead men simply meld into the status of all those remembered beings who are absent for any reason. The death of Hennessey, someone known and close, changes this attitude. Martinez realizes that "once he could have looked ahead at war with repugnance for the toil and misery of it, and a dour acceptance of the deaths that would occur. But now the idea of death was fresh and terrifying again."[31]

Gallagher's wife, Mary, dies in childbirth, and he continues to receive letters mailed weeks before like ghostly messages from the tomb. In his misery he "begins to think of the dead soldiers in the draw, only his mind pictures Mary consecutively in each of the postures their bodies had assumed." Despite these moments of singular personal loss, death reduces each of them to insignificance. One soldier complains about dying in the hospital, "What the hell's another guy to the Army? Those quacks get their orders to be sonsofbitches from the top."[32]

The novel offers verbal snapshots of the degradation of death. There are bodies "swollen to dimensions of very obese men; they have turned green and purple and the maggots festered in their wounds and covered their feet." And along with the physical distortions of death, there is the undisguised pleasure of killing. Croft "hungered for the fast taut pulse he would feel in his throat after he killed a man." "On impulse Croft fired a burst into him, and felt a twitch of pleasure as he saw the body quiver." In response to his sudden physiological tides, Croft kills an unarmed Japanese prisoner and remarks, "Goddam, that Jap sure died happy." In the final mopping-up operation when the island is taken, "the killing lost all dimension, bothered the men far less than discovering some ants in their bedding."[33]

The dark underside of war surfaces predictably in the problem of fate, in the puzzle about what determines life or death. Paul and his German companions in the trenches of World War I decided it was pure chance, as purposeless as a cast of dice. The men of the 460th Infantry Regiment have more varied reactions. Croft always seems to see some order in death—some purposive, malevolent intent. Whenever someone from his company is killed, he somehow feels a sense of justice in it. What bothers him is the possibility that this whole intricate system might even now be contemplating his fate. Roth, on the other hand, interprets matters differently: "It was so easy for a man to be killed; what he couldn't shake was his surprise." Red was shocked by his realization that man is a very fragile thing. "He looked at the corpse and didn't look, thought of nothing, and found his mind churning with the physical knowledge of life and death and his own vulnerability." The Americans are fascinated to discover in the diary of a dead Japanese major the same musings about ultimate purposes. He writes: "I am going to die. I am born, I am dead. I ask myself—why? What is the meaning?"[34]

They never discover any meaning larger than survival. The novel leaves them wondering what each will do when he returns home. The war goes on; death awaits in the unfolding of the distant miles. They have played their parts blindly as anonymous figures in a dark design of blood and mystery.

Captain Yossarian, the hero of *Catch-22*, by Joseph Heller, is a participant in the same war, but he is determined not to remain anonymous. In fact, after fifty missions he decides unilaterally that he has had enough! In this novel we have come many light years from the consciousness of Henry Wilson, who worries that he may not be able to measure up to the demands placed upon him by significant events, to the consciousness of Yossarian, who worries about preserving his life in the face of ridiculous and unjustifiable events. Although written in 1955, the book eloquently forecasts the mood of Americans through the turbulent sixties—a composite of radical individualism and extreme distrust of the policies of all large, complex organizations. Clevinger verbalizes the truism that must be accepted in order to conduct any war: " . . . it's not for us to determine what targets must be destroyed or who's to destroy them, or who gets killed doing it. We have no right to question." Yossarian counters: "Do you really mean that it's not my business how or why I get killed and that it is Colonel Cathcart's?" When Clevinger complains that such talk only gives aid and comfort to the enemy, Yossarian just as positively defines the enemy as "anybody who's going to get you killed, no matter which sides he's on."[35]

To his credit, Yossarian is not a recent recruit from bombardier training who arrives at the staging area on the imaginary island of Pianosa, takes a close look, and decides war is not for him. He has completed all the missions needed for rotation, but the number keeps increasing. The reason for this phenomenon is that Colonel Cathcart aspires to the rank of General and is convinced that only some dramatic gesture, such as having his men fly more missions than those of any other commander, will sufficiently distinguish him from the mob of other aspirants. Yossarian correctly perceives a bombing mission as a situation highly conducive to dying, and goes to great lengths to extricate himself and his comrades from that possibility. His acts include moving the bombing line on the official map and giving the whole camp diarrhea.

In a style so superficially facile as to belie serious content, Heller etches a portrait of men caught in an irrational context where events have slipped from human control and are directed by a self-contradictory system, of which "catch 22" is the symbol. As an example, concern for personal safety in a dangerous situation is the act of a sane mind. Therefore, anyone who asks to be grounded is sane. If a person is insane and flies missions, he doesn't have to. Or in another version: regulations specify that a person may be rotated after forty missions. Regulations also state that every order from a superior officer must be obeyed. What if the superior officer institutes a higher number of missions? The message of *Catch-22* is that war is a preposterous series of pseudo-heroic posturings in which the unwary individual may be annihilated.

The novel concerns death in a multitude of forms, from the bitterly tragic to the supremely ironic. Yossarian is vividly conscious of the threat of death, although it is from a source not recognized in the previous novels. Yossarian never comes within sight of the people he is assigned to kill. They are miles away behind the pinpoints of light in distantly seen cities. He kills merely by releasing a mechanism that contains bombs; he chooses not to see them to their destination. Yet even in this antiseptic situation Yossarian is terribly afraid "because strangers he didn't know shot at him with cannons every time he flew up into the air to drop bombs on them, and it wasn't funny at all."[36] Moreover, the ocean seen from his plane could swallow him instantly, disgorging his bloated body on some lonely beach weeks later.

To Yossarian death is not an alternative, not after the deaths he has witnessed. There was Kid Sampson, the ill-fated surfer who topped the wave just as McWatt swooped in for a low pass over the beach. Sampson was cut in half, and McWatt, horrified at his carelessness or terrified at what punishment might await, crashed his plane into a mountain. Idiot deaths they were, incidents without nobility or sense. To Yossarian the most terrible death was that of Snowden on the Avignon mission. "Yossarian climbed down the few steps of his plane naked, in a state of shock, with Snowden smeared abundantly all over his bare heels and toes, knees, arms, and fingers, and pointed inside wordlessly toward where the young radio-gunner lay freezing to death on the floor."[37] He remained naked for weeks out of a sense of grief and protest until the day General Dreedle stepped up to pin a medal on him and found him standing quietly in formation without a stitch of clothing.

Death can come almost as tragically when people simply become lost in the system. Doc Daneeka was scheduled to be in the plane with McWatt, and since he did not parachute out, was considered dead. He had changed his mind and did not take the flight, but the War Department is only interested in what the paperwork says. Mrs. Daneeka is notified of her husband's death, collects from various insurance policies, and attracts a group of male admirers. She and the children move out of the state, leaving Doc Daneeka without family, retirement pay, or job. He becomes a nonperson.

Yossarian muses listlessly over the meaning of all this death. He searches the skyline, thinking of Clevinger and Orr and wondering how they could just vanish. He goes to sleep counting the images of all the people he has ever known that are now dead. He senses an endless procession of death and dying. "Death was irreversible, he suspected, and he began to think he was going to lose."

To Yossarian not dying is the key to everything. An old Italian gentleman states his philosophy succinctly: "Italian soldiers are not dying anymore. But American and German soldiers are. I call that doing extremely well." The point is to keep from dying as long as you can. But why, if everyone has to die anyway? The trick, Yossarian would reply, is not to think about that. After all, as a subversive corporal once asked. "Who is Spain?" "Why is Hitler?" "When is right?" And Yossarian concludes, "Where are the Snowdens of yesteryear?"[38]

4

Voluntary Death

Dear Father, Mother, Brothers, and Sister;

I trust that this spring finds you all in fine health. I have never felt better, and am now standing by ready for action. . . .

Words cannot express my gratitude to the loving parents who reared and tended me to manhood that I might in some small manner reciprocate the grace which His Imperial Majesty has bestowed upon us.

Please watch for the results of my meager effort. If they prove good, think kindly of me and consider it my good fortune to have done something that may be praiseworthy. Most important of all, do not weep for me. Though my body departs, I will return home in spirit and remain with you forever. My thoughts and best regards are with you, our friends and neighbors. In concluding this letter, I pray for the well-being of my dear family.

Dear Father,

As death approaches, my only regret is that I have never been able to do anything good for you in my life. . . . On learning that my time had come I closed my eyes and saw visions of your face, mother's grandmother's and the faces of my close friends. It was bracing and heartening to realize that each of you wants me to be brave. . . . (Our) way of life is indeed beautiful, and I am proud of it, as I am of (our) history and mythology which reflect the purity of our ancestors and their belief in the past—whether width:1015px; height:1571px;

or not those beliefs are true. That way of life is the product of all the best things which our ancestors have handed down to us. . . . It is an honor to be able to give my life for the defense of these beautiful and lofty things.[1]

The idealistic fervor and selfless acceptance of death that suffuse the sections of two letters quoted above are typical of the personal philosophies of Japanese kamikaze pilots who so devastated American ships during World War II. The two ensigns who wrote these letters would have included fingernail clippings and a lock of hair in the envelope. They would have distributed their money and personal effects to comrades in the corps and waved bravely to those gathered to watch their takeoff. Such men were serious in their feelings of personal gratitude and obligation, in response to which their deaths seemed entirely appropriate. Though one might quibble endlessly about the political reality of such sacrifices, or enveigh against ambition in high places that would necessitate such loss of life, the young men themselves exhibit an abundance of the New Testament "greater love" for others that allowed them to volunteer their lives.

Auden reminds us in his poem "Musée des Beaux Arts" that, although there are "children who did not specially want it to happen," there are also the aged, "reverently, passionately waiting for the miraculous birth." Death is not always unexpected, unwanted, dreaded, or ignored. At times it is welcomed as the fulfillment, or perhaps the antidote, to life. There is a memorable speech to this effect uttered by an old man who is accosted by three young vagrants spoiling for a fight in Chaucer's "The Pardoner's Tale." To the query, "Why have you lived so long and grown so old?" the elderly man replies:

Because I cannot find a man in any city or any village, though I walked to India, who wishes to change his youth for my age. And therefore I must continue to have my age for as long a time as it is God's will. Alas, not even death will take my life. And so I walk about like a restless prisoner and knock both early and late with my stick upon the earth, which is my mother's door, saying, "Dear mother, let me in; look how I shrink, flesh, skin, and blood! Alas, when shall my bones find rest? Mother, I will trade my strong-box, which for so long has been my bedroom, for a hair shirt to wrap myself in!" Yet she will not do me that favor, and my face is therefore pale and wrinkled.[2]

The same combination of age, fulfillment, and longing appears in the story of Simeon in the second chapter of Luke. A devout man who had hoped for a messiah to deliver Israel, Simeon received a profound intuition that he would not die until his hopes were fulfilled. He was in the temple when the infant Jesus was first brought to be presented to the authorities. Simeon took the child in his arms and uttered that prayer which has become the "Nunc Dimittis" concluding Christian worship:

> Lord, now lettest thou thy servant depart in peace, according to thy word: For mine eyes have seen thy salvation, which thou hast prepared before the face of all people; a light to lighten the Gentiles, and the glory of thy people Israel.

The hymnody of the Christian Church abounds with longing for life's end, usually accompanied by hopeful references to some better alternatives. "Jerusalem, my happy home, when shall I come to thee?" is typical. Even devoid of transcendent reference, death can be the object of longing, as in Christóbal de Castillejo's poem:

> Some day, some day
> O troubled breast,
> Shalt thou find rest.
> If love in thee
> to grief give birth
> Six feet of earth
> Can more than he;
> There calm and free
> And unoppressed
> Shall thou find rest.
> The unattained
> In life at last,
> When life is passed
> Shall all be gained;
> And no more pained,
> No more distressed,
> Shalt thou find rest.[3]

Apart from such generalized expressions of weariness, there are renunciations of life that exemplify the heroic, sacrificial quality of kamikaze pilots. Death is deliberately chosen for the benefit of others. One memorable example is that of Lawrence Oates, a member of Robert Scott's expeditionary forces that reached the South Pole in 1912. Harsh weather descended on the return trip, and the necessarily lengthened journey resulted in illness, lack of food, and frostbite. Oates became a partial cripple and, believing that he would hinder the group's struggle for survival, walked out into the storm to disappear forever.

The mythology of tribal peoples includes such tales of heroic sacrifice. In his short story "Emperor of the Sea," Nigerian writer Obi Egbuna recounts the legend of Iza and Izadi. Two beautiful children of a destitute widow, they aroused the envy of the emperor, who thought of a scheme to get rid of them. He wined and dined them until they made rash vows that the Emperor proceeded to carry out. Izadi declared that for another such dinner she would gladly give her head to the axeman. The emperor soon saw that she got her wish. Iza vowed that for one night in bed with the princess he would willingly surrender his head. Having lost her daughter, the mother consulted with the most famous medicine man in the area, who reported that he could save the son. As in most African tales, there is a catch. The required magic potion must include one ingredient from the mother's head; to obtain it she must sacrifice her life. Though the son is outraged at the idea, the mother reasons that she will die of sorrow anyway if he is killed, and her sacrifice will insure one survivor. She says pointedly, "My life has become our suicide; my death your only hope." She plunges a knife into her heart; the son is saved and eventually frees the people from the oppressive emperor. The moral is drawn at the end of the tale that loving self-sacrifice is the most potent human force for good.

Quite a different, even a pathetic, effect is intended by Thomas Hardy in his tale of self-sacrifice in *Jude the Obscure*. Jude's wife, Sue, confesses to their oldest child that there will soon be a fourth born into their poverty-stricken family. Distressed, the boy replies:

> However could you, mother, be so wicked and cruel as this, when you needn't have done it till we was better off, and father well. To bring us all into more trouble! No room for us, and father forced to go away, and we turned out tomorrow; and yet

you be going to have another of us soon! 'Tis done o'purpose! 'Tis—'Tis![4]

Sue manages to quiet him and put the children to sleep for the night. She wakes early, goes to find her husband, and returns with breakfast. Jude and his wife open the door to the small room where the children are sleeping and find a pitiful scene.

> At the back of the door were fixed two hooks for hanging garments, and from these the forms of the two youngest children were suspended, by a piece of box-cord round each of their little necks, while from a nail a few yards off the body of little Jude was hanging in a similar manner. An overturned chair was near the elder boy, and his glazed eyes were slanted into the room; but those of the girl and the baby boy were closed. . . . Moreover, a piece of paper was found upon the floor, on which was written, in the boy's hand, with the bit of lead pencil that he carried: "Done because we are too menny."[5]

Surely, the reader thinks, such a sacrifice was unnecessary. They would have found some way to cope with their situation. The anger of little Jude and the possibly vengeful motive for these deaths is unsettling. But with the horror and regret there is also an element of admiration at the cool analysis the boy made of his situation and the courage required by his solution.

A similar poignant, but more clearly heroic, episode is recorded in Rodin's sculpture *The Burghers of Calais*. Created by the sculptor in 1886 as a commission from the City of Calais, France, the work memorializes the self-sacrifice of six men centuries before, when the city was besieged by the English King Edward III. According to the chronicles of Froissart, the city was on the verge of starvation when the king offered to compromise. He would release the city if six of its leading citizens would surrender unconditionally to him to be disposed of as he pleased. They were to leave the city wearing only their shirts and a rope about their necks, bearing the keys of the city and its fortress. The townspeople assembled to consider the offer, and six persons volunteered to be the hostages. They conformed to the king's specifications and were met by him and his executioner. Froissart ends his account of the episode with the intervention of the queen, who asked that their lives be spared. The king, it is said, agreed because his wife was pregnant.

Fig. 22 Auguste Rodin. *The Burghers of Calais.* 1884–95. Bronze, 82½ × 94 × 75″. The Philadelphia Museum of Art; gift of Jules Mastbaum. Photographed by Philadelphia Museum of Art.

Rodin chose to portray the moment of the departure from the city, when both the emotions of the participants and the uncertainty of their situation were greatest. Each one is living his last hour in his own way, resolving to face what may come. The work is full of gestures—resignation, farewell, anguish, determination. One is an old man with loosely hanging arms and dragging gait, bearing an expression of weariness and sorrow. Next to him a younger man carries the city key with an air of anger and defiance, his lips pursed and his hands clenched. A youth looks back wistfully, his face delicately composed as though singing to himself quietly. His brother stands at his side, hands spread in submission and head inclined as though for the executioner. Another man buries his face in his hands to compose himself and be alone briefly. The enigmatic gesture of the man who seems to turn back and walk forward at the same time reveals the inner turmoil of these volunteers. To tear oneself from life, even for a cause so significant, is no easy accomplishment. Rodin has made them ordinary heroes, reflecting their courage as a fundamental characteristic of the human species. He wanted to put the figures in the marketplace where the event began and where viewers could be part of the experience. These are not remarkably noble persons who, like Lawrence Oates, simply vanish without much ado. Nor are they pathetic in the manner of Hardy's hanged children. They are tragically real, and the truth of their situation is a parable for all such human occasions.

Suicide

Whenever Richard Cory went downtown
We people on the pavement looked at him:
He was a gentleman from sole to crown,
Clean favored, and imperially slim.

And he was always quietly arrayed,
And he was always human when he talked;
But still he fluttered pulses when he said,
"Good morning," and he glittered when he walked.

And he was rich—yes, richer than a king—
And admirably schooled in every grace:
In fine, we thought that he was everything
To make us wish that we were in his place.

So on we worked, and waited for the light,
And went without the meat, and cursed the bread;
And Richard Cory, one calm summer night,
Went home and put a bullet through his head.[6]

Sarah: Yes, I left you,
I thought there was a way away . . .
Water under bridges opens
Closing and the companion stars
Still float there afterwards. I thought the door
Opened into closing water.
. . . .
Oh, I never could!
I never could!

Even the forsythia beside the
Stair could stop me.[7]

The reader is stunned at the concluding lines of the first poem. What clue has been missed? Did Richard Cory lose his money? Was a loved one unfaithful? We search through the poem for some hint of the horror that sent Richard Cory to his unexpected death, and find nothing at all. In the same manner we fail to find anything that recalls Sarah from her determination to die as a result of unending tragedy. Why does one person resign life over seemingly nothing while another persists despite everything? The poets hint only that it is something inherent in the people, something beyond external conditions. There is no detectable series of reforms that present themselves as a solution to Richard Cory's blighted existence. Did he simply die of boredom? Sarah has no illusions that her life will be any better. Having lost all her children, her home, and every vestige of material security, she has no hope of realizing any meaningful life. She falls back entirely upon the emotional need she shares with her husband, JB. But she goes on and cannot explain how she is able to do so.

The web of personality and circumstance that eventuates in suicide is endlessly fascinating because there is some capacity for self-destruction within every person. As Camus remarked, "What is called a reason for living is also an excellent reason for dying." We struggle to rationalize the highly publicized suicides of the famous. Sylvia Plath left a long poetic trail of clues to her eventual fate. Her unassuaged grief at her father's death in her childhood is reflected in such poems as "The Bee Meeting," written after she had children. She imagines her hand held to the light with her life falling between the fingers. Her attempted suicide during her college years, as related in *The Bell Jar,* and her later brush with death in a car accident were part of a consistent chain of inner reality. Her poetry functioned partly to dissipate or ward off such suicidal thoughts, but she believed that her life could be verified only through escapes from death. This ritual escape was undertaken at intervals, consciously or unconsciously.

The circumstances of her life wove themselves into an ever-darkening design. She was separated from her husband and left with the responsibility for two young children. The winter was one of the worst on record; she had repeated bouts with influenza. Her poetry focused continually on images of death and calm resignation. At last she engaged a girl to care for the children, arranged breakfast for them, wrote instructions to contact her physician, and placed her head in the gas oven. Was her act a cry for help that fatally misfired, or the culmination of an unquenchable compulsion? Did she initiate this final ritual in hopes that it would free her once again from a deadly mental loop of despair? Speculations are endless and of significance, because it is estimated that at least a thousand persons throughout the world take their lives each day.

The painter Vincent van Gogh left a long, detailed record of his slow drift toward suicide in both pictorial and letter form. A person constantly frustrated by lack of meaningful relationships and professional rewards, Van Gogh came late to painting and created his memorable works in a ten-year period. He was for the most part supported by his brother, an art dealer. Any number of things, including poor nutrition, contributed to his bouts of mental illness and eventual commitment to a sanatorium. Fearing that increasingly severe attacks of depression would rob him of the only source of meaning in his life—his art—Van Gogh shot himself.

His late works reveal a great deal about his mental state. The dismal, threatening sky in *Crows over Cornfield* contrasts to his usual brilliant blue with whirling clouds or stars. Black birds spill out of the background as though pressing in upon the viewer. The corn is brilliantly colored, though it churns uneasily in varied directions. The most disturbing element is the conflict of paths through the pictorial surface. Three deeply rutted roadways lead in different directions without foreseeable destinations. The viewer is confronted with mysterious and unpleasant choices under an oncoming storm. As clearly designed and artistically controlled as Plath's last poems, the painting exhibits none of her calm resolve. It is a declaration of hopelessness.

Death caused by suicide has been regarded by society in markedly varied ways throughout human history. Suicide has been understood as a moral offence, a natural fact, an honorable choice, a crime against property or obligation, and even a spiritual duty. These alternatives do not emerge in some evolutionary sequence, but arise in random order according to the historic precedents and current needs of the group. Eastern attitudes often differ substantially from Western attitudes. The ideas of tribal peoples are sometimes remarkably similar to those of modern bureaucrats. There is, moreover, a constant gravitation between the strength of communal obligation and that of individual conscience, which causes changes in cultural attitudes toward suicide. Even the current tendency to regard suicide as a manifestation of mental illness is not new. As early as the second century A.D. the Mishnah, a collection of rabbinical discussions, directs that when a person of sound mind takes his own life, he shall not be bothered with. A sane man may well choose to take his own life honorably in situations of untenable pain, when otherwise forced to violate Jewish law, or to protect others in time of war. The link between mental state and suicide, then, is recognized very early in history.

Horror of suicide was quick to emerge among our earliest ancestors; tribal societies regarded suicides as spiritually unclean and apt to haunt the living. Bodies of suicides were sometimes mutilated in order to protect the living from their supposed power, or carried far away from the tribe so that their spirits could not find the way back. In his novel *Things Fall Apart,* African writer Chinua Achebe describes the reaction of those who find the body of a suicide hanging from a tree. They send for strangers from another village to take the body down and bury it, explaining:

> We cannot bury him. Only strangers can. We shall pay your men to do it. When he has been buried we will then do our duty by him. We shall make sacrifices to cleanse the desecrated land.[8]

Ancient Greeks were equally contemptuous of those who killed themselves by violent means; their anger was motivated more by the loss of a useful member of the city-state than horror of the deed itself. The same indignities were inflicted upon the bodies of suicides as those reported from more primitive societies. Irresponsible violence was particularly in disfavor. Indeed, self-inflicted death by slow starvation was exempted from punishment by some governments on the ground that it was a calm, reasoned act. Some communities had tribunals to hear the appeals of anyone who contemplated suicide; those which agreed with the reasons sometimes supplied the dose of poison. Suicide because of disgrace or loss of dignity was as well appreciated among the Greeks as among traditional Oriental cultures. The most poignant suicide in

Greek drama arises because of just such a case. Its victim and perpetrator is Jocasta, the wife and mother of Oedipus. She understands before he does the terrible secret of their unsuspected relationship and warns him to cease his quest for additional information. But Oedipus refuses her advice and she departs, vowing to tell him nothing more forever. We do not witness her suicide but are told of it through a messenger's anguished description:

> But still, so far as I have memory you shall learn the sufferings of that wretched woman: How she passed on through the door enraged and rushed straight forward to her nuptial bed, clutching her hair's ends with both her hands. Once inside the doors she shut herself in and called on Laius, who has long been dead, having rememberance of their seed of old by which he died himself and left her a mother to bear an evil brood to his own son. She moaned the bed on which by double curse she bore husband to husband, child to child.

When Oedipus bursts in upon the scene, the messenger with him remembers that "there we beheld his wife hung by her neck from twisted cords, swinging to and fro."[9]

The cause of this suicide is rooted in family history and springs from a curse by the gods. These events were fated to occur and all the wiles of human enterprise could not turn them aside. Jocasta takes her life in response to an ancient debt of cosmic significance, as something she owes in penance. Her sacrifice restores relationships between gods and men and atones for past spiritual indiscretions. Even though the suicide is tragic, it is heroic necessity, transforming the grubby tale of incest into a parable of human dignity. Oedipus himself lives the rest of his life in penance as a blind beggar. To the Greeks these events were part of the nature of life in a precarious world.

Romans justified suicide as an appropriate remedy against the outrages of fate and the anguish of disgrace. One of the exemplars of virtue during the Roman Republic was Lucretia, the model against whom all women were measured. Livy begins her story in his history of the Roman people with a drinking party at which a group of husbands bragged about their wives and then set out to see what each was doing late at night. Lucretia was found tending to household tasks, while the other wives were socializing. Tarquin, the king, was overcome with lust for his friend's wife and came to her home some days later when her husband was gone. He threatened to kill her if she did not submit to him and found her quite willing to die rather than yield. Only when he threatened to kill her and place a murdered slave by her side as evidence of adultery did she submit.

Lucretia immediately sent messengers for her father and husband to come and bring a trusted friend. Upon their arrival she told them what had happened and asked them to swear to kill Tarquin and avenge her desecration. After they had done so, Lucretia acquitted herself from guilt but not from punishment. She declared that no woman would ever excuse adulterous behavior by pleading her example and stabbed herself with a previously concealed knife. The enraged men swore vengeance once more over the bloody knife, and led a popular insurrection that deposed Tarquin. The suicide of Lucretia was related as a sterling example of proper morality and a lesson against using the advantages of position unwisely.

During the first centuries A.D. Roman attitudes toward suicide became more pragmatic than exemplary, more personal than social. Slaves who attempted suicide could be returned to the seller as defective! Soldiers who died by suicide were considered deserters and their property confiscated. These were practical matters affecting defense or business and involving no particular religious or moral elements. Stoic philosophy became a popular guide to living among the educated classes. It adopted the view that serenity and reason were the best objectives of life. Death, certainly the most profound serenity of all, was considered a legitimate choice for people overcome by intractable circumstance. Given the rampant violence and constant danger in which these Romans lived, some avenue of relief was desperately sought; suicide became an honorable means of escape. Such men as Seneca and Cato were admired for centuries because of the noble manner in which they undertook their own deaths.

Romans justified suicide in the case of an individual faced with grievous and inalterable circumstance, particularly when done without violence (as in the use of starvation). In literature and art, however, Romans craved more dramatic forms of suicide. Vergil coined one timeless example in the story of Dido in his epic *The Aeneid*. The whole of book four is devoted to Queen Dido, founder of the Phoenician Empire at Carthage.

Aeneas and his fellow refugees from the fall of Troy, forced to land by stormy seas, seek shelter and provisions to continue their journey to Italy. They find a thriving kingdom administered by Dido, a paragon of moral strength and tireless energy. Inspired by a goddess, she falls in love with Aeneas. Though he returns her affection, their love is doomed. The gods order Aeneas to continue his journey, and he sadly prepares to depart. Dido, outraged and dishonored, swears eternal enmity between their peoples. For love of Aeneas she has ceased to build the city, deserted administrative duties, and lost much of the favor of her people. Now, having lost Aeneas too, there is nothing more to live for. She orders a great pyre built in the courtyard, and as Aeneas's ships sail from the harbor calls to them:

> Shall I die unavenged? At least let me die. Thus, thus! I go to the dark, go gladly. May he look long, from out there on the deep, at my flaming pyre, the heartless! And may my death-fires signal bad luck for his voyage! She had spoken; and with these words, her attendants saw her falling upon the sword, they could see the blood spouting up over the blade, and her hands spattered. Their screams rang to the roof of the palace; then rumor ran amok through the shocked city.[10]

So striking and poignant a creation was this death scene that the story was retold over the centuries and eventually inspired an opera, *Dido and Aeneas*, by the seventeenth-century English composer Henry Purcell. Dido's death in Act 3 is the dramatic high point and the most famous musical section of the composition. Dido, alone on stage after Aeneas has gone to his ship, thinks of her destiny, singing, "But death, alas, I cannot shun; Death must come when he is gone." The group of citizens watching the embarkation form a Greek chorus, summarizing and commenting upon the situation. Dido then begins her famous aria over a somber, repeated bass line: "When I am laid in earth, may my wrongs create no trouble in thy breast." With emotional intensity at the top of her vocal range she calls out, "Remember me! Remember me! But, ah, forget my fate." Like some tremendous dance of destiny, the slow triple beat and the ever-repeating bass line drive toward a somber conclusion, when Dido stabs herself and falls upon the funeral pyre.

As in a Greek tragedy, the collective voice of the chorus

summarizes the theme and emotional import of what has happened. The concluding section of the opera is extremely soft and elegiac, the voices beginning, "With drooping wings, ye cupids come," in the highest soprano range and falling slowly into the richest bass tones. In a more animated fashion they bid the cupids scatter roses on her tomb, and the voices sigh repeatedly with the words "Soft and gentle as her heart." In a more dramatic manner, using pauses for emphasis, the chorus concludes, "Keep here your watch, and never part," on a spare open fifth interval—a stark, simple cadence.

Heroic resistance in any form was appealing to Roman taste, even when exhibited by their enemies. The Gauls were a large group of tribal peoples who constantly threatened the Roman frontier in Western Europe. Known for their fierceness in combat (note *A Gaul Committing Suicide*), they preferred death to captivity. In a highly realistic portrayal, a Roman sculptor created a powerfully muscular Gaul who has just killed his wife and is in the act of plunging quite a large knife into himself. The body of the wife hangs listlessly, supported as she falls by her husband's hand upon her dangling arm. Even the drapery on her body crumples downward. The Gaul is a study in violent movement, his face strained and muscles taut as he puts all his energy behind the blow he is about to deal himself. The sculptor even indicates the insertion of the knife and the first drops of blood. As a portrayal of suicidal death the work is both anguishing and fascinating. The full psychic and physical vividness of the moment is fozen in time, a study in pain, resistence, and pathos.

The popular acceptance of Christianity in the first few centuries after Christ did not affect the equal popularity of suicide. The prospect of instant translation into heavenly bliss was an added incentive beyond simply the noncensorious Roman attitude toward such a form of death. Many early Christians died from such ascetic practices as starvation and self-mutilation. St. Augustine complained that killing themselves was becoming the Christians' daily sport. Tertullian defended these actions, pointing out that Christ died by his own decision, when and how he would. St. Augustine believed that whatever its motives, this suicidal mania was a tragic waste of useful life and he inveighed against it in his *City of God*. He argued that suicide was a form of homocide and thus is in direct violation of the commandment not to kill. Confronted by the high death rate,

Fig. 23 School of Pergamum. *A Gaul Committing Suicide.* ca. 230–220 B.C.
Roman marble copy after a bronze original, 83″. National Museum, Rome.
Photograph courtesy of EPA.

the church came to adopt his position, issuing its first official disapproval in 533 at the second Council of Orleans. In later pronouncements suicides were denied the burial rites and interment in consecrated ground. Desecration of the bodies of suicides was revived, along with a host of superstitions regarding their disposal.

Throughout the Middle Ages suicide rates were low, the exceptions being unfortunate women accused of witchcraft. Unlike the Roman situation, there were enough psychic mechanisms such as the assurance of heaven, and enough social stability to render this ultimate escape less necessary. To be sure, there were occasional outbreaks in such guises as the dancing manias, which led to death by exhaustion. It is possible that the relatively short life span made existence more bearable.

The treatment Dante invented for suicides in the *Inferno* segment of *The Divine Comedy* reveals something of the regard in which suicide was held. He places them in round two of lower hell in the vicinity of sins of violence against neighbors, God, art, and nature. The suicides are gnarled trees with black foliage bearing poison thorns instead of fruit. Together they form a dense forest wherein dwell the mythical Harpies, who cry prophecies of disaster. The air of this forest resounds with moans of anguish. After Dante breaks a branch from one of the trees he discovers that it is a human being. Blood forms in the torn wood, and a voice from within the trunk begs for mercy. Dante and Vergil learn that the tree had been Pier delle Vigne, a minister under Frederick II, who was falsely accused of treason, imprisoned, and tortured. In fear and despair he took his own life to escape further torment. Pier delle Vigne reveals the origin and ultimate fate of the suicides in hell:

> when out of the flesh from which it tore itself,
> the violent spirit comes to punishment,
> Minor assigns it to the seventh shelf.

> It falls into the wood, and landing there,
> wherever fortune flings it, it strikes root,
> and there it sprouts, lusty as any tare,

> shoots up a sapling, and becomes a tree.
> The Harpies, feeding on its leaves then, give it
> pain and pain's outlet simultaneously.

> Like the rest, we shall go for our husks on Judgement Day,

> but not that we may wear them, for it is not just
> that a man be given what what he throws away.

> Here shall we drag them and in this mournful glade
> our bodies will dangle to the end of time,
> each on the thorns of its tormented shade.[11]

Dante is clearly concerned with the generic capacity for evil in the human species; his individual encounters are pointed examples of this cosmic vision. Yet this suicide because of tragic circumstances evokes his sympathy rather than horror. It is hard to align with the justice imputed to God. Dante even volunteers to clear the record for the accused among the living.

Shakespeare, a writer deeply influenced by the Renaissance philosophy of man, emphasizes the variety of personal circumstances rather than the cosmic system of justice with regard to such things as suicide. In his dramas he often expresses the spirit of ancient thought. The conclusion of *Julius Caesar* is a veritable panorama of suicides. First Cassius kills himself because he mistakenly believes a strategic battle has been lost. Pindarus, his servant, is enlisted as his accomplice with the promise that he will be set free as his reward. Ironically, the sword with which Cassius kills himself is the same sword used to kill Caesar and set in motion a train of tragic events. Brutus finds the body of Cassius and his friend Titinius, who has killed himself as a demonstration of loyalty. He reacts not with horror but with sorrow and respect. He declares that they were the last and best of the Romans, whose like shall not be seen again.

Brutus soon realizes that his cause is lost. The murder of Caesar has accomplished nothing except useless bloodshed; his vision of society will not come to pass. He enlists his servant, Strato, to hold his sword so that he may run on it and end his life. His last words declare his relief in surrendering his life in view of these tragic events. Again, those who discover his body are overcome with the pathos and nobility of the death. Antonius declares: "This was the noblest Roman of them all," and procedes to list his virtues. Nor is there any hint of dishonorable treatment of this body of their enemy. Octavius states:

> According to his virtue let us use him,
> With all respect and rites of burial.

Within my tent his bones tonight shall lie,
Most like a soldier, order'd honorably.[12]

The suicides provide a satisfactory end to the play. No anguish of imprisonment or torture lingers beyond the concluding action. No violent confrontation between victor and vanquished mars the final moments. There are heroism and healing, carrying the suggestion that this was an honorable choice that noble men can make.

Quite a different justification is established for the suicide of Othello, the unjust, suspicious, violent man who kills his innocent wife. Desdemona is young, confused, and deeply in love with the strange Moor who won her from a father so shocked by the affair that he died of grief. Iago, because of jealous vindictiveness, succeeds in convincing Othello by circumstantial evidence, innuendo, and pure luck that Desdemona is having an affair with his trusted second in command. Not until after Othello has killed his wife in a blind rage does he discover the truth. Othello considers himself "an honorable murderer" because his motive was not hate but personal honor. But he also feels blighted by fate and terribly fearful for his soul. He says to Desdemona's body: "When we meet on judgement day, this look of thine will hurl my soul from heaven and fiends will snatch at it." Othello makes it plain that he considers suicide the only appropriate act of justice. Bystanders rightly place the blame for these events upon Iago, who is led away to whatever tortures may satisfy the audience's imagination. Othello has demonstrated the ultimate in repentence, surrendering his life for his tragic mistake.

The death of Ophelia in *Hamlet, Prince of Denmark* reveals something of the moral, social stigma surrounding suicide, in contrast to Shakespeare's occasional suspension of such dicta for his own dramatic purposes. Ophelia has become increasingly irrational because of the disappointing way Hamlet has treated her and the shock of her father's violent death. Her last appearance is as a singing madwoman, strewing blossoms and leaves from the garland she holds in her arms. Her thoughts are constantly with her dead father. In the last scene of Act 4 her death is poetically reported by Gertrude:

There is a willow grows aslant a brook,
That shows his hoar leaves in the glassy stream;

> There with fantastic garlands did she come
> Of crow-flowers, nettles, daisies, and long purples
> That liberal shepherds give a grosser name,
> But our cold maids do dead men's fingers call them:
> There, on the pendent boughs her coronet weeds
> Clambering to hang, an envious sliver broke;
> When down her weedy trophies and herself
> Fall in the weeping brook. Her clothes spread wide;
> And mermaid-like, awhile they bore her up:
> Which time she chanted snatches of old tunes;
> As one incapable of her own distress,
> Or like a creature native and endued
> Unto that element: but long it could not be
> Till that her garments, heavy with their drink,
> Pull'd the poor wretch from her melodious lay
> To muddy death.[13]

It is difficult to ascertain from this description if the incident was a conscious suicide. The remarks of the priest at the funeral procession leave no doubt as to his interpretation or the usual treatment accorded one in her circumstances. Since there is doubt, Ophelia will be allowed burial in sanctified ground, but she shall not have a requiem or other rituals given those whose souls have departed in peace. Her brother is incensed, asserting: "I tell thee, churlish priest, a ministering angel shall my sister be, when thou liest howling." Here is an evident conflict between human feelings and ritual forms, which grows more bitter in ages to come.

In the nineteenth century the cult of Romanticism inspired interpretations of human life akin to those of Shakespeare. The works of that master became the focus of great interest and the inspiration for new works of art. Delacroix painted his version of the death of Ophelia, following closely the description of her death given in the play. She still grasps the remains of her garland, her white dress swirling out into the river. She regards the viewer with a sense of wonder and puzzlement. The most dramatic element is her gesture of clinging to the branch above her. We seem to be witnessing a supreme moment of decision, not knowing how she will choose. The anguish of the decision and her innocent perplexity are the themes of the painting. She hangs forever in the dark water between life and death, helpless to rescue herself. The Romantic sense of lost innocence and inner torment are perfectly suited to Ophelia's situation.

Fig. 24 Eugène Delacroix. ***The Death of Ophelia.*** 1844. Oil on canvas, 9 × 12″. The Louvre, Paris.

Another Shakespearean play, *Romeo and Juliet,* inspired many a Romantic transformation into art or music. In the original tale their double suicide is precipitated by social pressure and the frustration of their earthly love. Romeo's final speech states his ultimate commitment and his suspicion that fate has destined events as they are to be:

> I will stay with thee;
> And never from this palace of dim night
> Depart again: here, here will I remain
> With worms that are thy chamber-maids; O, here
> Will I set up my everlasting rest,
> And shake the yoke of inauspicious stars
> From this world-wearied flesh.[14]

Romeo's suicide is poignant and leisurely, rising from a steady mind and some prior preparation. Juliet's is quite different. Refusing to run for freedom when the friar comes for her, Juliet catches sight of Romeo's dead body and makes an instant decision. Since he has left no poison for her, she snatches his dagger, saying passionately: "O happy dagger! This is thy sheath; there rust and let me die."

In the concluding action it is made plain that these deaths are vengeance from heaven for the hate between the two families of the dead young people. Through their deaths the anger is dissipated in mutual sorrow. The families pledge to end their hostilities and together mourn their losses. Suicide as divine recompense for social ills is certainly a new rationale for the act and a sympathetic interpretation of it.

The standard Romantic adaptation of the tale in music is the opera *Romeo and Juliet,* by Gounod. The suicide scene differs considerably from Shakespeare's version, but in a manner that thereby achieves greater musical effectiveness. The style is typically Romantic, featuring a large varied orchestra and wide-ranging lyric melodies. There are loud and soft juxtapositions, eloquent silences, and many tone color effects. Following the sequence of the play, Act 5 is the tomb scene. Romeo's aria is beautifully adapted from the Shakespearean soliloquy in which he describes Juliet's appearance in death. Embracing her one last time, Romeo drinks the contents of a small flask. Unlike the Shakespearean version, he does not die immediately but starts back amazed as Juliet, awakened by his embrace, rises from her bier. The orchestra leaps and soars as the lovers embrace and plan to escape together. Suddenly the mood darkens as Romeo, realizing that he has drunk poison, sings that his destiny is to enter the gate of heaven. To a spare, pensive orchestral accompaniment Romeo consoles Juliet with the thought that their life is infinite and will survive even death. He sings to harp accompaniment of the nightingale, who watches over their love. A dramatic tremolo underscores the emotions of Juliet as she discovers that there is no more poison and takes his dagger. A similar tense sound heralds Romeo's outcry: "Juliet, what have you done?" To a descending melodic line their bodies sink to the floor, and to a steady underlying pulse of strings they sing their last lines, "Lord, Lord, forgive us!" The orchestra swells into the love theme, rapturously repeating the intense mood and ending in somber, low-pitched unison.

True to the original version of the play in most regards, the opera heightens the suicide scene by the extended duet between the two lovers in their simultaneous expiration. The last lines append a concern not previously present for the possible sinfulness of this act. It is quite possibly a belated recognition of the rift between social convention and artistic preferences common in our own time as well.

The peculiarly intense fascination that suicide exerted over the Romantic imagination is generally believed to have been initiated by Goethe's morose tale *The Sorrows of Werther*. A melancholy, inactive, self-centered youth, Werther is hopelessly in love with a woman who has married another man. Instead of sensibly removing himself from a situation that can only cause him pain, he abandons all activity besides visiting Charlotte and writing about how badly it affects him:

> How her image haunts me! Waking or asleep, she fills my entire soul! Soon as I close my eyes, here, in my brain, where all the nerves of vision are concentrated, her dark eyes are imprinted. Here—I do not know how to describe it; but if I shut my eyes, hers are immediately before me; dark as an abyss they open upon me, and absorb my senses.[15]

After many pages of this self-torment, Goethe forms in his hero the resolution to die. Werther pictures that eventuality with wonder and hesitation:

> One lifts up the curtain, and passes to the other side—that is all! And why all these doubts and delays? Because we know not what is behind—because there is no returning—and because our mind infers that all is darkness and confusion, where we have nothing but uncertainty.[16]

Werther's anguish in this life eventually conquers his uncertainty about the next, and after writing any number of suicide notes, he shoots himself with pistols obtained, ironically, from Charlotte's husband. He is found hours later rapidly expiring, and Goethe pictures the scene as a mayhem of emotional display. His servants throw themselves upon his dying form, and one has to be extricated forcibly. The tale ends with a few cryptic comments: "Charlotte's life was despaired of. The body was carried by laborers. No priest attended." In such spare phrases Goethe delineates the powerful but forbidden attractions of suicide within the society of his time.

Overwrought as it may seem a century later, the novel established a style of thinking that prized the extremes of emotional experience—love and death being the polarities.

Worldweariness became a fashionable pose. So many suicides were found with copies of the novel on their bodies that its sale was banned in various cities and Goethe was denounced from pulpits as a murderer. Goethe himself thought that the work had delineated the frustrations and disappointments that reside in all of us so effectively that it overwhelmed imaginative readers.

Suicide epidemics such as that sparked by the story of Werther are not uncommon to Western culture. There have even been associations founded for the purpose of helping the membership escape life. Robert Louis Stevenson's short story "The Suicide Club," fantastic though it seems, was based upon historic precedent. A member of the club explains to the heroes of the story that many people are heartily sick of life and hold to it only because their families would be shocked or they are too cowardly to put an end to it themselves. The Suicide Club, then, is the convenient way to quit life. Their meetings are convivial and confessional, members sharing the deeds and disappointments that brought them together. They toast the memories of famous suicides. Then cards are dealt. One person receives the ace of spades and becomes the victim. The one receiving the ace of clubs is designated the murderer. As the tale proceeds, the heroes pursue the president of the club across several continents, finally killing him in a duel. As part of a collection called *New Arabian Nights,* the tale had that typical energetic, bizarre, exotic combination that was the hallmark of Romanticism. Yet casting the leader of the club as a villain mollified social opinion concerning such lawless activities.

The epitome of the exotic suicide might well be the conclusion of the opera *Aïda,* by Verdi. The action is placed in Memphis and Thebes during the time of the ancient Pharaohs, lending the effect of mystery and opulence. Through a long series of plots Rhadames, a captain in the Egyptian army, is wrongfully declared a traitor. His loved one, Ethiopian captive Aida, also faces imprisonment for her part in a revolt. In the last scene of Act 4 the jury of priests leads Rhadames to the statue of Osiris, the god he has offended by his acts, and prepares to place him in a crypt, shut it with a stone, and leave him to suffocate. The final scene begins with a somber orchestral chorale. Rhadames, now enclosed in the tomb, reflects upon his fate in a melodic line that hovers about a single tone until his thoughts of Aida send him into lyricism. A sudden tremolo of strings indicates Rhadames' perception of a figure moving out of the gloom. "Heaven! It is Aida," he cries. To the low-pitched, steady pulse of a martial rhythm Aida tells how she secreted herself undetected in the tomb. Rhadames extols her act and laments its consequences. "You are too lovely for death," he sighs. In a responding aria of almost Mozartean jollity Aida pictures the gates of heaven opening to them, angels welcoming them, and eternal love awaiting them. From another level of the stage the voices of the priests and priestesses are heard in their ritual chant to the god Ptah. "It is our death chant," respond the lovers. A final moment of struggle with the rock that seals the tomb, expressions of fear, and then resignation bring the music to the concluding aria:

> Farewell, O earth! farewell, thou vale of sorrow!
> Brief dream of joy condemned to end in woe!
> See, brightly opens the sky, and endless morrow
> There all unshadowed eternal shall glow!

The ritual chanting of the priestly chorus forms a monotone for the wide-ranging lyricism of this final duet. The orchestra concludes with the high, sweet sound of strings as the lovers expire. The essential pathos of this death, largely compelled by social circumstance, is much like that of Gounod's setting of *Romeo and Juliet*, with the added interest of the exotic setting and vaguely Near Eastern flavor to some of the music.

One suicide that provokes not pity but the spontaneous approbation accorded a heroic act is found in the concluding moments of the opera *Tosca*, by Puccini. Though his music seems to contemporary listeners to possess all the vocabulary of idealistic Romanticism, Puccini thought of himself as a realist who portrayed life as it is. In essence, Baron Scarpia, infamous chief of the Roman police, lusts for Tosca. In order to break down her resistence, he captures and tortures her true love, Mario. Unable to bear his agony, Tosca agrees to satisfy Scarpia in exchange for a mock execution of Mario and letters of passage out of the country. When Scarpia completes the letters and comes to take her, Tosca stabs him fatally. She grabs the letters and runs to his cell to tell Mario of the plot and his role in it.

The final, climactic scene of the opera opens with Mario being led to the wall facing the firing squad and Tosca nervously pacing in the background. The music is a steady march tempo, as though ticking off the minutes. As the squad prepares, the music becomes intense, and the sound of shots rings out. Agitated, Tosca calls out: "There! Die! Oh, what an actor!" Immediately the sound level falls as Tosca creeps stealthily toward the motionless figure, cautioning him to remain still. When all the soldiers have gone, she bends over him in complete silence. The orchestra bursts in dramatically as she finds that Mario is dead and that Scarpia has betrayed her. The soldiers return noisily, having just discovered Scarpia's body. As they push forward shouting, "Tosca, you will pay dearly for his life," she rushes to the edge of the tall fortress. At the very top of her vocal range she sings defiantly, "With my own! Oh Scarpia! Before God!" and plunges to her death. With drumrolls and cymbal clashes the orchestra concludes this astonishing sequence of events. The audience, breathless with the pace of action, is stirred to approval at Tosca's choice. It is the ultimate statement of resistance against heartless fate.

A more earthy type of Romanticism is exemplified by Dostoevski's analytical novel *The Possessed*. Two suicides conclude the novel, both perpetrated by incipient revolutionaries in Russia during the late nineteenth century. The suicide of Kirillov is largely spurred by a conflict of social ideals and a desire to demonstrate ideologically that the assertion of human will is the secret to happiness. The suicide of Nikolay Stavrogin concludes a life of supreme alienation and oppressive guilt. Through their stories Dostoevski expresses his fear of nihilism and his concern for the social fabric of Russia. The same existential questions about the nature of God and the import of belief dwelt upon in *The Grand Inquisiter* surface in the conversation of Kirillov and Piotr Stepanovich, and with the confession of Nikolay Stavrogin to the monk, Tihon. Though the plot of the novel is based upon an actual murder and the subsequent trial evidence, the darkly tangled human tapestry that Dostoevski unfolds wanders far from fact, portraying with deadly accuracy in the light of events of this century the degredation of the individual in the interests of the group.

The two suicides represent different relationships to the collective life. Stavrogin is unable to love, to distinguish between good and evil, to belong to anything or anyone. Kirillov believes himself to be the discoverer of the new life, signing his death statement, "Gentleman, seminarian, Russian, and citizen of the civilized world." The man who emerges whole from this tale of subterfuge and corruption is Pyotr Stepanovich, the manipulater without conscience whose purpose is his own advancement. Kirillov has accepted money from the revolutionaries, promised to help them, and then had a change of heart. He realizes that they will try to eliminate him. The group decides to kill another disillusioned individual and induce Kirillov to write a confession to the murder, following this document with his suicide.

Besides his disappointment with the course of the reform movement, Kirillov is obsessed by an existential puzzle. As he puts it: "God is necessary and so must exist. But I know he doesn't and can't. Surely you must understand that a man with two such ideas can't go on living?" Kirillov concludes that the conflict must be resolved in human decision. He explains:

> Can it be that one in the whole planet, after making an end of God and believing in his own will, will dare to express his self-will on the most vital point? . . . I want to manifest my self-will. I may be the only one, but I'll do it. . . . I am bound to shoot myself because the highest point of my self-will is to kill myself with my own hands.[17]

Kirillov decides to shoot himself not for a cause, but for no cause at all—simply as a demonstration of his place in the universe. Man has invented God, he believes, in order to have some reason for continuing to live. Kirillov refuses to invent God. "Let them know it once for all," he cries. He is the supreme nihilist, asserting that the laws of nature spared not even Christ, so the basis of this planet is a lie. Kirillov is himself a god against his will. He adopts the cause of freeing mankind from his former God, and with this last heroic gesture shatters his skull with a bullet.

Nikolay's suicide is precipitated by years of idleness, dissipation, and anguish over his sexual indiscretions with a child who later hanged herself. He has joined many groups and lived various kinds of life, hoping to find some sense of personal fulfillment. His growing anguish leads him to consult a sympathetic bishop living presently as a monk and to present him with a written synopsis of his life and thought. Fits of passion and impulses toward violence pepper the pathetic document. The bishop, Tihon, tries to assure him that such a document represents true repentence, and that he must forgive himself. His assessment of Nikolay is blunt: "evil passions and the habit of idleness render you really callous and stupid." Tihon urges Nikolay to place himself under some spiritual discipline and begin to work toward a solution for his inner life. Nikolay agrees not to publish the confession, but Tihon, sensing some ultimate evasion within the man, dismisses him with words of intense grief: "never, poor lost youth, have you stood nearer to a new and more terrible crime than at this moment."

In his letter to Darya Pavlovna just before his death, Nikolay writes of his estrangement from those human connections which stabilize life. He has become a citizen of the canton of Uri, not to begin a new life, but without hopes of any sort. He feels estranged from his own country; he feels a terrible responsibility for his wife's death. He desires both good and evil, deriving equal pleasure from both. He cautions Darya, if she should decide to join him, to expect no return for her love. "From me nothing has come but negation, with no greatness of soul, no force." He even fears suicide, though he feels obligated to do it, because it will turn into a sham once again. Yet by the time Darya and his mother reach him, Nikolay has indeed hanged himself, leaving a note that reads: "No one is to blame, I did it myself." Perhaps ironically, Dostoevski records in the concluding lines of the novel: "At the inquest our doctors absolutely and emphatically rejected all idea of insanity."

The artist Manet, using the same criteria of contemporary realism, created a painting called *The Suicide*. It is as uninspiring and anti-heroic as possible. The scene is a shabby room resembling a hotel more than a home. The furniture and accoutrements are minimal and rickety. A man, rather well dressed for this environment, lies uncomfortably braced upon the edge of the bed. His carefully cuffed white shirt reveals an obvious red stain upon the chest, and his hand still clutches a revolver. The scene is intensely precarious, with the unbalanced body, the disheveled surroundings, and the peculiar perspective relationships. The painting is almost colorless, seeming more grimy than hued. It is a statement of things as they generally are, free from the pretensions of Romanticism or the grace of nobility.

The twentieth century has witnessed no slackening of interest in suicide or curiosity about its motives. Psychological perspectives are prominent. There is renewed interest in universals of human experience found in classical mythology. There is a reconsideration of the relationship of death to life and concern about death as a legitimate option. Camus, the philosopher of suicide, has dealt extensively with the rationale of this act as a response to conditions of human existence. He stresses the individual, rather than the social nature of the act, and believes that its inspiration, like that of a work of art, rises involuntarily within the person. Suicide is a confession that a person has recognized the absence of some obvious reason for living. This new perspective, often stimulated by catastrophic events, leads to a divorce between a person and his life.

What holds us to this life is, initially, the habit of living, which the body assumes before the mind acquires the habit of thinking about it. One grows used to eluding death and evading decisions about ultimate matters. Life as lived offers uncertainty and inconsistency. The question of the true nature of our existence is unanswerable. In short, our lives are absurd. But does the absurdity of our lives justify self-inflicted death? "There is but one truly serious philosophical problem, and that is suicide," Camus declares in the opening lines of his essay "The Myth of Sisyphus." Reason of the traditional sort is of little help in responding to such a question, and because of this Camus believes that the attack on reason has been particularly violent in our time. Can we live without appeal to all the conventional certainties, Camus inquires? Does life have to have a meaning to be lived? Camus's answer is that it will be lived all the better if it has no meaning. Life then becomes a state of permanent revolution, necessitating a total acceptance of flux. Suicide represents a final attempt to settle the absurdity, to stop the enrush of events. But our conscious revolt from this kind of certainty gives contemporary life most of the value it has, asserts Camus. Doctrines that explain ourselves and our universe also debilitate us. "It is essential to die unreconciled and not of one's own free will. Suicide is a repudiation."

Contrary to this view, suicide has been seen as the ultimate revolt. In the Broadway play *It's My Life, Isn't It?*, the revolt is against living a life that has been forced into the value systems of others. Is the initial body habit of sustaining life to be honored long after the mind has ceased to participate in a world of its choice? The protagonist, a paralyzed patient without hope of recovery, argues against being imprisoned by others in a life he does not want. There are no solutions offered, merely an eloquent presentation of the questions. Camus's preposition remains: can life be lived without a purpose? If life could be accepted as a totally purposeless state, would the paralytic's situation change?

A quite different, yet decidedly contemporary, alternative is taken by Eugene O'Neill in his play *Mourning Becomes Electra*. He returns to ancient Greek premonitions of fate with a highly psychological overlay. The Mannon family seems cursed in the same manner as the family of Oedipus. Each character is doomed to assume the hated qualities of the others. Their personalities have been formed by relationships in childhood; the anger and jealousy hoarded from that dim past burst into vengeance and self-destruction. In the Greek sense of the term, the basic "sin" of the family is the loveless marriage between Christine and Ezra Mannon. This lie at the heart of their relationship leads to Christine's rejection of Vinnie, their daughter, the everly protective relationship between herself and the son, Orin, and to the death by poisoning of Ezra. Once that death has occurred, the whole family is fated to perish by violence to body or psyche. Life as preached by O'Neill is not simply without intrinsic meaning but full of the most terrible and unyielding meaning. The same sense of unimpeachable universal laws recognized by the ancient Greeks asserts itself in the psychological relationships between characters.

Learning that Christine's act of poisoning their father stemmed from her desire to marry her lover, Brant, Vinnie and Orin murder Brant. Their arrangement of room and body to indicate a robbery is so interpreted. To Orin, just returned from war with a head wound, their act is another nightmare:

> This is like my dream. I've killed him before—over and over. Do you remember me telling you how the faces of the men I killed came back and changed to Father's face and finally became my own? He looks like me, too! Maybe I've committed suicide![18]

These are fateful words, for Orin is never again out from under the shadow of these deaths. He confronts his mother with his knowledge of her affair with Brant. It becomes apparent that Brant was really his rival for his mother's affections and that he wants his mother all to himself. To his horror she runs into the house and kills herself with her husband's pistol. Orin screams:

Why didn't I let her believe burglers killed him? She wouldn't
have hated me then! She would have forgotten him! She would
have turned to me! I murdered her! She's gone—how can I ever
get her to forgive me now?[19]

In truth, he cannot, and the collective weight of that anguish
and guilt drives Orin to madness and suicide in the same manner as his mother.

Vinnie, whose strength has come from her belief that she
is an instrument of justice to avenge her father, now faces the
knowledge that she has unintentionally driven someone to his
death. Her future with a man she loves is irretrievably blighted.
"I'm bound here—to the Mannon dead," she tells him. "I'm the
last Mannon. I've got to punish myself." She enters the house
and has the shutters nailed down, swearing to remain there for
the rest of her life. She will let.the dead hound her until the
curse is paid out, and she is sure that they will compel her to
live a long time.

Certainly one of the most dismal assessments of suicide in
all contemporary literature, *Mourning Becomes Electra* seems a
clear case of Camus's warning about living life against a back-
drop of immutable law. Yet these characters gain whatever
memorability they achieve because of the way they fulfill, even
against their wills, the dictates of this law. It is the kind of irony
the twentieth century seems supremely capable of rediscover-
ing.

A famous operatic suicide of this century is as quiet and
suggestive as the Mannon family suicides are noisy and obvious. Composed by Benjamin Britten and derived from a poem
by George Crabbe, the opera *Peter Grimes* is an account of a
particular social context and the blighted relationships within
it. The opera opens at a trial in a small English fishing village in
the early nineteenth century. The testimony of the accused,
Peter Grimes, fails to stop the gossip about the death of his
apprentice. His naturally reserved manner, mystic yearnings,
and unpredictable physical outbursts of temper have made
Grimes feared and resented by the townspeople. The loss at
sea of his young, badly treated apprentice has focused their
disapproval and further alienated him. With aid from Ellen
Orford, whom he hopes to marry, Grimes obtains a new apprentice. Soon the boy is found to be bruised, and the villagers
sing cynically, "Grimes is at his exercise." Realizing that the

gossip has begun again, Grimes accuses the new apprentice of talking, and decides to leave immediately for the fishing grounds. In their haste to depart the apprentice falls from a cliff above the sea and is killed.

Grimes's hopes of marrying Ellen, buying a home, and winning the respect of the villagers are doomed. After three days at sea he returns to find himself a hunted criminal. The final scene opens in a dense mist matching Grimes's despair as he wanders through the deserted streets. The orchestra provides a kaleidoscope of wispy sounds over sustained strings. Fragments of memories drifting through his brain are projected as melodies in the tonal fabric. Distant voices hum intermittently. Without accompaniment Grimes sings erratically of his shattered dreams, becoming increasingly unintelligible. He is startled by the voices of Ellen and a friend who hope to join him. He repeats their voices calling his name, as though in a nightmare.

Ellen sings, over a distant blending of voices intoning Grimes's name, "We have come to take you home." He does not understand her and returns to his fancies of peace and love in lyric flights of tone. Ellen's companion finally commands him in a direct speaking voice, "Sail out till you lose sight of land. Then sink the boat. D'you hear? Sink her. Goodbye, Peter." He leads Grimes to the boat and helps him push it away from shore.

The sound of the sea is heard in flute runs as dawn breaks. Stragglers from the manhunt return and life begins again. A villager stops to sing of a boat sinking far out at sea, beyond their rescue. The ceaseless movement of the orchestral tide sweeps over them, and in a full chorus the villagers sing of their work and the joys and sorrows of their lives. The body of Peter Grimes floats far away in the dark streams, as expressed by the soft flowing arpeggios in the orchestra as the curtain falls.

Though the literature of suicide in this century has partaken fully of expressionist, idealistic, and even satiric frames of reference, autobiographical realism has enjoyed a particular vogue. An illustrious member of this confessional genre is *The Woman Said Yes*, by Jessamyn West. The first half of the book recounts the refusal of Jessmyn's mother to accede to Jessamyn's seemingly unavoidable death from tuberculosis, and her successful restoration to health. The second part relates quite a different outcome in the case of Carmen, Jessamyn's sister. Carmen, fatally afflicted with cancer, has determined to take her own life before her disease kills her. Jessamyn is called to help her carry out that intention. Their first problem is philosophical—how to determine the rightness of this intention. Carmen reasons that the cancer is the cause of her death rather than her own unilateral decision. Now the only problem is that of suffering. Is she required by some cosmic principle or being to suffer? Jessamyn describes Carmen's conclusion:

> She had not chosen death: fate or genes or God, which is perhaps the name we give that combination, had made the choice. She at least intended to have some voice in the matter. Why should she spend two or three months in agony? Or so drugged to avoid the agony that she no longer had any existence as a human being? What God would want His children to die in that way? What child of God would so malign his Creator's nature as to believe that such a death was His choice?[20]

The sisters are bolstered by the Knowledge that their grandmother died in extreme agony, and their mother regretted for the rest of her life not finding a way to end the torment. But when does one choose a time that is appropriate? Carmen's physician is very skeptical about suicide as an option for anyone:

> We are born with an instinct to survive, not to die. . . . Life is all we've got. Not a thing more. It takes a lot of courage to throw away all you've got. Even if it's only one rational hour a day. So they postpone until they're too weak and too drugged to do what is necessary.[21]

Indeed, his description of the limits of endurance are what Carmen finally accepts. It is time, she decides, when there is not even one good hour each day left to live. She gives away her clothes, arranges her funeral, dresses as though preparing for some significant event, and swallows the pills she hopes will kill her. After nearly a full day, they do. Jessamyn, filled with sorrow and pride, speaks to her dead sister in the very imagery of the Roman Stoic:

> My darling, you did it. You had the courage. It was a great gift to all of us. To depart like a courteous guest. You did not wear out

your welcome. You did not linger to cause us all to suffer. All as you planned. Nothing more to worry about now.[22]

Martyrdom

The line separating suicide from martyrdom is neither darkly drawn nor deeply etched. Recall Tertullian's observations that Jesus knew what awaited and could have avoided it, and thus his death was suicidal. Most of the major martyrdoms that have subsequently changed societies went unrecognized at the time. Death was simply a way of ridding those in power of a particular human nuisance. The hallmark of martyrdom is some cause for which an individual gives his life. His associates must know and believe in that cause, and the cause must be significant to human life. Further, the cause must eventually triumph and be widely respected. Many are the martyrs in embryo such as Savanarola, whose cause did not prosper and whose example failed.

Martyrs are not necessarily likeable persons. They tend to divide society radically and polarize attitudes. They often precipitate institutional disintegration and long-lasting social upheaval. They are generally pugnacious, intractable, and inordinately complex. It is almost impossible at the time to distinguish a true martyr from a blamed nuisance. As John Stuart Mill wisely remarked, if we today were confronted with Socrates or Jesus, we would probably react precisely as their contemporaries did. Nor are martyrs always verifiable historical persons. A large contingent of Medieval martyrs are utterly devoid of historical veracity. They simply suited the urgent psychological and social needs of the time.

Undoubtedly the current favorite martyr of the ancient world is Socrates. During his lifetime he seems to have been either completely admired or utterly vilified. His teachings about the gods, the nature of truth, and the meaning of human existence were quite out of step with the norms of that time. His very innocence and spirit of open inquiry subjected men in high places to revelations of their own faulty reasoning, unfortunately in the presence of witnesses. Clearly something had to be done about the ugly old man who was misleading young citizens.

Socrates was no help at all to himself, if we believe the

recollection of the trial that survives. Far from being repentant, he asserted his value to the state as a necessary corrective to sloppy thinking and intellectual laziness. He placed his hope in the workings of democratic discussion, which he relied upon to culminate in a just verdict. Alas, the process failed him, and he was condemned to death, albeit in the dignified manner of self-administered poisoning. The most complete account of his last hours is recorded in Plato's *Phaedo*. Socrates spends his last hours speaking about the relationship of philosophy to death. A philosopher is always pursuing death, which is the separation of the soul from the body. Certainly he will not unlawfully take his life, but will live so as to prepare his soul to be without his body. True existence consists of thought alone, Socrates asserts, and true knowledge of absolute things can only be attained after death. He looks forward to attaining wisdom, that state of unerring immortality which he believes to be available after death to those who have prepared themselves for it. The pains and pleasures of the senses chain us to the corporeal world and prevent many souls from attaining the realm of pure thought. Never fear, he comforts his followers, that a soul nurtured by thought and reason will be scattered into nothing.

At the end of their discussion Socrates bathes, bids his farewell to his family, and accepts the cup of hemlock from the jailor. With it in hand he offers a prayer to the gods to prosper his journey and cheerfully drinks it down. He walks about until his body grows numb and then lies down, covering himself with a sheet. Thus he expires peacefully and relatively painlessly, with great effect among his followers. His habits of rationality were to have marked effect upon Western civilization for centuries to come through the work of his students.

One example of that influence may be found in the portrayal of his last moments in David's painting *The Death of Socrates*. Created during the Napoleonic Era in France, the painting was part of a revival of classical themes that at the time (1787) expressed civic virtue and the heroic pursuit of collective ideals. Socrates is sacrificed in the cause of class justice, the inference being that each citizen should be proud to do likewise. The high emotion of the participants and the moral message of the theme unite in a moment of singular pathos.

True to its classical basis, the painting is constructed according to specific theories of form and space. There is conscious suppression of all extraneous detail and complete

Fig. 25 Jacques-Louis David. *The Death of Socrates.* 1787. Oil on canvas, 51 × 77¼". Metropolitan Museum of Art, New York; the Wolfe Fund, 1931.

fidelity to the fundamental images and their logical relationships. At the extreme this method achieves the effect of posed statuary. Taken more loosely as in this example, the approach achieves a power and dignity appropriate to the subject. The red, blue, and yellow of drapery relieves the barren setting of the dungeon. The powerful light source focuses upon Socrates with theatrical effect. The twelve friends in attendance are not historically accurate but symbolically effective in the light of Christian tradition. The jailor is overcome with emotion at his task, and he and the friend leaning in anguish upon the wall balance the calculated stance of figures with an emotional display. Nobility and sacrifice are well projected in the powerful, alert figure of Socrates, indicating the path his soul will take. The centuries have not dimmed the grip this unique man has upon our imagination.

A later martyr, cast in nearly the identical mold from which Socrates sprang, is Giordano Bruno, a sixteenth-century Italian Dominican priest accused of heresy. Much of the constitution of his character and of the path of his life is foreshadowed by the ancient Greek. Bruno was, like Socrates, a philosophical martyr whose error was thinking clearly and far beyond the speculative range of the people of his time. He reflects in his writings upon ideas that are, indeed, wondrous for that century. He says that nature constantly unfolds in never-repeating motion; planetary life in any sidereal system is derived from the heat and light of a central sun; worlds without end move through space guided by their own intrinsic energy. All cosmic bodies share the same basic elements, and there are many worlds besides our own. Only the universe is eternal; worlds perish and are reconstituted. To be sure, Bruno missed the mark in such cases as his doctrine that simple numbers represent the constitution of the universe and his incorrect estimations of planetary distances.

Besides his cosmological interests, Bruno was fascinated by new ideas regardless of the source from which they came. He visited with Protestants, conversed with heretics, and traveled widely outside the confines of the monastery where his education began. He shared with Socrates the fatal belief that men are reasonable, and that they can be brought to share a liberal regard for exciting ideas. After many skirmishes with the Roman Church, he was formally accused of heresy by his employer, who was motivated by monetary profits. A judicious mixture of oddly interpreted versions of his writings, along with much nonsense, formed the list of charges. Bruno's fundamental defense was that his field was science and philosophy rather than religion per se. He was perfectly willing to repent of all religious misadventures, but not to stop speculating about ideas outside a purely canonical context. The statements attributed to him were, in many cases, quotations that he was citing from other sources for the sake of argument. He was not so obnoxious as Socrates in telling his judges that they should be grateful to have him keep them on their toes. But he made it plain that he could not be kept from thinking or discussing his thoughts.

An inordinate amount of time was spent in collecting and examining his writings, time that Bruno spent in prison. He wrote nothing for seven years, was fetched up and examined again, and placed for more years in prison. Appeals to the Pope failed and after twelve years, according to the best estimate, Bruno was scheduled to be burned at the stake. Records of the Brotherhood of Pity of St. John the Beheaded, clerics assigned to accompany the condemned to the stake, furnish the only authoritative details of Bruno's death. He was burned early one morning in the Field of Flowers in Rome during a jubilee year. He was chained by the neck and accompanied by a group of priests exhorting him to repent, which he refused to do. His ashes were scattered to the wind. His writings never achieved popularity. His memory disappeared for centuries.

At length nineteenth-century German philosophers discovered portions of his writings and were so struck by their range and power that a wave of enthusiasm for Bruno spread across Europe. Italian presses issued his collected works in new editions, and Spinoza heralded him as the ideological ancestor of his own philosophy. Typical of the polarization he caused in life, an ironic repetition occurred in the wake of the dedication of a statue to his memory on the spot of his martyrdom. Pope Leo XIII issued a denunciation of Bruno as a "man of impure and abandoned life." He was, according to this pope, a degraded materialist whose writings were full of errors, and whose only accomplishments were insincerity, lying, and selfishness. Be that as it may, no modern account of the Renaissance and its history of ideas is complete without inclusion of Bruno's life and thought.

The central martyrdom of Western civilization is that of Jesus, who divides the entire course of history. His resemblance to both Socrates and Bruno is more that casual; it is his impact upon vast numbers of people in a specifically religious sense that is different. Jesus, too, was condemned for teaching a large, consistent body of doctrine that was tremendously innovative and, at points, blasphemous, in the estimation of his fellow Jews. The various accounts of his trial give evidence of the characteristic firmness and calm of most martyrs. Like Socrates, Jesus taught that death was not the end but the occasion of a new and richer life. Unlike Socrates, he suffered a most cruel death and left a group of disorganized working-class people to share his memory and start a spiritual fellowship, a Church.

One of the uses of a martyrdom is to lend itself to reinterpretations according to social changes and varied artistic visions. Through the ages the martyrdom of Jesus has been expressed in almost every stylistic alternative except outright satire. The first portrayals were highly symbolic representations of the human body, denaturalized in order to dramatize the more than human significance of his death. Throughout the

Middle Ages touches of naturalism crept in until the Renaissance summarized centuries of artistic convention, producing works memorable even today.

In the sixteenth century the German realist painter Grünewald produced his version of the crucifixion. The body of Jesus is rendered in exaggerated realism, knobby, skeltal, and hacked. The crown of thorns is nail-like in its unyielding lines and bloody penetrations. The fingers are eloquently raised toward heaven in a last anguished appeal. The face projects suffering and despair, and the dark sky with the eclipsed sun and barren horizon present a forbidding spectacle. About this figure are gathered the figures of his mother, Mary Magdalen, and one of the disciples, their feelings of sorrow and foreboding readily apparent in their gestures. The absence of clearly indicated space thrusts this parable of suffering directly upon the viewer. The ragged edges of the clothing heighten the effect of unrest, reflecting analogously the inner state of the wearers. Though entirely conventional in subject and form, the Grünewald *Small Crucifixion* is unusual, perhaps even repulsive, in its style of realization.

At the opposite pole is the idealized presentation of the *Raising of the Cross* by the seventeenth-century painter Rubens. The body of Jesus is portrayed like that of a Greek god in its muscularity, pose, and even mannerisms. The pearly skin glows in a light from heaven, toward which the central figure looks appealingly. Vibrant action suffuses the scene, which includes playful tangles of vegetation and a small dog. Powerful bodies lean backward with the weight of their burden, their informal drapery emphasizing their heroic proportions and dramatic gestures. Even the background is not the dismal one of Grünewald's choice but a lush green bank. It is a scene couched in terms that remove pain and torment and replace them with theatrical effects and sensual appeal. Needless to say, such an idealistic alternative is always a stylistic favorite with the viewing public.

The twentieth-century painter Rouault takes a highly expressionistic approach in the *Head of Christ,* emphasizing both physical suffering and emotional despair. The face is almost unrecognizable behind the slashing lines that rip across the pictorial surface. The two black points of eyes are the central forces, and their direct stare seems almost accusatory. None of the actual details of the face in their normal proportions are

Fig. 26 Mathis Grünewald. ***The Small Crucifixion.*** 1519. Oil on panel, 24½ ×
18½″. The National Gallery of Art, Washington; Samuel H. Kress Collection.
Photograph courtesy of the National Gallery of Art, Washington, D.C.

Fig. 27 Georges Rouault. **Head of Christ.** 1905. Oil on paper, 39 × 25¼″. The Chrysler Museum, Norfolk; gift of Walter P. Chrysler, Jr.

Fig. 28 Salvador Dali. *The Sacrament of the Last Supper.* 1955. Oil on canvas. The National Gallery of Art, Washington; Chester Dale Collection. *Photograph courtesy of the National Gallery of Art, Washington, D.C.*

given, yet the reference is recognizable, and the emotional element assumes the dominant position.

A symbolic, metaphysical approach to the same subject is taken by Dali in his version of *The Last Supper*. The work has all the conventional inclusions, but is assembled to give an illusive, meditative effect. Floating above the live Jesus sharing this repast with his disciples is the transparent figure of God, First Person of the Trinity. In a familiar Daliesque double entendre, the Holy Spirit is hidden in a lock of Jesus' hair. The room containing the scene is itself transparent to the surrounding harbor and the men at their daily fishing tasks. The moment is full of symbol and ceremony, gesture and contemplation. Yet it is open to the ordinary world; through it we see the commonplace with greater clarity. Each element is presented with studied realism, though the context is not readable on that level. The painting describes the transformation of life by the power of ultimate meaning.

One of the most moving of all versions of the crucifixion is that by Velásquez. Its freedom from pretension is its strongest quality. The somber, unfigured background forces the viewer to attend without distraction to the quiet figure facing us directly. No symbols of power indicate its other than human aspect. No exaggeration of line or juxtaposition of context enables one to escape into another frame of reference. The simple, unadorned realism lends to the scene a remarkable dignity. Despite cruel slander, torture, and treachery, the person has survived with self-contained dignity. He will be taken from this place not as one confiscates a brutalized animal, but as one who exemplifies ultimate integrity.

One martyrdom can be used to comment upon another, less-recognized, instance. This is the approach taken by Chagall in his *White Crucifixion*. The subject is immediately located in the center of the painting, attached to a disturbingly chaotic space. It is these surroundings that give this portrayal its power as social commentary. We note various accoutrements such as the candles and scroll, which refer to Jewish tradition. The figures resemble conventional images of European Jews, while the background describes intense destruction, flight, terror, and death. Flaming houses and tumbled buildings are created in the same visual shorthand used so effectively by Picasso. These are the Russian Jews whose many persecutions Chagall portrays under the guise of the older crucifixion. His identification of his own people with another historic act of cruelty lends a deeper reference to his immediate subject.

Musical works centered upon that sequence of events which culminated in the crucifixion also exhibit stylistic traits that introduce different meanings into their common subject. The style that forms the current point of reference remains that of the eighteenth- and nineteenth-century oratorio. A combination of sung narration, reflective arias, instrumental interludes, and memorable choruses gives this traditional form a particularly flexible and emotionally convincing format. Bach's musical setting of the trial and crucifixion as recorded in the Gospel of John is one example of the genre. The episode is structured to give the story first from the perspective of bystanders, then from immediate participants, and finally from the view of contemporary listeners wondering about the significance of these events.

The sequence begins with the sung statement by the narrator that Pilate delivered Jesus to the multitude to be crucified and that he was led away, carrying his cross, to a place called Golgatha. The ensuing bass aria urges us as members of the

Fig. 29 Diego Velásquez. ***The Crucifixion.*** 1631–32. Oil on canvas. The Prado Gallery, Madrid. *Photograph courtesy of Alinari/EPA.*

group of bystanders to hasten to that place on the wings of faith, not as the callous mob. The rapid tones of the melody portray the mood of urgency, and the chorus punctuates the forward flow by inquiries, "Ah, where?"

A simple recitation concludes the episode with the information about the persons at the scene and the cynical epigraph, "The King of the Jews," that Pilate had placed on the cross. The chorus, as the mob, remonstrates with the Roman leader about the interpretation of the message, and the soloist representing Pilate declares that it will remain as written. The congregational hymn that follows engages the participation of the listeners and transfers these events into the realm of contemporary life, asking that the incident "shine within my vision as comfort in my need." The narrator describes the soldiers casting lots for Jesus's clothing and puzzling over his seamless coat. The ensuing chorus casts listeners into a mob discussion of the matter. The words "Do not rend it or divide it" ring out like hammer blows on a single pitch, resolving into a boiling tangle of melody lines winding to an energetic climax.

This series of turbulent events concluded, our attention turns to the more intimate participants in this martyrdom. The narrator introduces Jesus' mother, her sister, and Mary Magdalen along with a favorite disciple, all standing under the cross. In a sweetly modulated lyric melody Jesus commends them to one another's care. A chorale reflects on this familial scene and mirrors its import for contemporary life:

> O, Man, set your life aright,
> Love thy God and neighbor—
> Death no more will thee afright,
> Sweet thy rest from labor.

The ensuing aria also juxtaposes two different moods. There is the mournful "It is fulfilled," sung to a slow, lyric melody full of painful tonal suspensions. In the middle section is the joyous "The King of Judah triumphs now," with its rapid strokes of sound in a trumpetlike motif. The narrator proceeds to conclude the crucifixion episode of the oratorio with a simple declaration, "And he bowed his head and was gone." No musical punctuation ends this statement; it is left eternally dangling. The bass aria again pulls these events into contemporary life, asking, "Am I from death forever freed? Am I, since Thou in woe hast ended, to heaven's realm commended?" The certainty of the music belies the questioning of the text, lilting hopefully in counterpoint with a cello melody. In its idealistic frame of reference, which occasionally wanders into theatricality, the Bach *Passion According to St. John* is an appropriate match for the Rubens *Raising of the Cross*.

The *Passion According to St. Luke*, by the contemporary Polish composer Penderecki, takes the austere metaphysical approach of Dali's *Last Supper*. His account ranges outward from the narrative supplied by Luke and includes (in Latin) selections from the Roman Breviary, the Psalms, and the Roman Missal. Emphasis is placed equally upon straight narration in a speaking voice, sung interchanges between characters, the collective expressions of the chorus, and highly evocative orchestral effects. These elements alternate in perfect balance during the trial scene before Pilate, the mob contending with the dramatic bass melody of the soloist, and finally triumphing with the shouted, "Crucifige, crucifige illum."

The actual crucifixion scene is prefaced by Psalm 22:15, "Thou dost lay me in the dust of death." Extraordinarily slow, nonrhythmic melody lines set the mood for the simple narration describing the walk to Golgatha. The sound increases in pitch and intensity, falling disconsolately to a rumble of bass strings. Extreme tonal tensions pull these melodic strands about, twisting them painfully, and slowly dissipating. Violent hisses and shouts of the mob break through; strange sound effects whistle through the interludes. "O my people, what have I done unto thee? Or in what have I offended thee? Answer me." This section ends with a prayer for mercy and an extremely low-pitched, somber orchestral meditation. "There they crucified him, and the criminals, one on the right and one on the left," declares the narrator simply and directly.

An extremely wide-ranging, tonally erratic soprano solo describes the woodland origin and role of the cross, based upon a Good Friday hymn from the Roman Missal. A soaring interlace of upward-lifting string melodies accompanies this section, as do interjections of the chorus. A lightly accompanied, sweetly lyrical plea of Jesus for their forgiveness is followed by a richly chorded meditation on Psalm 22. We return to the mob around the cross in a section resembling chaos, out of which the voice of one of the crucified thieves begs for salvation and receives assurance of it. The message of Jesus to his loved ones concludes with the ancient sequence, "Stabat Mater." The modal, chantlike choral setting recalls the medieval origin of the text.

The narrator describes the time and surroundings of Jesus' last words. The soloist begins on a high pitch and falls steadily downward with, "Father, into thy hands I commit my spirit." A profoundly gloomy orchestral interlude moves from lowest strings into the chorus, culminating with a final surge of hope, "Thou has redeemed me, O Lord, faithful God." The work ends, uncharacteristically enough, on a massive major chord. Highly emotional and highly abstract at once, this Passion story is as strangely unforgettable as the Bach version.

Another contemporary setting of the crucifixion describes itself as a "rock opera," and though it leans heavily on popular styles, has not floundered upon the seedy commercialism typical of such offerings. *Jesus Christ, Superstar*, by Tim Rice and Andrew Lloyd Webber, is a strange mixture of ultra-realism, stream-of-consciousness, and near satire. Ranging freely over the Gospel accounts, the work picks up such themes as secular materialism and heterosexual love only incipient in the original documents. Jesus is portrayed in the crucifixion episode as alternately strained, perplexed, and pugnacious. He shouts at Pilate in their confrontation; the mob responds with "crucify," and the twenty-nine lashes are counted off rhythmically to a driving rock beat. Pilate concludes the scene by screaming at Jesus that if he wants to die and won't defend himself, he'll get what he deserves.

A brassy section based on the title song expresses dismay at how Jesus has botched his job. What does he think his life has been about, the chorus inquires? "Don't get me wrong. I only want to know," they reiterate to the energetic dance rhythm.

The actual crucifixion scene is an imaginative combination of the spoken words of Jesus expressing his abandonment and thirst. A wordless choral undertone, an electronic tape of sardonic laughter, and a jazz combo lace through the confusion. At his final words, "Father, into your hands I commend my spirit," the sound conglomerate suddenly ceases. A pensive, sentimental string meditation sets in, trailing off into a flute melody and two summary chords.

The martyrdom of Jesus set in motion those influences which inevitably led others to the same fate for the same cause down to the present day. The roll of Christian martyrs seems endless. Some, like St. Sebastian, are exceedingly obscure historically but widely popular. Martyrs are believed to intercede in heaven on behalf of others. Their relics are venerated. A picture of St. Sebastian, accompanied by the requisite prayer, was believed to ward off the plague during the Middle Ages. The motive for martyrdom was to absolve personal sin and assure one a place in heaven. Their example of triumph over adversity and steadfastness in suffering is their legacy to human culture.

St. Sebastian was a victim of the persecution under Roman rulership. A soldier in the service of the Emperor Diocletian, Sebastian defected to Christianity and was condemned to die by being shot with arrows. According to legend he miraculously survived, reproached the Emperor about his treatment, and was promptly clubbed to death. Martyrs are as often remembered for their outlandish or grisly deaths as for their life work, and the conditions of St. Sebastian's death fairly cried out for dramatic portrayal. Hence he became one of the most popular figures of Christian iconography.

In the painting *The Martyrdom of St. Sebastian*, Renaissance artists Antonio and Piero del Pollaiuolo chose a highly idealized version of the tale. The martyr is placed upon a low series of branches of a truncated tree, his executioners gathered in a circle about him. True to the new anatomical inquisitiveness of that age, these figures are veritable essays in the nude and clothed human figure. Revelling in the newly discovered principles of aerial perspective, the artists provide an intricate background that vanishes into distant space. Only the scale of the figuration keeps this background from overwhelming the main subject. The destination of the arrows is realistic but not gory. The body of the the martyr is classic in its proportions and posture, his eyes aimed appealingly to heaven. This work is typical, though only a single example, of the array of works dealing with this martyrdom.

More than four hundred years later these events were set into the form of a mystery play by poet Gabriele d'Annunzio and furnished with incidental music by Debussy. As a theatrical work, *The Martyrdom of St. Sebastian* is realized in the symbolic style of early twentieth-century impressionists. In the first scene Sebastian witnesses the martyrdom of two brothers, and their manner utterly transports him until he dances toward them over a field of fire. The heavenly seraphim join their ecstatic hymn, the crowd bows to earth in terror, and the heavens open for the souls of the two martyrs.

The second scene is equally metaphysical, centering on a confrontation with the mystery cults of the ancient world. Sebastian tells the worshipers of Apollo and Dionysus the news of Christ, and vows to destroy their magic chamber. By the power of the Savior's shroud the bronze doors swing open and a dim vision of the Virgin appears inside. Sebastian, overcome, kneels on the threshold.

In the third scene Sebastain is offered wordly success by the Emperor Augustus and refuses it, telling him instead the Passion story in an elaborate dance-mime. The women in attendance mistake him for the god Adonis and throw themselves upon him in a frenzy of devotion. Revolted by such sacrilege, Sebastian throws the awards the Emperor gave him to the floor.

The fourth scene is the martyrdom episode in which Sebastian, tied to a laurel tree, is riddled with arrows. A flourish of trumpets begins the scene with a strong, clear martial sound. A male chorus of soldiers repeats their instructions to "shoot until your quivers are empty and his body is like a wild hedge-hog." A pensive orchestral meditation reflects upon this fate as an apparition of the Savior carrying a lamb, appears, and vanishes. The voices of the women disciples of Adonis mistakenly lament his coming death in the form of Sebastian. Their high wails float in wisps over the orchestra, "Weep, oh women of Syria. Cry out: Alas! My dear Lord." Their anguish grows more intense and ends the scene in a rush of sound.

Section five begins with a quiet orchestral interlude based on a short questioning melody as though the import of the death were in doubt. At length a more secure lyric sweep dominates, leading to a resounding major chord as the heavens open. In the concluding hymn choruses of virgins, martyrs, apostles, and angels welcome the soul of Sebastian to paradise. The overlay of male and female voices forms shafts of multicolored sound, gathering at the end of each verse to a climax of joy on the name "Sebastian." The voice of the martyr himself rises from the midst of this hymn with the exclamation, "I am a soul, O Lord, in thy bosom." A rhapsodic choral finale praises God to the text of Psalm 150, concluding with "Alleluia, alleluia," in massive chords.

Artistic interpretations of the lives of martyrs have varied from the sublime, as in the Debussy score, to the "cheeky," as in the case of Bernard Shaw's play *St. Joan*. Joan of Arc lived at a critical time at the birth of modern Europe and unknowingly precipitated some of its major changes. Her canonization early in the twentieth century revived interest in her life and brought to light many documents that detailed her activities. Her brief career has been the subject of several films, an opera, a dance composition, statues, and iconographic paintings. Of them all, Shaw's play has been the most successful and controversial.

Rejecting the image of Joan as the "dear little girl with the holy bob face," he shows a woman of indomitable energy and pretensions to revealed truth that stunned sensible people of her time. After the triumph at Orleans even her close friends wished that she would return quietly to her farm. High officials trembled at the potential effect of her example.

Shaw came to grips with the character and habits of Joan in ways that are consistent with his opinion that she was a person of extraordinary good sense and resourcefulness. In the play she defends her appropriation of male attire by stating the obvious—that she was acting like a soldier and needed to dress like one. To Robert de Baudricourt's assertion that the supposed voices of the three saints guiding her "come from your imagination," she replies quite openly, "Of course, that is how the messages of God come to us." To accusations that her leap from her prison tower was suicidally motivated, she replies scornfully that anybody with any sense prefers to try for freedom instead of remaining in prison. Yet she is fearfully ignorant of the machinations of politics and the power of self-interest. The whole point of her trial escapes her; the Inquisitor himself declares afterward, "She did not understand a word we were saying. It is the ignorant who suffer."

The underlying humor of Shaw's interpretation of Joan is established in the first scene with the dilemna of chickens that refuse to lay eggs. At the conclusion of the episode after the astonished military commander has agreed to give her horse and passage to the king, eggs miraculously appear. This essentially light manner enables a few bitter truths to be impressed upon readers. Supposing, Joan inquires in the epilogue, she should come back to life again so that her accusers might have a chance to make things right? Bishop Cauchon responds for all of them, "The heretic is always better dead. And mortal eyes cannot distinguish the saint from the heretic. Spare them."

What did Joan believe that was so intolerable to the powerful men of the fifteenth century? As a simple country girl she was often turned out of her bed to cower in terror as the English invaders raided the countryside. She saw her French countrymen fight under outmoded Medieval concepts of battle, using what armaments they had unskillfully. She simply had enough and decided to do something about it. Cauchon perceives her philosophy: "To her the French-speaking people are what the Holy Scriptures describe as a nation. Call this side of her heresy Nationalism if you will." Over this collection of French persons Joan envisions a legitimate titled head. As Warwick complains: "It is a cunning device to supercede the aristocracy, and make the king sole and absolute autocrat." Though he recognizes that nominally his lands are vested in him by the king, nevertheless he really owns and defends them. "Now by the Maid's doctrine the king will take our lands—our lands!—and make them a present to God; and God will then vest them wholly in the king." With this much self-interest at stake by so many influential people, Joan would be a prime candidate for martyrdom on this issue alone.

It is another pattern of belief that actually leads her to doom; Joan asserts that she deals personally with God through three saints and that her acts are a response to His directives to her. Cauchon reflects cynically:

> I know the breed. It is cancerous: if it be not cut out, stamped out, burnt out, it will not stop until it has brought the whole body of human society into sin and corruption, into waste and ruin. . . . What will the world be like when the Church's accumulated wisdom and knowledge and experience, its councils of learned, venerable pious men are thrust into the kennel by every ignorant laborer or dairymaid whom the devil can puff up with the monstrous self-conceit of being directly inspired from heaven?[23]

Warwick terms this heresy Protestantism, and allies Joan with Huss, Wycliff, and others of the early Reformation divines. Joan is utterly baffled by this attitude. She is completely above reproach in the moral and liturgical requirements of the church. She will gladly obey the reverend fathers in all their counsels, but they are not acting as holy men when they counsel her to ignore the direct voice of God. "That's plainest common sense," as Joan would say. Charles, the king she has had crowned, puts the case succinctly." "It always comes back to the same thing. She is right; everyone else is wrong."

Aside from these suspicious beliefs, what did Joan do that was beyond the bounds of toleration? Besides her pretensions to God's guidance, the articles of confession she signed at the close of the trial listed wearing an immodest (male) attire, clipping her hair, engaging in battle "even to the shedding of human blood," and inciting others to follow her. Clearly Joan transgressed that not always formally stated boundary between acceptable and unacceptable behavior. Only through recognizing her errors and placing herself in the discipline of the church could she hope "after all this wickedness" to be redeemed. Her trial is before a church court, the aim of which is to save her immortal soul. But to Joan the state of the body is of quite essential importance and, learning that she is to be imprisoned until the end of her life, she revokes her confession, crying "Light your fire: do you think I dread it as much as the life of a rat in a hole?"

So she was burned, cautioning those who held the cross out for her solace to stand back lest they be singed. Whatever was left of her ended at the bottom of the river, and the executioner assured the trial officials that that would be the last of it. But Joan's personality was far too powerful. She had established a new political order; she had polarized public opinion. The causes that she represented, of which she may have been only dimly aware, represented the leading edges of a massive change that was sweeping over European culture. Joan stood with one foot in the Middle Ages and one in the Renaissance; her death was the symbolic separation of these eras.

The closer one draws to one's own time the more difficult it is to recognize a true martyr with any certainty. After all, the recognition of Joan of Arc as a major martyr accumulated over a five-hundred-year period. The qualities of Martin Luther King and the results of his life activities have been absorbed into the social fabric and received some initial projection into the arts and literature, all of which forecasts the possibility of martyr status. For best effect, people identified as part of the power structure should have been responsible for his death instead of merely an errant gunman. John F. Kennedy was not a candidate because of lack of a controversial social, political, or religious policy to split the nation. His death, also, was out of character. Even some regrettable instances of persecution lack specific hallmarks of martyrdom. The "witches" of Salem were victims of hostility against persons of their age and sex agitated by a wave of superstitious hysteria. They had no well-defined collective cause, except perhaps the right to be left alone. Even the most memorable heroes of our Revolutionary War were not objects of that peculiar brand of social guilt which forms the foundation of martyr status.

The case of Sacco and Vanzetti is a marginal but interesting one that contains most of the qualities of martyrdom. The one lack is that of a strong, highly vocal and persistent following sharing a well-defined cause. The two men were Italian-born immigrants living in Boston and organizing support for their political philosophy of anarchism. They became centers of agitation between various immigrants and the older white, Anglo-Saxon, Protestant settlers who held powerful social positions. On April 15, 1920, the Slater and Morrill Shoe Company in South Braintree was robbed and a paymaster and guard shot to death. A few weeks later Sacco, who worked in another shoe factory, and Vanzetti, a fish peddler, were arrested while carrying pistols. A year later they were put on trial for murder, initiating one of the most divisive controversies of this century. Marginally admissive evidence about a bullet and their whereabouts at the time of the shooting were discussed with the jury. The judge was publicly accused of prejudice. The men were convicted and executed on August 23, 1927.

In their letters to their families, published after their deaths, the men maintained their innocence. The evidence was never more than circumstantial. The suspicion grew intense, and their partisans declared that the conviction was based upon their radical politics rather than their criminal guilt. Thousands of persons, including well-known figures in the literary world, demonstrated on their behalf before and after their execution. The matter is still volatile after fifty years. When officials in Boston and New York sought to set aside a day to commemorate the anniversary of their deaths, the mayor of New York was pressured into retracting the proposal and the Massachusetts governor was censured by the state senate.

The American artist Ben Shahn created the most vivid

Fig. 30 Ben Shahn. *The Passion of Sacco and Vanzetti.* 1931–32. Tempera, 84½ × 48″. Collection of Whitney Museum of American Art; gift of Edith and Milton Lowenthal in memory of Juliana Force.

memorial of those trying events in his painting *The Passion of Sacco and Vanzetti*. The dead men are exhibited in their coffins with gray complexions and sharply outlined, somewhat exaggerated features. The painting greatly resembles a caricature, collecting suggestive images unrelated to a specific naturalistic scene. Over the coffins hover three dignified figures representing the social constituencies the artist holds responsible for the deaths. The uniform of scholarship effectively indicts the intellectual community in the central figure. The flanking figures of the elegantly dressed, top-hatted men suggest those in social power. The judicial system is castigated in the form of the background figure of the judge, his hand raised swearing to uphold the law, and surrounded by courtroom trappings. Shahn's painting is a rogues' gallery lined up for our inspection. The incident itself may well fade into obscurity, leaving stacks of newspaper reports and one unforgettable painting.

The singular martyrdoms of individuals are particularly compelling to the imaginations of the general public. One person serves to focus or particularize an issue, giving us an example of a philosophy lived through to the end. However, martyrdom can be applied to groups as well. Certainly the self-slaughter of the Jews at Masada to avoid capture by the Romans has become a significant part of the history of the Middle East. The inhabitants of the island of Melos probably missed achieving a place in the cumulative memory by surrendering to the Athenians after years of siege. They were killed or enslaved anyway, and a mass act of resistance in the form of self-inflicted death might well have enshrined their cause of neutrality forever. On the other hand, the infamous deaths at Jonestown that shocked the world in recent years achieved nothing but universal horror. What factors lead an entire village or social unit to do away with itself? Is such an act incipiently heroic or merely a misguided waste; what basis is there for judgment in such matters? The fascination with such acts and the questions that surround them have proved irresistible to creative artists and writers.

Moussorgsky's opera *Khovantchina* is based upon just such an incident. The time is that of Peter the Great (1682), and the situation is the Khovansky uprising. In a land long dominated by powerful political factions, the Tsar is trying to achieve unity and extend his power into every province. He has hired German mercenaries to help him discipline regional revolutionaries. But the people are close to their old traditions, jealous of their freedom, and protective of their own leaders. Khovansky and Galitzen have managed to put together an effective coalition of peasants and soldiers of the region to resist subjection. They are aided by a group of religious fundamentalists who call themselves the Dissenters, and whose spokesman is Dosifei. Throughout the opera the noose tightens around the resistence fighters, and at last the main leaders are duped and murdered by representatives of the Tsar. The Dissenters realize that their only options are conquest or death.

At the opening of Act 5 their leader, Dosifei, meditates upon the melancholy turn of recent events and formulates their next plan of action. He sings plaintively a wandering melody, even-paced like steady thought, and accompanied by a spare background of flute and cello dialogue. As he sings sorrowfully the Dissenters walk toward him slowly and assemble around him. With each richly enunciated syllable of Russian he announces to them in a powerful base the tragic fate of their movement and its leaders. He concludes with great energy, "We are caught in the ambush of Antichrist. We will not give ourselves up to him, brothers. We will perish in flames rather than surrender." His aria is lengthy and dramatic as the people cluster about this charismatic figure.

It is time for action. The people respond in separate choruses of men and women with assurances of loyalty. Dosifei excitedly directs them to put on white shrouds, light and holy candles, and await their glory. The Dissenters chant to the tolling of a bell their intention to cleanse themselves in the sacred fire. Within this sweep of sound two lovers, Marfa and Andrei, sing in remembrance of the past. "Death is near," Marfa warns. "I shall kiss you for the last time." The bugles of the Tsar's soldiers announce their approach. "The trumpets of salvation," Dosifei cries dramatically. To a firmly accented march tune, Marfa sings of the ways of fate and her determination to join the sacrifice, tempering the vows of her love for Andrei in the flames. The bugles ring out again. The Dissenters join the heroic march tune as Marfa lights the great pyre around the community house. Violins trill like leaping flames, combining with the resounding hymn of the Dissenters and the bugles of the Tsar's soldiers. Against the background of this rich tapestry of sound the fire consumes the community in one enormous holocaust.

A work with the same theme of group martyrdom but using entirely different stylistic means of expression is the *Dialogue of the Carmelites,* by Poulenc. It is set in 1789 during the French Revolution and opens in the home of the Marquis de la Force, who relates some terrifying encounters he has had with the French mobs. His daughter, Blanche, having grown quite somber over certain portents she feels, has decided to become a nun. The world, she explains, has become an alien place, and she wishes to detach herself from it. She is examined by the Mother Superior of the Carmelite Order and promised not peace but many trials. Indeed, the Mother Superior in her death from old age has terrible visions of the convent's destruction. A young nun, reflecting upon that difficult death, utters words filled with premonition: "We do not die for ourselves alone, but for each other. Or sometimes even instead of each other. Who knows?"

Drastic changes in the convent life occur rapidly. Their priest is forbidden to say Mass. Fear descends upon the whole countryside, and the new authorities appear to dissolve the religious order and confiscate its property. Standing in their devastated chapel, the nuns decide to take the vow of martyrdom. In the confusion that follows, Blanche, the chaplain, and Mother Marie escape the mob. The rest of the community is imprisoned and condemned to death.

In the final scene the Carmelites are brought to the scaffold at the Place de la Revolution. A darkly hued march tune announces their arrival, its tense rhythm and slightly dissonant chords underscoring the tragedy of the scene. The nuns walk through the crowd singing the *Salve Regina* to that tune. From time to time their song is interrupted by a tremendous "thwack" as the guillotine descends. One by one their voices cease. Out of the crowd Blanche appears to join her sisters in their final praises to God. Blanche mounts the scaffold, and in counterpoint with the vanishing hymn begins the *Veni Creator.* After another thud she alone is left, her voice soaring upward in ecstasy until it too ceases after the last fatal thud. The orchestra dissolves into a tissue of spectral sound.

The Renaissance painter Dürer was fascinated by the story of the mass deaths of Christians ordered by the Roman Emperor Diocletian, and carried out by the King of Persia against those religious adherents in his land. Frederick the Wise commissioned a painting on this theme, a woodcut version of which had been produced ten years earlier. So complex and detailed is the painting that one is tempted to count to ascertain if all ten thousand are actually present. Though ostensibly his setting is Bythnia in 343, Dürer complicates our reference by placing the crucifixion of Christ in the left foreground. His companions, the two thieves, already hang upon their crosses, and Jesus is being prepared to join them. The Persian King, resplendent in a huge turban and gold-threaded robe, watches from his horse. The rest of the composition features, surprisingly enough, the Teutonic countryside and dress of the painter's own time. Dürer even portrays himself in a new cloak bought in Venice, pointing disconsolately at the mayhem before him. An aged Bishop is waved toward a long line of bound captives being herded up the side of a wooded cliff, from the crest of which they are leaping to their deaths. The scene is a tangled mass of dismemberment, methodological torture, and despair. Dürer could have turned his *Martyrdom of the Ten Thousand* into propaganda against the pagan East. With the mixture of historic references and change in clothing and setting, he chooses instead to use the occasion as a metaphor for the bloody religious conflict between Protestants and Catholics that blighted his own time.

Untold millions of persons have chosen voluntarily to set aside their lives. Their characters have varied from the calm nobility of Socrates to the shabby failure of Manet's painted victim. Their causes have ranged from the core concerns of human civilization to some idle bother that was too much to deal with. Some deaths have caused profound changes in the stream of history. Others have caused not the slightest ripple of effect. However and for whatever reason it may occur, voluntary death exerts continuing fascination and is a permanent theme in the cultural traditions of the world's peoples.

5
Immortality

Oh, had I the wings of the morning,
I'd fly away to Canaan's shore;
Bright angels should convey me home,
To the new Jerusalem.

"Where do you suppose new Jerusalem is, Uncle Tom?" "Oh, up in the clouds, Miss Eva." "Then I think I see it," said Eva. "Look in those clouds! —"they look like great gates of pearl; and you can see beyond them, —far, far off, —it's all gold." . . .

"Uncle Tom," said Eva, "I'm going there." The child rose, and pointed her little hand to the sky; the glow of evening lit her golden hair and flushed cheek with a kind of unearthly radiance, and her eyes were bent earnestly on the skies. "I'm going there," she said, "to the spirits bright, Tom. I'm going before long."[1]

*I*N her conversation with Uncle Tom, Eva delivers this detailed account of the conventional Western mythology of immortality. Later conversations between Uncle Tom and Simon Legree reveal the relationship of Eva's vision to Christianity in general and justice to one's fellow man in particular. New Jerusalem is, indeed, a reserved space attainable only by the pure in heart. The conviction of its existence enables Uncle Tom to achieve true saintliness and a death worthy of martyrdom. Within the context of these fictional events, the reader

163

can hardly remain unconvinced of the actuality of this vision. But do we truly persist in some recognizable form with our characteristic recollections beyond the event of death? Answers come in many varied responses, all of which may be grouped into a few mutually exclusive alternatives. Maeterlinck concluded that, outside the realm of religious doctrine, there are four imaginable solutions to the problem of immortality. There is either total annihilation; survival with our consciousness of today; survival without any sort of consciousness; or survival with some more universal consciousness different from that known in this world.

Another fundamental analysis of the possibilities for the human species after death rests on the very nature of that species. If mankind is considered as a monism—a completely unified being in which all elements of character and physical qualities combine inextricably into a single entity—then there can be but two possibilities. This being may be extinguished entirely at death, all aspects of its nature perishing completely and forever. Or this being may be miraculously reconstituted— resurrected— in some version of its original earthly form. If mankind is thought of as a dualism—a being separable into distinct and perhaps even mutually antagonistic characteristics such as body and soul—there are, again, several possibilities. This being may sustain one portion in a disembodied form in the earthly realm of its origin, perhaps maintaining certain recognizable qualities that constitute personality. Or one portion of the being may persist in an unimaginable form in a location quite different from the earthly realm. Allowing for freely embroidered extrapolations of each of these alternatives, imaginative creations in literature and the arts have tended to follow these four interpretations throughout much of human history.

Extinction

Quite unexpectedly as Vasserot
The armless ambidextrian was lighting
A match between his great and second toe
And Ralph the lion was engaged in biting
The neck of Madame Sossman while the drum
Pointed, and Teeny was about to cough
In waltz-time swinging Jocko by the thumb—

Quite unexpectedly the top blew off;
And there, there overhead, there, there, hung over
Those thousands of white faces, those dazed eyes,
There in the starless dark the poise, the hover,
There with cast wings across the canceled skies,
There in the sudden blackness the black pall
Of nothing, nothing, nothing—nothing at all.[2]

Archibald MacLeish pictures the end of the world in terms of sudden extinction, in which the most terrible of all apparitions is simply the "nothing at all." Any something would be better than this, the poem implies, even that which we expect to be revealed hovering with "cast wings in the black pall." We are unprepared for the absence of everything; nothingness must be repeated three times to convince us it is true. Extinction, on a personal or cosmic level, is the most unthinkable fate of all.

On the other hand, in Milton's *Paradise Lost* Adam muses over the alternatives waiting for him at death. His reflections lead him to a surprising attitude toward utter extinction: "It was but breath of life that sinn'd; what dies but what had life and sin? The Bodie properly hath neither. All of me then shall die: let this appease the doubt, since humane reach no further known." But he reflects again and becomes suspicious that God could draw out our punishment indefinitely to satisfy his sense of justice. "That death be not one stroke, as I suppos'd, Bereaving sense, but endless miserie" becomes his absorbing fear.[3] Extinction, then is a viable alternative that may be interpreted as an ultimate horror or a blessed relief.

The modern argument for the probability of extinction rests on the identification of mind with brain. According to this rationale, while the terms *mind* and *brain* have different meanings, they refer to the same object. As a scientific hypothesis the proposition is stated that consciousness is a brain process; thoughts and brain processes are the same things, and one does not exist without the other. Though thoughts and electrochemical phenomena seem to belong to quite different orders of reality, advocates of extinction accept a complete correspondence, instead of simply a correlation between the two. There is at present no conceivable experiment that might verify this hypothesis. Even complete brain mapping could demonstrate correlation rather than identity.

Bertrand Russell in an essay entitled "Do We Survive

Death?"[4] argues against the probability of survival after death largely on the basis of brain-mind identity and the nature of reality as change. Our memories and habits, all the things that constitute personality are, he argues, bound up with the structure of the brain. His analogy is that of a river of thought following the channel of brain grooves. When the organism dissolves at death, there is no sense in which the river of thought can proceed. We, as total mental-physical structures, act and feel and think; there is no such mediating entity as mind that does it for us. All that constitutes a person is a series of experiences connected by a memory of those experiences, which grows increasingly dim as they receded into the past.

Besides the completely physical nature of mental events, Russell points out the influence of change on both types of phenomena. The body constantly changes—its continuity is a matter of appearance and behavior, not of actual substance. Nutrition, excretion, and replacement of cells is always occurring. Reciprocally, mentality is constantly forming new habits and accepting new stimuli. Injury or lack of proper chemical nutrients may change entirely the character of the mentality. Russell concludes that it is very unlikely that under these conditions the memories and habits that compose personhood can continue after death in an entirely new set of circumstances. He confesses that belief in life after death is an important psychological defense against fear of the unknown, a key weapon in the struggle for life of our species, and essential to military ventures. Admiration for the human species and an assumption that its creator would not countenance its dissolution constitute another rationale. However, Russell dismisses these observations as not logical arguments with scientific credentials.

The Roman philosopher Lucretius argues from precisely these two points of mind-brain identity and change in his own advocacy of extinction. Following the teachings of the Greek philosopher Democritus, he accepts the idea that all things are physical compositions of only two basic properties, atoms and space. Though he observes the distinction between body and soul, Lucretius believes that they share a common atomic nature. Soul atoms are merely exceedingly round and small so that when a person dies these soul atoms, which immediately disassemble, register no loss of body weight after their passage. He explains the identity between body (brain) and soul (mind) in the imagery of the unity between redness and a rose. Souls could outlast their bodies only if waves could outlast the sea, he asserts. Yet these atomic structures we identify as ourselves are not lost, destroyed, negated. Nothing atomic can be lost, because that unit is eternal and indivisible. At this point the process of change becomes intrinsic to his view. Life lives on, disunited and reassembled in varied forms, though a specific existence may end. Consciousness is the victim of this theory of extinction. Nothing of us dies (since everything is atomic) but there is no continuity of memory between our present state of atomic assemblage and any future state. Thus Lucretius lifts the voice of science against superstition, offering freedom from irrational fears of imagined torments in a nonexistent afterlife.

The consolation of extinction is elaborated in D. H. Lawrence's poem "The Ship of Death":

> Have you built your ship of death, Oh have you?
> Oh build your ship of death, for you will need it.
>
> Now in the twilight, sit by the invisible sea
> Of peace, and build your little ship
> Of death, that will carry the soul
> On its last journey, on and on, so still
> So beautiful, over the last of seas.
> When the day comes, that will come.
> Oh think of it in the twilight peacefully!
> The last day, and the setting forth
> On the longest journey, over the hidden sea
> To the last wonder of oblivion.
>
> Oblivion, the last wonder!
> When we have trusted ourselves entirely
> To the unknown, and are taken up
> Out of our little ships of death
> Into pure oblivion.
>
> Oh build your ship of death, be building it now
> With dim, calm thoughts and quiet hands
> Putting its timbers together in the dusk,
> Rigging its mast with the silent, invisible sail
> That will spread in death to the breeze
> Of the kindness of the cosmos, that will waft
> The little ship with its soul to the wonder-goal.
>
> Ah, if you want to live in peace on the face of the earth

Then build your ship of death, in readiness
For the longest journey, over the last of seas.[5]

Drawing from the ancient imagery of a water journey to a land of the dead separated from that of the living, D. H. Lawrence ends the journey in oblivion. Yet this destination is urged upon us as a pilgrimage of beauty. It is undertaken purposefully, for we must construct our conveyance out of our deepest contemplation. We are using invisible sails to navigate an invisible sea on a totally subjective voyage. We can conclude our journey only when we have learned to trust the unknown; only then do we leave our psychic vessels and vanish into pure oblivion. There are no alternatives; we must build that ship because we will need it. Yet neither D. H. Lawrence nor Lucretius regards the prospect of oblivion as a dismal eventuality. Their language is elevated, allusive, even mystic. The process they describe is of the very nature of reality and therefore ultimately trustworthy.

A similar intuition is shared by Ivan Ilyich at the end of a prolonged agony of dying.[6] Out of long periods of introspection, terror, and regret, Ivan Ilyich arrives at last at the end of his life. He wishes only to stop his torment and that of his waiting family. He is in terror both of death, which is to come, and pain, which is unrelentingly present. His dark mental state is deepened by his own estimation of his life as a disappointment. He has left behind nothing that truly represents the depths of himself. So he is dying after many months of suffering, without hope or even the comfort of human companionship. At the last moments he realizes that death is not to be feared. He hears someone say "It is all over," and realizes that it is. Death does not exist any more, thinks Ivan, as he stretches himself and dies. That which he has feared has vanished; Ivan has met death and found it bearable. Surrender to the simple nature of reality, to origin and cessation, has become a joy.

The viewpoint of extinction at death is not one from which an abundance of detailing has poured forth. It is an alternative far too spare to inspire artistic elaboration. Most creative solutions based upon an acceptance of extinction spring from avoidance of this inevitability. Extinction is the basic philosophy of much of Western culture—not that there is active promulgation of monism of this sort, but that there is a profound lack of conviction about any other version of our state after death. No mythic tradition has risen to replace the dispirited Christian mythology, hence extinction is more grudgingly than enthusiastically embraced. Goethe's character Faust exemplifies modern man, whose whole stake is in this life and who is unconcerned about any existence beyond this plane of reference. Mephistopheles offers Faust infinite freedom, youth, power, in return for infinite reverse service when Faust dies. Faust barely hesitates in accepting the offer. He asserts that what lies beyond doesn't worry him; his whole meaning as a human being springs from this earth. From this life comes all the joy he is likely to know.

Immortality here on earth, in avoidance of extinction, has become the absorbing concern of our century. Immunization, replacement of body parts, and discovery of certain keys to the aging process have in turn provided some element of hope that life on earth might be extended indefinitely. The potentials and limitations of this ultimate response to extinction have been the subject for some stunning works of literature. In *The Immortalist* Alan Harrington puts the matter squarely: "that insight into doom, once the priviledge of certified thinkers, has now been brought home to nearly everybody who can read. . . . the gut realization that the void is waiting for everybody and that each of us is going to vanish into it. . . . Salvation by whatever means—and quickly. It has become the central passion that drives us, a need rapidly turning into an imperious demand to be rescued from nothingness."[7]

The quest for immortality has taken some bizarre forms in our time, Harrington asserts, pointing to publicity of any kind as a mode of perpetuation for which some people are driven to kill. The hippie subculture is seen as a means to achieve immortality now in freedom from time, social systems, and the past in any form. The communal immortality of violence is represented by the Hell's Angels and Chinese Red Guard. The central question of our time, says Harrington, is whether medical advances to arrest the aging process will prevail over mass psychosis and military destruction. In response he urges the immortalist thesis that the time has come to go after the problem at the heart of all these lethal phenomena, our desperate need for an immortality achievable through medical engineering. Although no specific biological entity may be guaranteed eternal life, the inevitable process of aging and death can be eliminated, he believes.

One might legitimately hesitate to live endlessly in a human society marked by violence, greed, and all the normal faults endemic to our species. Harrington believes that the absence of death would change much within our nature. Evil is the direct result of death. We offend our neighbor out of a need to reinforce our own claim to immortality at his expense. The natural order seems bent upon doing away with us, and as a result we see ourselves as rivals for advantage in some state beyond death. If evil is simply one attempt to get around death, then the elimination of the inevitability of death should make the world a much less evil place in which to live.

In the same manner the frantic sexual liaisons characteristic of our age are regarded as attempts to halt the flow of time and hold onto something of eternity. "The lovers step off the moving sidewalk that carries everyone else toward death." Lying is a result of the need to evade death. The liar distorts reality in order to validate his existence, hoping to fool the presumed balance sheet that constitutes one's immortality card. Even contemporary arts Harrington regards as experiments in maneuvering time so as to make available multiple zones of action. Participants escape fear of nothingness by living multiple lives all at once vicariously through the spell cast by the creative act or work.

Believing that only the achievement of an effective earthly immortality can solve the moral dilemma of mankind, Harrington procedes to indicate how this state might be brought about. He catalogues a multitude of experiments underway, including cryonics, replacement of parts, cellular duplication, and injections of one's own DNA newly grown in a test tube. "Only by subduing the processes that force us to grow old will we be able to exempt ourselves from death, the lot of beasts, and assume the status of gods, our rightful inheritance."[8]

What would a person do with such a life as an option? Harrington envisions time out from single lives, hibernations of self-determined lengths, after which one would assume a life chosen from numerous possibilities. Relationships could be renewed or dropped from one life to the next. One would be free to reject such rejuvenation, age and die; or there is the alternative of self-elected suicide. There is always the risk of accidental death to add edge to such an existence. The central message emerges clearly. Extinction has always been the normal fate of mankind, causing despair that results in a wide range of human evils. The only remedy against extinction lies in technological conquest of the process of aging, with death as its inescapable conclusion.

This is the stuff of which science fiction is made, and Harrington's book is first cousin to that genre. Rejuvenation in some form is, indeed, a significant theme in contemporary science fiction writing. Nikolai Amosov's novel *Notes from the Future* celebrates earthly immortality with much of the gusto encountered in *The Immortalist*. Amosov's hero, a Russian scientist dying of leukemia, has himself frozen, awakens in 1991, and is cured. He begins life anew with another full cycle of learning, love, children, and contact with the existent world. Harrington warns us that the transitional generations will experience great difficulty in adapting to immortalist potentials and reordering society to encompass eternal individuals. The "between" generations and the social chaos resulting from the presence of the first immortals are the focus of two well-known science fiction novels.

In *Methuselah's Children*, Robert Heinlein envisions the year A.D. 2136 and a widespread group (100,000 strong) of extremely long-lived persons descended from the Howard family genetic chain. They have achieved a life span of several hundred years through a slow process of natural selection, aided by hormones, symbiotics, gland therapy, and some psychotherapy. Senescence is inevitable, but can be indefinitely postponed. When at last it appears, the person dies within ninety days, though most choose euthanasia once they are sure of the diagnosis. Because the family is mutually supportive as well as intelligent, they have amassed a large fortune, which enables most of them to live comfortably. They share a psychic sensitivity that allows them to communicate without being detected. The near planets of our solar system have been colonized on a limited basis, so there are many places to go and a great deal to do.

Although the Howard families would seem to be in a most fortunate state, actually they are in quite a dangerous situation. Eve Barstow explains:

> it is clear to me now that our mere presence, the simple fact of our rich heritage of life, is damaging to the spirit of our poor neighbor. Our longer years and richer opportunities make his best efforts seem futile to him—any effort save a hopeless strug-

gle against an appointed death. Our mere presence saps his strength, ruins his judgment, fills him with panic fear of death.[9]

Because of this quite accurate perception of their effect on society, the Howard families have kept their existence a secret for many generations. During periods of civil upset they have created new identities or altered their age records to better fit their appearance. At last human culture reached a point of great stability; the age records of the family were becoming indefensible; and it was decided to allow up to ten percent of the family members to reveal their actual status. This was a mistake. The result was a smoldering resentment against these persons, which at the time of the story is about to burst into flame.

Society has mistakenly decided that there is an instant solution to the mortality problem and that the Howard families have it and treasonably refuse to share it with others. Political pressure has forced the head Administrator to have all members of the family arrested and tortured, if need be, to extract the truth from them. The Administrator talks with the chiefs of the family to try to find some way to avoid the massive persecution that seems inevitable. The solution they hit upon is to allow mass immigration via a huge cargo spaceship to some place outside the solar system. With true Buck Rogers spirit and engineering genius they manage to orbit past the sun. Overcrowding and boredom lead to many volunteers for cold storage, which alleviates problems of space and food supply. Years pass.

The travelers take up residence on two different but seemingly hospitable worlds. Each proves lethal for human habitation. On the first the dominant life forms on the planet wish to turn the earth people into domesticated animals and, finding them unsuitable, cast them back into space. On the second the collective personhood of the inhabitants totally absorbs one of the earth people and begins genetic transformations to improve the stock with a newborn child. Disillusioned, the space voyagers decide to return to earth in hopes that after a seventy-five-year absence they may be welcome.

Earth has by this time discovered the secret of immortality, achieved basically by continuous blood exchange. The departed are welcomed because in their absence everyone has become like them. But an earth with a nearly immortal population has become an inhospitable place. The people of the North American continent number nearly 700,000,000 and the demand for housing is almost insurmountable. Official permission must be obtained to bear a child. People have come to wonder about the value of living such an extended life:

> What is the purpose of our long lives? We don't seem to grow wiser as we grow older. Are we simply hanging on after our time has passed? Loitering in the kindergarten when we should be moving on? Must we die and be born again?[10]

The returnees have a different perspective. Lazarus declares: "Earth men never have had enough time to tackle the important questions. Lots of capacity and not enough time to use it properly." From one of their planetary adventures they have returned with a starship drive that will enable mankind to colonize the great star systems. With an unlimited life span and technical means to achieve freedom in space, humans begin the greatest era of their species.

The Immortals, by James Gunn, is a much more pessimistic assessment of the impact of earthly immortality in conflict with extinction. A genetic mutation of the blood has made one man, Cartwright, immortal. The fact is discovered when he sells his blood to a blood bank and the recipient reverts to a thirty-year-previous state of health. The physician who traces the donor reveals the nature of his heritage and urges him to propagate himself through children as widely as possible, and also to avoid detection so as not to be bled to death by wealthy elderly people wanting a reprieve from their own deaths. Eventually a Dr. Russell Pearce discovers a way to create limited amounts of elixir based upon the original Cartwright blood sample, and medicine begins to offer the assurance of immortality once reserved for religion.

The novel concentrates upon the tragic effects of this discovery upon human culture. As Dr. Pearce remarks before his defection from medicine: "They've added a few years—just a few—to the average lifespan, and our society is groaning at the readjustment. Think what forty years would do! Think what would happen if we never died!" He believes that such a phenomenon must come slowly by mutative spread, and to some extent through rediscovery of mental alternatives in healing. Dr. Pearce himself claims to be almost two hundred years old without having had a transfusion of Cartwright blood or an elixir injection. The effective mind, he has discovered, can control the very cells that make up the blood stream and the body.

Meanwhile medicine has become the obsession of the population, consuming 52% of the nation's wealth. The technology of health has become stupendously complex and staggeringly expensive. The wealthy form a cadre of cartels in the medical market, supporting physicians with enormous endowments and perquisites. Physicians in turn endow their financiers with the potions that keep them alive, abandoning people without the vast sums required for the treatment of various common diseases. The National Research Institute grows constantly stronger by inheriting the estates of clients who do finally die. Hijacking of medications is common; head hunters capture and sell human bodies, which are permanently anesthetized to be used for organ banks. One young intern asks impatiently: "Why are a hundred million people without adequate medical facilities, condemned to a lingering death in a sea of carcinogens, unable to afford what the orators call 'the finest flower of medicine?'" The cost of living is always given as the reason, along with the observation that "we can be too healthy." Either the too old or the too young are most often the objects of vastly expensive medical treatment. Medical staffs are saving the lives of people at the margins of existence for lives of perpetual care, and placing the final burden of this attention upon society at large. Is there an optimum beyond which medicine consumes more than it produces in benefits, the young intern wonders? Is this why medicine has become a monster, devouring the society that produced it? What allowed this to happen except the terror of extinction? The wealthy have a morbid fear of death and disease. The huge mass of society has nothing more to look forward to.

In the end of the novel we meet one of the immortals, who has received all the advantages of the medical-political complex. He is the governor-dictator of what was once Kansas. He is attached permanently to nutrient tubes that keep him alive, a gigantic maggotlike entity of sagging white flesh who has not moved from his filthy bed for half a century. He has married a Cartwright and bled her and her mother regularly to supply himself with continuing life. He represents the ultimate degradation of medicine, a compilation of physical inadequacies that under normal circumstances would have caused a merciful death. Here is the immortal we will get by technological means, and here is the price our whole culture will pay to sustain his miserable life.

Acceptance of the probability of extinction forcuses the quest for immortality squarely within the context of the present and considerably broadens the very definition of eternal life. There is, for example, one case of physical immortality that has become part of medical folklore. HeLa, acronym for a name inaccurately recorded as Henrietta Lacks, Helen Lane, or Helen Larson, is very much alive in cellular form in laboratories all over the world. Her history as an immortal begins in February of 1951, when a biopsy specimen from her cancerous cervix was given to Dr. George Guy of Johns Hopkins Hospital. Though many others had failed, her malignant cells multiplied in his roller tubes and established subcultures. He was able to transplant some original cells into new tubes where they proliferated grandly. Samples were shipped to cancer research centers nationally and then worldwide. These cells became the standard basis for diagnostic comparison, yielding important data about the metabolism and growth characteristics of cancer. They have been exposed to environmental pollutants, drugs, and chemicals to measure resulting physiological disturbances. Thus for thirty years HeLa the woman has been physically alive and of great value to society.

After several thousand years we have come full circle back to Lucretius, finding that, after all, we are most obviously alive in particulate form. Such a philosophy seems appropriate to the painting by Miró entitled *Maternity*. No beatific mother-and-child of the Christmas advertisements appears before us. We are presented with the germ plasm itself, the minuscule elements out of which organisms are formed. They swim in a multitude of cheerful squiggles, clean etched on a bright color field. If there is anything enduring, agree Lucretius and Miro, it is the basic genetic code that gives the directives to existence. Beyond consciousness, beyond time, these seedlings float into the stream of life, forever corporeal, part of the stuff of the universe.

Resurrection

Acceptance of the monistic character of human life does not require a parallel acceptance of extinction as its sole conclusion; however, avoiding this ideological link seemingly necessi-

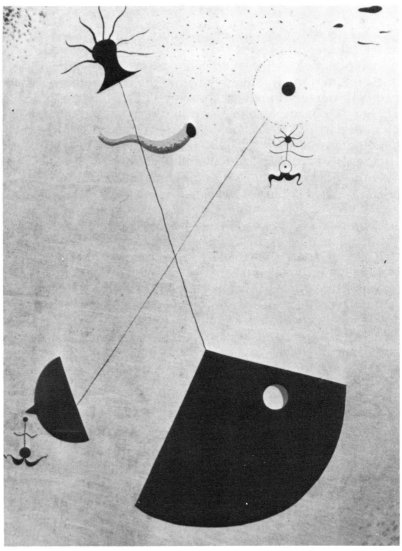

Fig. 31 Joan Miró. **Maternity.** 1924. Oil on canvas, 35¾ × 28¾″. Collection of Sir Roland Penrose, London.

tates recourse to the miraculous. Gibbon, in his *Decline and Fall of the Roman Empire,* attributes the origin of the resurrection image to the Egyptians and describes the Islamic version of this idea. God the Creator reanimates the breathless clay and recollects the scattered elements of our corporeal forms. But between the moment of death and the moment of resurrection, all is mysterious.

In the Western tradition the resurrection motif is firmly embedded in the narrative of events after the cruxifixion, though there is quite a variation of interpretation among the extant accounts. The Gospel of Luke contains the most physical orientation. Not only does Jesus appear to his disciples after his death and burial, but he invites them to touch him and even eats a fish in their presence. However, in another account he cautions the women who have come to anoint his body not to touch him because he has not yet ascended to his Father. Jesus himself spoke in physical terms of the "temple" of his body, which he would raise up in three days (John:18–22). Yet on another occasion he spoke as though the physical conditions of our earthly lives had no similarity at all to our state after death (Mark 12:18–27). The Gospel of Matthew elaborates upon the purely physical reality of the resurrection by relating that at the moment of Jesus' death many bodies of saints who had died were raised, came out of their tombs, and were witnessed in Jerusalem by many people. There is no "natural" explanation for this concept of immortality in the sense of the case argued by Lucretius and Russell for extinction. Such an eventuality is understood to be far beyond the range of the expected or the attainable by natural means.

Other, less physical, versions of the Resurrection also existed from the beginning of the Christian tradition. Luke 24:31 relates Jesus' appearance within a locked room and his disappearance in the same manner. The earliest (ca. A.D. 50) account of the Resurrection in 1 Corinthians 15:3–8 is expressed in terms of a series of visions, the last of which occurred to Paul himself on the way to Damascus. He does not refer to a physical presence, rather a blinding light and a voice speaking to him. The nature of this revelation to him personally is the basis upon which Paul claims his firsthand experience of the Resurection; thus it is incumbent upon him to present the incident carefully and accurately. In Romans 6:3–11 Paul uses the Resurrection in a highly metaphoric manner as something in which all believers participate. We die to sin and are resurrected in holiness.

In whatever interpretation it may appear, the doctrine of resurrection did not originate with the death of Jesus. Gibbon may be correct that the idea is evident in ancient Egyptian culture; certainly it was prevalent in mainstream Judaism before the time of Jesus. Linked to it inextricably was the myth of the Last Judgment along with several interpretations as to when this event might take place. In the parable of the sheep and goats Jesus pictures a culmination to earthly events in the coming of the Son of Man in his glory; the Last Judgment occurs at that time. But in the parable of Dives and Lazarus the poor man is carried by angels to Abraham's bosom, and the unrighteous rich man finds himself in torment. Judgment occurs in this instance at the moment of death, and prior to resurrection in the general sense. These two versions combine uneasily in the historic development of Christianity.

John H. Hick, H. G. Wood Professor of Theology at Birmingham University, England, suggests one way in which the concept of resurrection can be thought of intelligibly today.[11] He offers a "replica" theory, in which an exact psychophysical concretion of a deceased person appears in a presently unobservable space. It is logically possible, he points out, for there to be any number of partly contingent worlds, each in its appropriate space, all observable at once by Universal Intelligence. This interpretation is substantiated by Norbert Wiener, the cyberneticist, who divorces bodily identity from physical matter. The living human body is a pattern of change, and that pattern can be coded and translated much as radio signals and video signals are. It is theoretically possible to transmit the "self" in coded form to some hypothetical receiving instrument. One need only extend the analogy to transmission outside the world with which we are familiar. Thus resurrected persons would retain identity, memory, and recognition. They would know that they were replications only by recognizing the incompatibility of their time-space assumptions with their present situation. In fact, the time assumnptions might actually be workable; events might transpire in quite different spaces at the same markable moment in a single time flow. Our whole concept of "the same person," Hick confesses, has not been developed to cope with such a situation. There are conceivable situations in which personal identity would cease to apply, but the principle, he maintains, is a logical possibility.

Resurrection as a motif in visual art has both highly concrete and metaphoric aspects. Preceding that of Jesus, the raising of Jairus's daughter, a widow's son at Nain, and Lazarus all figure prominently in the Gospel accounts of his ministry. The Book of Acts records Peter's raising Tabitha from the dead. Thus resurrection was early a major manifestation of the miraculous within the Christian faith. To be sure, these incidents are not restorations of the flesh long after it has fallen to dust, as is implicit in the belief in the coming of the Kingdom of God. But they are restorations to life of both physical and mental facilities in a publicly recognizable form of the original person. Though the Gospel of John alone relates the story of the raising of Lazarus, the very detail with which it is rendered has made it a popular subject for artistic realization. By the time Jesus arrives after being summoned by the sisters of the dead man, he has been four days in the tomb. Jesus explains that he is the resurrection and the life, and that he has power to overcome death. Jesus stands before the tomb and calls out, "Lazarus, come forth." The once-dead man soon appears, dressed in the burial wrappings and quite obviously alive. The drama of the situation and its extremity have given to this episode an enduring iconographic importance from the early third century on. Some forty representations survive in the catacombs alone. The scene is repeated in manuscript paintings, ivory ornaments, sarcophagi, and altar decorations as well as formal paintings or murals. It has been transferred into the material surroundings and style preferences of widely differing cultural traditions.

However significant, the raising of Lazarus is understood as a metaphor for the Resurrection of Jesus himself, which has been rendered in a variety of styles from the abstractly symbolic to the sensuously idealistic. This subject is the basis for the most famous fresco by Renaissance painter Piero Della Francesca. Since the Resurrection is not described anywhere in the Gospels, Piero chooses his own setting, the countryside around the small Italian town where the painting was placed. The gray dawn is breaking over the barren hills and through the small clearing in the woods. Four soldiers in varied positions of sleep are arranged at one side of a massive stone sarcophagus. Jesus is placed still standing within this tomb, one leg raised so that the foot rests on the stone top. One arm rests easily on the knee, while the other holds a tall pole to which is attached a flag with a symmetrical cross emblem. His wounds still visible, Jesus looks directly at the viewer in an attitude of sorrow and contemplation. A clean, timeless piece of geometry, the very form of the picture invites close inspection of such subtle symbolism as the bare trees to the left and the fully leafed trees to the right of center.

A Northern Renaissance painter, Grünewald, takes quite a different approach in his Resurrection panel of the Isenheim Altarpiece. A huge ball of brilliant yellow-orange surrounds the head of Jesus, who is shown suspended above his tomb, which has just been blown apart by the force of his exit. The sleeping guards have been thrown backward into the air and are caught in mid-flight by the artist's brush. The striking color and broken lines make the work sizzle with energy, as though this singular event were seen in the brief space of a lightening flash.

Michelangelo's drawing for his planned Resurrection mural is midway between these extremes. Choosing the mode of idealization, the artist portrays Jesus in a classical body style emerging deliberately from a low stone sarcophagus and reaching upward in joy and expectation. One figure beside him matches his gesture in an opposing manner, falling backward in astonishment. The other figures of the guards place their nude forms about decoratively in a variety of eloquent poses. The contrast of expressive musculature and gesture of the two bodies and the languid poses of the others give the work a balanced level of tension.

A modern version of the Resurrection by Jacob Epstein in the nave of Llandaff Cathedral, Cardiff, returns to a pre-Reformation level of abstract symbolism. The sculpture is largely a plain bronze tube from shoulder to ankle. The highly realistic face is as contemplative as the Piero version. Hands and feet still bear the wounds of crucifixion. The most visually lively portion of the work is the yards of clothlike bronze falling in levels from shoulder to wrist like burial sheets. The work is fashioned to be wall mounted, and thus, like the Grünewald version, to appear suspended as though in a vision.

The Resurrection of Christ is one specific instance of a more universal ideology, which includes a summary of earthly history, a resurrection of the human species, and a final judgment and dispersal of individuals to their eternal states. This

Last Judgment is the subject of some of the most unrelentingly terrifying iconography throughout the world. In the Buddhist-Taoist system Yama, the king of the dead, administers ten law courts, which judge crimes and allot punishment. Yama is shown as a Chinese judge, red-faced and angry generally, with occasional lapses into leniency. He examines each mortal with the aid of a mirror that reflects their deeds and of a staff with accusing faces carved upon it. Medieval cathedrals exhibited equally frightening scenes often directly above a main church door. On Bourges Cathedral angels weigh souls while demons stand close by with sharp prods in case the scales show some imbalance. In other similar surfaces giant hands are sometimes shown plucking the dead from the earth in preparation for this climactic judicial process. The style of exaggerated realism is all too convincing.

The most famous Last Judgment scene, painted by Michelangelo on the altar wall of the Sistine Chapel, is equally unrelenting. It is based upon the version of the second coming in Matthew, which pictures Jesus descending from heaven in great glory. His angels, with a sound of trumpets, gather his elect throughout earth and the heavens. From the level of the altar, figures rise from the earth in all conceivable states, fleshed and unfleshed. In a vast array they ascend to circle around the central figure of Christ and sink slowly downward toward hell. A full range of emotions, excluding those of joy and hope, is exhibited. Wonder, awe, fearfulness, dread, even utter stupefaction, combine to a pitch of terror. It is a scene unrelieved by any significant color except that of human flesh against a slate blue sky. A massive figure of Christ assumes the central position, his right hand raised in condemnation of those who fall back into hell, and his left hand gesturing more gently in benediction to the blessed.

Michelangelo's is certainly a graphic version of the Last Judgment, but it emphasizes the inner spiritual factors as well as purely physical ones. There is, to be sure, a representative faction of demons, a glimmer of the fires of hell, and some bodies in skeletal form; mostly there is the human form in all its beauty, matching on a lesser scale that of the very angels. The torment is that of the guilty soul rather than that of the ravaged body. The power of the work lies in its massive visionary quality rather than in gruesome details. It is one cultural revolution removed from the entire medieval mentality of cathedral art.

Fig. 32 Michelangelo. ***The Last Judgment.*** 1534–41. Fresco. Sistine Chapel, Rome. *Photograph courtesy of EPA.*

In massiveness and power the Michelangelo version of the Last Judgment is matched in music by the *Dies Irae* sections of the two most famous requiems of the Romantic period, those by Verdi and Berlioz. The sonic resources employed are of the scale of the Sistine Chapel altar painting. Spatial means used for the three works share the gigantic forward pull moving intensely through time or space. The use of Latin lends to the music the same authority gained in the painting by the use of classical anatomical structure and pose. The vigor and firm definition of Michelangelo's individual figures are paralleled by the sectional contrasts in the music.

Verdi begins his *Dies Irae* with four abrupt, heavily accented chords played with full orchestra. The huge chorus responds with a unison melody that becomes a virtual wail of anguish to the text, "Dies irae, dies illa," picturing the day of wrath and mourning prophesied long ago. A series of string tremolos threads through the outcry of the chorus in a line that wends from the top to the bottom of their sound range. Suddenly a quiet, mysterious passage with the hollow resonance of a clarinet repeats the message of the prophet's warning, lending an air of certain doom. The "dies irae" text is repeated sorrowfully again and again. A swift alteration in texture leads to a deep-toned, gloomy march rhythm over which the chorus declaims in a spare stroke of sound a vision of heaven and earth burning and mankind trembling in fear.

The brilliant sound of a trumpet introduces the middle section. It is immediately joined by other brasses from various positions around the audience until the sound reaches a peak of brilliancy and energy. Batteries of drums intensify the racket, and the chorus declares "tuba mirum," portraying the last trumpet sounding through earth's sepulchers and summoning all before the throne of judgment. In contrast to the sheer noise of this section, a baritone soloist declaims the "mors stupebit" as death is struck down and all creation awakes. The melody is a slow, dramatically sustained line that the orchestra, as though fearful of such a proclamation, punctuates very sparsely. The word *mors* is repeated sorrowfully and concluded with a single chord.

A soprano soloist gives the "liber scriptus" (in the book all is recorded) a pleading, lyric melody with a soft upturning phrase. It is a patch of bright color against a virtual death march in the choral background. As though frightened, she sings in swift, widely spaced tones the warning that judgment shall be meted out. The chorus has followed her sadly, intoning the "dies irae" as response. After one last soaring outcry from the soprano, the chorus bursts in, as at first, with the wild anguish of sudden realization, "judex ergo" (when the judge has taken his seat and every hidden deed is revealed, nothing will be left unpunished). It is a merciless conclusion, a vision of cosmic violence.

The Berlioz *Dies Irae* is every bit as expansive and dramatic, using the same general sound resources, but with quite different detailing. It is a predominantly masculine effort, using divided parts to make a men's chorus provide a vigorously heroic, or expressively dark-hued sound. Berlioz begins, quite unlike Verdi, with deep, soft, string tones in a unison melody reminiscent of the orginial Gregorian Chant version of the text. In high contrast, a delicate lyric soprano melody floats above the constant intonation of "dies irae" by the male chorus. The texture changes at the beginning of "quantus tremor," the women joining the men in an uneasy sea of moving lines that resemble the anguish of fear. Suddenly the entire orchestra joins a grand upward tremolo passage, and the "quantus judex" idea receives a strong march rhythm. Bass viols pluck ominously on the offbeat. Another upward-sweeping tremolo thrusts out a strong, steady soprano line accompanied by a mass of swiftly moving bass and tenor lines. A third dramatic orchestral sweep concludes the section.

The "tuba mirum" most closely resembles the treatment given by Verdi, for it too features massed fanfares of brasses. The resulting enormous blast of sound sustains for many measures, underlining the text with an air of pure terror. The tenors sing the "tuba mirum" in full heroic sound with the power of a single clean-etched melody. In contrast, the basses respond with a soft, ominous pedal point on the text "death is struck down and all creation wakes." The trumpets return in full force, along with a division of male voices to portray the reading from the book of records. At the word *judex* the bass drums roll and the women's voices join in the expression of fear at this inevitable event. What seems like the absolute summary of the section is reached with brasses, choir, drums, and orchestra. From the depths of total silence following the massive cadence a sad, meditative melody quietly laments over the last bit of text, "nothing will be left unpunished."

A most imaginative and detailed literary version of the resurrection motif is conceived in Philip José Farmer's award-winning science fiction novel, *To Your Scattered Bodies Go*. His hero is Sir Richard Francis Burton, the famous explorer, who becomes conscious seemingly immediately after his death. All the old familiar pains of his worn body are gone. As soon as he can see he notices a multitude of floating forms in an infinity of space. He realizes that they are all human forms of great variety, naked and hairless, spinning slowly and guided by metal rods that radiate some sort of force. Slowly they are being reconstituted into healthy young versions of themselves with all their earthly elements of personality intact. He loses consciousness and wakes in a space that closely resembles earth and carries all its time-space assumptions. His companions in this new place are extremely varied as to time and origin. One is a nonhuman space traveler; another is a subhuman precursor. The same antagonism and dissension prevails as on earth, and much of the time of Burton and his companions is spent in defending themselves. There is plenty of food sent to them, all prepared daily at feeding stations, and plenty of room to inhabit. But the burning question of the meaning and origin of the place hounds Burton into seeking some answers.

Their geographical circumstances are fascinating in themselves. There are zones with varying patterns of vegetation and climate, all related to but not exactly duplicating those on earth. In the center, having access to all zones, is a river that Burton and his friends estimate to be twenty million miles long. Based on their observations they conclude that there must be thirty-five or more billion people living in the various zones. The subhuman, having attained some functional language skill, conveys to Burton's circle his perception that a very few inhabitants of this world are distinctive in that they do not wear the internal device that all the rest have behind their foreheads. These individuals are revealed as the directors of this strange world, the Ethicals. One of them, under considerable duress, is pressed into giving information about the purpose and origin of the world. The Ethicals are distant human offspring, the time being approximately A.D. 7,000. These far advanced versions of *homo sapiens* have learned to recover the past quite literally. They have located, by visual means, every human who ever lived and, using some process of energy conversion drawn from the planet's molten core, have recreated these persons in their biopsychical entirety. They have not only re-juvenated the flesh but corrected deformities and abnormalities. Complete recordings are made of the newly re-surrected persons for storage in some vast memory bank. In addition, agents of the Ethicals mingle with the resurrected persons, recording their languages, mores, and even indi-vidual biographies. But what about their eventual disposition when they have provided all the information needed? The Eth-ical recoils from the question, saying only that they must re-habilitate themselves; he then promptly dies from self-inflicted thought energy.

The companions are left with the vast puzzle of how this can be. As Frigate reasons:

> I *know* that I am Peter Jairus Frigate, born 1918, died 2000 A.D. But I also must believe, because logic tells me so, that I am only really a being who has the *memories* of that Frigate who can never exist again. Not flesh of his flesh, blood of his blood, but mind of his mind. I am *not* the man who was born of a woman on that lost world of Earth. I am the by blow of science and a machine. Unless there is some entity attached to the human body, an entity which *is* the human being. . . . So that, if the body were to be made again, this entity, storing the essence of the individual, could be attached again to the body. And so the original indi-vidual *would* live again. He would not be just a duplicate.[12]

The answer to this puzzle hinges on our initial view of human-kind. Are we a monism or a dualism? This resurrection does not provide absolute clarification. To complicate matters, Bur-ton finds that when a person dies, he revivifies shortly in another area of the vast river continent. This resurrection with-out permission angers Burton, and he determines to get to the end of the river, find the headquarters of the Ethicals, and wrench the final bits of truth from them.

Resurrection as a conceivable alternative is particularly de-pendent for its affective surround upon the nature of God or other resurrector. In the Christian tradition, this form of im-mortality is fortunate depending on the judicial decision of the Creator. Burton finds a darker possibility to the motives of the Ethicals when a renegade member of that band asserts that there is no "church of the second chance." Humans are merely the objects of a scientific experiment. When they have served their purpose, back to the dust they shall go. The Ethicals are immortal; time hangs heavy on their hands, and toying with humans is the most absorbing project they have come across. The renegade enlists Burton and others he has selected to plot against this decidedly unethical treatment of life forms and to find a way to end their dark design.

Shall we some day find our way back to our scattered bodies? Will the battered hulk of our well-used frame reconstitute itself on some basis and house the memory chain that defines our personhood? The belief in this eventually is one of the longest traditions in human history,. Its motifs are varied, but at its heart the concept expresses the urge toward self-consistency and the persistence of those traits that compose our individuality. Resurrection is both a cosmic puzzle and a psychic demand.

Earthly Survival

The idea of a single individual composed of material and spiritual aspects, the latter surviving the death of the former, is a late arrival on the human intellectual scene. Traditional tribal life assumes without question the endurance of some definable substance after death. The widespread cult of ancestralism is based upon this assumption; a vast array of tribal art is devoted to the imagery of those members who have passed into the state of death. These persons are believed to remain in the same area they inhabited in life, carrying on an existence closely related to that of their former states. Their very being is contingent upon the memories of family and friends, with whom they may consult when summoned. After this memory link is broken by the passage of generations, individuals become part of a collective of anonymous spirits hovering over and around the tribal vicinity. In this view time runs steadily toward the past, the dead being closer to the Creator who began time. One's destiny, except for a short period after death, is to be absorbed into that great company of anonymous departed.

The emergence of the unique individual with a specifically determined experiential context awaiting after death took many centuries to develop. The ancient Hebrews accepted the belief that for the most part a person's afterlife was completely absorbed by the continuing life of the people as a whole. Hopes for a glorious postexistence were not available to be used as factors in political control. Very rarely was the belief that the soul gains by passing out of this world in evidence. The unquestioned assumption of some form of existence is, then, coexistent with humankind, often validating itself through vivid appearances in dreams of persons who have died.

The first hints of individual immortal identity, at least in the Western tradition, derive from Greek kings and heroes, and Hebrew prophets. In the *Odyssey* King Menelaus is told he will on his demise go to the Elysian plain at the world's end, where life is easiest for men. He is destined for this earthly paradise not because of great deeds or moral virtue, but merely because he married Helen, who is a descendent of the gods. Anyone familially related to the gods was automatically granted immortality, as was the habit in Egypt. Among the Hebrews certain major prophets such as Enoch and Elijah were taken into heaven before their physical deaths. The masses sank into the shadow world of oblivion, alive only in the collective memory of their people. The soul was there, but it was the soul of the group, which outlives every generation of its members.

It is currently thought that under the influence of the teachings of Zoroaster the Hebrews of the seventh and sixth centuries evolved the idea of the autonomous responsible individual. Jeremiah rejects the inheritance of moral corruption from one generation to another, stating that each soul is responsible for itself. Historians have noted that the Babylonian conquest of Judah in the sixth century, the exile, and the effective disappearance of the Hebrews as a nation psychologically threw the individual on his own. The single person had to be held in existence, possibly in the mind of God, until the group that gave him immortal continuity could be reassembled. As a result a variety of immortalist doctrines arose at this point and became incorporated into the religious traditions of the West.

The mystery cults added the next bit of imagery to the developing idea of personal immortality of the soul. The initiated were promised a privileged fate after death, and such hopes drew thousands of worshipers to the Eleusinian festivals. The hypnotic trances and ecstatic emotional states elicited by the rituals of the mystery cults projected masses of people into altered states of consciousness, which seemed to them like a sample of postlife existence. The Orphic Mysteries were propagated in literate fashion by Pythagoras, whose teachings nourished Socrates, Plato, and the philosophy of Idealism. From these roots developed the concept of the immortal soul realizing in unlimited time its highest potentials of knowledge and moral responsibility.

Supposing the existence of an individually recognizable spiritual essence, the location and activity of that entity assume strategic importance not only for the dead but for the living. One long and highly developed tradition that responds to both issues is the myth of the ghostly return. The African poet Birago Diop portrays the relationship of these ghostly forces to the world of the living:

> Listen more often to things rather than beings,
> Hear the fire's voice,
> Hear the voice of the water,
> In the wind hear the sobbing of the trees,
> It is our forefathers breathing.
>
> The dead are not gone forever.
> They are in the paling shadows
> And in the darkening shadows.
> The dead are not beneath the ground,
> They are in the rustling tree,
> In the murmuring wood,
> In the still flowing water,
> In the lonely place, in the crowd;
> The dead are not dead.
>
> Listen more often to things rather than beings.
> Hear the fire's voice,
> Hear the voice of the water.
> In the wind hear the sobbing of the trees.
> It is the breathing of our forefathers
> Who are not gone, not beneath the ground,
> Not dead.
>
> The dead are not gone forever.
> They are in a woman's breast,
> A child's crying, a glowing ember.
> The dead are not beneath the earth.
> They are in the flickering fire,
> In the weeping plant, the groaning rock,
> The wooded place, the home.
> The dead are not dead.
>
> Listen more often to things rather than beings.

Hear the fire's voice,
Hear the voice of water.
In the wind hear the sobbing of the trees.
It is the breath of our forefathers.[13]

Why do the spirits of the dead gather about the places of the living? Why do they breathe in the wind and mutter about the fires? The answer, coming from the indeterminate past, is to warn and to counsel those who need their superior knowledge, and occasionally to ask for the performance of necessary rituals in their behalf. It is in this latter role that the ghost of Patroclus appears to the warrior Achilles just before the fall of Troy. As Homer describes the incident, the soul of Patroclus appears in a dream to his friend Achilles, standing by his head and speaking sorrowfully. He accuses Achilles of having forgotten him now that he is dead. His body must be buried so that he can proceed to the world of the dead; because he lies unburied he is prevented from fulfilling this natural destiny. He reminds Achilles that he, too, will fall eventually before the gates of Troy as the war draws to a close. Finally, he asks that his bones be placed with those of Achilles in one urn when death at last claims his friend. In his disturbed sleep Achilles promises to carry out the wishes of this spirit and tries to embrace him one last time, but his soul vanishes like smoke. Achilles wakes and cries out in amazement at what he has learned about life after death. There is something about the human being that lingers in the realm of hades, he asserts, but no life in any real sense though there may remain a profoundly convincing personal essence.

Vergil makes frequent use of the ghostly appearance for warning and prophecy in the *Aeneid*. One of the most touching is the scene at the end of Book 2 between Aeneas and his wife. She has been lost in the flight from Troy, and Aeneas returns to search frantically amid the destruction in hopes of finding her. She appears to him in a form larger than life, and he reacts with terror at her appearance. Using the greater range of understanding assumed by the dead, she counsels him that her death is part of the complexity of destiny. Aeneas is fated to wander about the world until he finds that site which will become the foundation for Rome. Marriage with a bride from that new land awaits; his family line will prosper. She conforts him further with her own gratitude that she is not a captive to work as a slave for the conquering Greeks, and that she is safe under the protection of the goddess Venus. Though Aeneas tries to embrace his wife's shade, it vanishes like a wisp of wind. But it has given him vital clues to his future action.

Such an appearance on a subtler level features prominently in James Agee's novel *A Death in the Family*. Jay has been killed quite suddenly in an automobile accident, and his wife and her family have gathered to share their sorrow. Aunt Hannah silences them momentarily, stating that she hears or feels something and asking them to verify her intuition. As they wait quietly the rest also feel a strong presence about them. Mary, the wife, traces the focus of the energy to the children's room upstairs where they are sleeping and recognizes it as her husband. Believing that he has returned to see that they are alright, she assures him that they can survive his death, and begs him not to be troubled. The energy that is his presence is full of the sorrow of this separation. Mary holds him with her a few moments above the sleeping forms of their children and then tells him good-bye. The pain seems to vanish from his presence; he fades slowly from the room and from the house. In trying to find some rationale for their strange experience, Hannah decides that Jay's death was so completely without warning that the shock left him unable to ascertain what had happened to him. Only when he was able to see that his family was cared for could he begin to consolidate his own situation and move on.

The ghostly appearance and its attendant message is handled imaginatively by Larry Rubin in his poem "The Druggist":

> He came to me last night, as if there had never been a box.
> Routine, no tales of Hell to tell, he worked on a prescription,
> And I watched, as I used to when I was a boy, and stifled
> My eyes, and from the corner of his eye
> He saw me and asked why. But all that dirt, I said.
> How did you get up past all that dirt?
> I can pull pegs out with my teeth, he said, and went on
> working.
> Later, just before the third cock, he handed me the jar.
> Son, he said, I want you to deliver this before you go.
> Is that all, I said, mustn't I avenge your death so you can rest?
> I knew being sealed up like that had turned his wits because
> I saw he made the label out to me.[14]

The various elements of the funerary realm leave no doubt that the encounter is with a ghost. As in the previous examples, either the appearance or activity of the apparition adequately identifies it to the observer. A message is the object of the encounter; in this case the nature of that message is unclear. It is seemingly a warning, but whether concerning the inevitable shortness of life or the need for corrective action on some particular issue is not defined.

A most entertaining interpretation of the ghostly return is Noel Coward's play *Blythe Spirit*, which he subtitles "An Improbable Farce." Charles, a writer presently married to Ruth, endeavors to obtain data for a new book by arranging for a seance with Madame Arcati, whom he assumes to be a fraud. Much to his chagrin, the evening's labors produce the ghostly materialization of his first wife, Elvira. Unperceivable by anyone but Charles, Elvira proceeds to make his life miserable. She even plans to kill him so that he can join her; ironically, Ruth is the one killed in the rigged automobile. With aid from the maid, who is a natural and unrecognized psychic, Madame Arcati succeeds in ridding Charles, at least visibly and audibly, of his two wives' presences.

Within this plot structure a number of details about life after death are sketched in. Although the presence of the deceased is rarely audible or visible to a living person, it is able to affect the physical environment to the extent of carrying flower bowls about, sawing ladders partway through, dropping pictures from the walls, and the like. However, it cannot cross water, and cannot go and come without restraint; Elvira often nags Charles to take her to a movie. Ghosts are a uniform gray color right down to skin, hair, and clothing. In the contemporary period there are few ways to exorcise ghosts, because the decline of faith has made all the old rituals ineffective. Seemingly, all the earthly emotional responses persist after death. As Elvira explains to Charles:

> I sat there, on the other side, just longing for you day after day. . . . I went on living you and thinking truly of you . . . that's why I put myself down for a return visit and had to fill in all those forms and wait about in draughty passages for hours—if only you'd died before you met Ruth everything might have been all right—she's absolutely ruined you—[15]

After delivering herself of this diatribe, Elvira bursts into tears—only ghost tears, as she explains, but painful anyway.

When questioned as to where she has come from, Elvira confesses to having forgotten most of it. She remembers only playing backgammon with a sweet old Oriental gentleman (Genghis Khan, if her memory serves) when Madame Arcati's ghostly child contact rushed in to say that she was wanted by Charles. Though Elvira can manipulate physical things, she cannot be touched. The best physical contact that can be made is slightly ruffling the hair of someone alive, or blowing in his ear. There is a physical separation between the realms of the living and the dead, though Elvira has been completely aware of Charles's activities since her death.

Though it is pure fantasy, *Blythe Spirit* is based upon an occurence that has achieved common belief as far back as human tradition can be traced. Do human manifestations really live on after death? Investigations of parapsychology have not yet been able to separate influences emanating from transferred thoughts of living persons from those possibly transferred from the dead. If it were possible to do so, what would serve to explain such a phenomenon? The theologian John Hick speculates that there may be persisting psychic traces or mental fragments left behind by the dead. These "psychic husks" may well contain enough energy to communicate with a talented medium, though they will refer only to memories of this life. Indeed, most often those spirits which speak through mediums give the impression of still being engaged in earthly life. They refer to all the usual paraphernalia of earthly existence. They speak of persons known to them during their lives and reveal information gained through earthly experience.

According to ancient tradition, some psychic traces have a long and exceedingly restless postdeath history. Those who are not ritually laid to rest are, in the imagery of classical literature, wanderers upon the earth, unable to pass into the realm of hades. One poignant version of this theme is the tale of the sailor who is doomed to sail the seas forever in a ghost ship until the spell is broken. Such is the framework for Wagner's opera *The Flying Dutchman*. A variant of the Wandering Jew motif, the story Wagner settled upon came from several sources. A Dutch captain out of anger and frustration swore to sail around a certain cape if it took him until Judgment Day. The devil condemned him to that fate unless he could be redeemed by the faithful love of a woman. One day each seven years he was allowed to come ashore to seek that woman. Thus the presumptions of mankind and his struggles against fate, along with self-sacrifice as the way to redemption, form the essential themes of the opera. The main musical motifs reflect these concerns. There is the dramatic power of the intervals of a fifth, which portray the ghost ship with its blood-red sails, feared by sailors everywhere. The theme of redemption is Senta's song, in which she expresses her pity and love for the condemned Dutchman. Struggle and torment in the grip of fate are in the dark string tremolos that underlie the Dutchman's soliloquies.

In Wagner's version of the tale a storm drives the Dutchman and other local sailors ashore by a Norwegian port town where his story is well known. Dazzled by the precious cargo the ghost ship carries, one sailor gives permission for the Dutchman to marry his daughter. The daughter, Senta, in turn has spent much of her life singing the ballad of the wandering Dutchman and gazing at his picture on the wall of their home. She has decided that she is destined to be the woman who saves him from eternal voyaging. When they meet, each recognizes in the other something they seemingly have felt most of their lives; they arrange to be married.

Tragedy occurs when Eric, who loves and wishes to marry Senta, complains that she once declared her love for him and now has changed her mind. In the middle of Act 3 his "Cavatina" reminds them of happier times: "Don't you remember how your father entrusted you to my protection when he went off to sea, and how you twined your arms about my neck and said you loved me?" It is a warmly lyric aria with wide-ranging melody, exuding assurance and contentment. Hardly the music for a disappointed lover, Eric's song gives the impression that he is in full possession of his heart's desire. Unfortunately, it is overheard by the Dutchman, who realizes that if Senta once gave her love to Eric and changed her mind, she could do so with him. In extreme anguish he shouts "I am forever lost." The orchestra underlines his outburst with jagged rhythm and the rumbling strings that are part of the theme of despair. Senta, Eric, and the Dutchman confront each other in a trio of energy and intricacy, with each separate emotional state carried through the interwoven vocal lines. Eric is terrified by the appearance of the Dutchman; he fears that he is a manifestation of the devil come for Senta. The Dutchman sings, "To sea forever. My hope is shattered. Your pledge is ended." Senta for her part affirms her decision, begging him not to be so blind and doubtful.

As though to close this painful confrontation, the Dutchman details the destiny Senta has escaped by not vowing formally before God to be faithful. He reviews his torment as an eternal voyager in a spare recitative with only occasional trombone interludes, dramatic and dark-hued. All who vow solemnly and then break faith with the wanderer are damned eternally. Senta will be saved, but the Dutchman returns to his dismal life. He runs toward the waiting ship as Senta calls out in an aria bursting with anguished lyricism: "I knew who you were from the beginning. I am the true love through whom you will find salvation." Unable to restrain her, Eric and her family call as she climbs the cliff above the harbor. As the ghost ship with the blood-red sails turns into the wind, Senta sings in a high, sweet voice the theme of redemption: "Here I stand, true until death." She leaps into the sea surrounding the ship, which sinks into a whirlpool with the whole ghostly crew. As the entwined themes of the overture close the opera, the transformed images of Senta and the Dutchman are seen drifting into the evening sky.

Possibly the most famous operatic ghost story of them all is Mozart's *Don Giovanni*, a work that has been in almost constant production somewhere in the world for 150 years. The individual of its title is a thoroughly amoral member of the lower nobility, whose life moves from one amour to another between bouts of drinking and fighting. Behind him lie a string of broken hearts and the dead body of the Commendatore, who has lost a duel in defending his daughter. Act 3, Scene 3 finds Don Giovanni and his long-suffering servant Leporello hiding out briefly in a cemetery after a narrow escape from the latest amorous adventure. As Don Giovanni brags about his evening's conquest, a slow, dignified voice chants gloomily as from a distance, "You will stop laughing before morning." Mystified, the two men sing quickly in recitative style about their speculations on the source of the voice. The nervous, rhythmic music is interrupted once more when the same slow, dramatic voice commands them to let the dead alone.

The mystery is solved when Don Giovanni discovers a marble statue of the recently interred Commendatore and identifies the voice as his ghost. He commands Leoporello to read the inscription at the base. To the tune of a lilting waltz Leporello ironically reads the grim legend: "For the impious one who brought me to this extreme state vengeance waits." The reader is terrified, muttering, "Did you understand? I'm trembling." But the Don with utter disdain offhandedly tells Leporello to invite the ghostly figure for supper that next evening. Terrified, Leporello again begins his aria and addresses the statue in most obsequious terms. With many interruptions and pleas not to be compelled to complete his message, poor Leporello finishes his song. To their amazement the statue nods its marble head in assent. The scene concludes with rapidly sung exchanges between the men, Leporello begging to leave and Don Giovanni mentally making preparations for the supper.

Act 2, Scene 5 is set in the dining room of Don Giovanni's palace. After the meal is presented and music played, Leporello races in to announce the appearance of the stone figure and beg them to lock the door tightly. Unable to budge Leporello, Don Giovanni himself lets the ghostly figure in and invites him to share the food. In the same slow, dark-hued baritone of the cemetery scene, the statue declares that he has other business. His song is spaced between the suave lyricisms of Don Giovanni and the terrified whimpering of Leporello. Much of the music of this section is based upon a slowly ascending scale accompanied by rapid runs in the strings, which accent the rising tones. "Will you come to have supper with me?" the statue inquires ominously. Fearlessly Don Giovanni assents and offers his hand as pledge, crying out in surprise as he grasps the ice-cold appendage of the statue. "Repent," demands the statue. "Yes, of course," responds Leporello. "No, no," Don Giovanni responds defiantly. "Ah, the time has flown," says the statue. A cymbal crash announces the spirits of darkness, who sing as the flames of hell begin to rise. Thoroughly frightened at last, Don Giovanni sings frantically of the terrible vision of punishment he sees before him. With a scream he is swallowed up in the great chorus of demonic voices.

Ghosts, the psychic husks of the living that seek to inform or perhaps avenge, are sometimes manifestations of the mind alone rather than the shared social context. Sometimes the creator who envisions them maintains their reality as an open question. This is the case with Gian Carlo Menotti's opera *The*

Medium. As in *Blythe Spirit,* the situation centers about the work of a fraudulent medium who has made her living duping unsuspecting relatives with approximations of their dead loved ones. But at one seance the medium, Baba, is terrified when, completely outside of the elaborately controlled staging, a cold hand touches her throat. She accuses her daughter and the mute boy who helps her of deliberately trying to frighten her. Completely undone by the unforeseen experience, Baba refuses to conduct seances and falls to drinking.

In a drunken reverie she sings strangely, interrupting herself occasionally to shout, "Who's there?" She decides that the best course is to try to laugh about it, and so howls with raucous humor. Abruptly her mood turns again and she pleads to God for forgiveness for her aged, sick self. Suddenly she hears a real noise but doesn't see the mute boy, who has returned to the house for his few possessions. Warning that she will shoot if the noise fails to identify itself, she kills the boy who could not respond. Hearing the shots, the daughter pounds on the door, begging to be let in and then leaving to summon help. Was there ever a ghost? Was the episode a result of Baba's fatigue and bad conscience? Are ghosts in the mind as deadly as ghosts that walk about in statues?

Henry James's *The Turn of the Screw* responds with a powerful affirmative to the destructive potential of subterranean ghosts. He is also powerfully evasive as to whether these phenomena exist as the psychic perception of two children, or only their governess, or whether they are publicly verifiable to some extent. The reader is, in turn, alternately convinced of each possibility. There is no uncertainty about the interpretation of the ghosts as remnants of Quint and Miss Jessel, until recently valet and governess at the estate. They were believed by the housekeeper to be thoroughly evil and to have transmitted their ways to the children placed in their care. The new governess, without knowing the details of their tenure, encounters the ghostly form of Quint staring at her from the top of a tower at the roof level of the great house. He appears to her again, staring in the window in the twilight. A third appearance suffices for the governess to describe the apparition exactly to the housekeeper—red hair, whiskers, wide mouth, thin lips, and borrowed clothing.

Not only is the governess sure now that the ghosts are perceptible phenomena, but she is positive that the children see and speak to them. They are continuing their morbid relationship, and catching the children late at night in the area where she has seen the figure confirms her belief that the children are aware of their existence. The children, in turn, seem to hint in their sparse conversation of some mutual awareness of the ghosts, but never directly show any such recognition even when questioned by the governess. The boy once tells her directly to leave him alone. At the end, when the governess confronts the boy with the image of Quint that she sees through the window, he asserts that he sees nothing. But immediately he utters a terrible cry and dies. Hence the question of the shared reality of the ghosts is left an open issue.

The fact that the housekeeper recognizes the images the governess describes and is her confidante in their mutual struggle to rectify their former influence on the children is the one foundation of sanity the present governess clings to. The housekeeper's lack of imagination and practical orientation are stabilizing. But in another dimension of reality the governess is sure that the ghosts are almost constantly among them. They harass her so that she can hardly refrain from trying to force some admission of their presence out of the children. In a climactic attempt to verify her perceptions, she takes the housekeeper to the lake, across which is distinctly perceived the figure of Miss Jessel. Though she looks carefully and dutifully, the housekeeper reports that she sees nothing; it is all a mistake and a needless worry. The child who is with them reacts with fear, not at the apparition but at the governess herself. The tension between shared perception and private vision has been strained to the limit in the novel.

Earthly survivial of some spiritual aspect has another tradition as old as that of ghosts—namely, reincarnation. The spirit survives not by retaining merely some perceptible psychic husk but by adopting a new physical mechanism into which it is born in the normal process. So intrinsic to Hindu, Buddhist, Jain, Parsee, and Sikh religious doctrines is the concept of reincarnation that it has not developed a base of philosophical argument. What really might continue in this way of thinking? A memory stream would be the most logical choice, though in actuality memory of verifiable details of a former life are exceedingly rare. The continuity of physical growth and development, intrinsic to our concept of identity throughout life, is eliminated by the rebirth process. All that is left that could serve as continuum from one life to the next is a pattern of mental and emotional dispositions. Such a broad description seems highly unlikely to match any two persons with shared specific life contexts. If there is a more specific, largely unconscious memory thread connecting successive lives, its value to our present situation seems negligible. Only if the whole of existence were collected in the mind at some point would the separate episodes assume any experiential reality.

Reincarnation is, among other things, an attempted response to the problem of justice. The vast discrepancies in physical and intellectual conditions into which humans, seemingly beyond any control, are born are incompatible with the concept of a moral element in the universe. A naturalistic point of view would posit a beginningless process of recurrence neither just or good, but simply the way things are. A theistic point of view must accept a responsible moral force whose purpose directs the universe. The gross inequities obviously inherent within it cannot be logically attributed to a loving creator; therefore humans must deserve the state in which they find themselves. Since a small infant has done nothing to deserve who or what he is at this time, logic demands a prior existence when the conditions of the present life were determined by the nature of that experience. Of course, this merely postpones the issue, since at some point in the succession of lives a creator had to make an initial choice of life situation.

Leaving aside the philosophical verifiability of reincarnation, the idea has had a long and fruitful imaginative history in both East and West. It was firmly embedded in Western mysticism with the infiltration of the Orphic Mysteries into Greece. The monastic community founded by Pythagoras held the migration of souls as an element of fundamental belief. Socrates taught that the living sprung from the dead and the souls of the dead are in existence. He notes that everything has an opposite; if everything dies there can be ultimately a state without any opposite. Based upon what we know of the laws of earthly existence, such a state cannot be; therefore what is dead must turn again into its opposite. Nevertheless, Socrates does conceive of a state of incorporeal, unembodied existence, which he hopes to attain. Thus death does not have to turn into life in an embodied form exclusively. Plato continues this line of thought in the *Meno* dialogue, endeavoring to demonstrate that certain types of knowledge are simply present in the soul and need no teaching. Such knowledge has been acquired in a previous existence and can be recovered by skillful questioning. Even Lucretius recognizes the possibility of reincarnation, though he has many objections to it and says that without specific memory of past lives the process serves no purpose.

One of the most elaborate historical allegories is constructed by Vergil in Book 6 of the *Aeneid,* using reincarnation as the vehicle. Aeneas's father is revealing to his son the destiny that awaits the great kingdom he will found. Along the riverbanks of the underworld where the scene takes place, hordes of people are gathered. "They are souls who are destined for reincarnation; and now at Lethe's stream they are drinking the waters that quench man's troubles, the deep draught of oblivion." But why, inquires Aeneas, should one who has escaped life desire to return to earth again? His father explains:

> The life-force of our seeds is fire, their source celestial,
> But they are deadened and dimmed by the sinful bodies they
>   live in—
> The flesh that is laden with death, the anatomy of clay:
> Whence these souls of ours feel fear, desire, grief, joy,
> But encased in their blind, dark prison discern not the
>   heaven-light above.
> Yes, not even when the last flicker of life has left us,
> Does evil, or the ills that flesh is heir to, quite
> Relinquish our souls; it must be that many a taint grows
>   deeply,
> Mysteriously grained in their being from long contact with the
>   body.[16]

After a thousand-year period in which the dead are disciplined and pay the penalty for old evils, they are summoned again to the river of forgetfulness. Having been washed of all memory, they may again be born into the world. As each waiting soul is pointed out, Aeneas is told his future identity and the role he will play in the formation of Roman culture. Some are to be his grandchildren; others, lawgivers; others, rulers over Rome's golden age. Standing at the center of the mystery, Aeneas receives this mystic revelation from the spirit of his dead father and comes to understand the process of the universe.

The ministry of Jesus occasionally reflects the popular acceptance of reincarnation among the mass of Jews during his lifetime. The controversy over the identity of Jesus is reported by Matthew, Mark, and Luke to include speculation that he is Elias or another of the venerable prophets of the past come again. With the Gospel of John, Jesus acquires an eternal past and an eternal future: "Before Abraham was, I am" (John 8:59), and "I will come again, and receive you unto myself; that where I am there ye may be also" (John 14:3).

During the first centuries after the death of Jesus, when the theology of the church was in the shaping, not only the heretical groups but many well-respected Christian theologies entertained the notion of reincarnation because, as one historian commented, of its antiquity and universality. The great Origin derided literalist views of heaven and hell, conceiving a series of world orders through which spirits, created pure, return at last to their original perfection. The preexistence and future embodiment of souls is assumed by this rationale. Though in his official writings he denied a theology of reincarnation, Augustine in his *Confessions* wonders if he had a history prior to this earthly one. He admits to being much taken with the question but having no evidence of his own on which to proceed. Yet it was he who introduced the doctrine of predestination as a prominent element of Christian thinking.

Though never a major stream of thought, reincarnation bubbled along just beneath the surface of official Western ecclesiastical doctrine, and burst into view with every schism. Such heretical sects as the Cathars, who flourished during the late Middle Ages, believed in reincarnation as the means to final deliverance from earth. St. Francis openly taught the union of all creatures in a universal soul. The Renaissance brought a brisk traffic in Eastern writings and for a time a significant upsurge in speculative mystical thought. The dread hand of the Inquisition ended this flowering and made such speculation dangerous for many generations. The eighteenth-century Rationalists, not impressed with mystic doctrines, nevertheless knew of and considered the concept of reincarnation as a serious explanatory principle. No less an empiricist than David Hume confessed in his essays that if one were to reason about a soul from the common course of observed nature, reincarnation would be the most logical conclusion. The nineteenth-century Transcendentalists and Theosophists broadened the appeal of reincarnation in the West, and world communications in the present century have made some rapprochement between Eastern and Western concepts of the afterlife inevitable.

Contemporary literature is full of imagery reminiscent of reincarnation motifs. There is Robert Frost's "Swinger of Birches," who wheels forever from heaven to earth and back again. There is Yeats's poem "Under Ben Bulben," written three months before his death, with its memorable second stanza:

> Many times man lives and dies
> Between his two eternities,
> That of race and that of soul
> And ancient Ireland knew it all.
> Whether man die in his bed
> Or the rifle knocks him dead,
> A brief parting from those dear
> Is the worst man has to fear.
> Though grave-diggers' toil is long,
> Sharp their spades, their muscles strong,
> They but thrust their buried men
> Back in the human mind again.[17]

Hesse's Siddhartha learns at the end of a long spiritual adventure the secret that there is no such thing as time. Sorrow, fear, and all evil exist in time; as soon as one conquers time through death, these things exist no more. In Hesse's *Glass Bead Game* students train their imaginative faculties by conceiving themselves in different lives, learning to wear their present persons as one might a costume for a temporary role. In a much more highly formulated sense the doctrine was the organizing factor for "The Cambridge Reincarnationists," philosophers James Ward, G. Lowes Dickinson, and John Ellis McTaggart. Out of this welter of references and allusions have come two popular, though stylistically different, books whose very structure is dependent upon reincarnationist ideology.

The Reincarnation of Peter Proud, by Max Erlich, resembles *Oedipus Rex* in its combination of the quest for personal identity with a rousing detective story. The reader is plunged into events in the middle of a disturbing dream that eventuates in the death of the dreamer, Peter Proud. An even more disturbing fact is that when investigated in the sleep laboratory, the dream does not record as such. The research director can only assume that the dream is a psychic phenomenon. There are many such dreams; together they reconstitute a complete environment and tableaux of human relationships. Dr. Proud, a scholar of Indian Culture, is reminded of the widespread belief in Ondinnonk—a secret desire of the soul embodied in a dream. Moreover, he suffers from chronic, unlocatable pain, which comes and goes mysteriously. After trying other avenues of explanation, Peter Proud confers with a psychic who tells him about innumerable lives he has lived, one as an Indian who was wounded in precisely the spot where his present physical pain is located. But of the world of his dream she can tell him nothing.

The next link in the search for the dream source is provided by a chance television report from Riverside, Massachusetts, which Peter recognizes instantly as containing the relevant physical appurtenances of his mental imagery. There he finds newspaper reports of the very tragedy his dream confirms. He realizes that he was killed by his wife, now an alcoholic, and survived by a daughter now his own age, with whom he subsequently falls in love. In hopes of breaking the visions that hold him to this vanished life, he decides to reenact his swim in the lake that took his life. Because of an unfortunate incident in which the former wife hears his dream voice, she believes that he is her husband come back to haunt her. As though doomed by some tragic fate, the two meet as before in the middle of the lake. Peter knows enough to stay away from the oar with which he was previously clubbed to death; he does not recognize the pistol until it is too late. Once again he sinks to the lake bottom, destination unknown.

Roger Zelazny's *Lord of Light* is a much more complex and highly imaginative science fiction interpretation of reincarnation. Its characters are drawn from the realm of gods who have learned to surmount time; humans who contest with the gods for their power; subhumans such as Tak who strive toward greater consciousness; and demonic forces that have acquired the power to become disembodied. Time and place are the great variables through which these characters move, sometimes visible and sometimes invisible. There is a real death, and it is greatly feared. But there are feasible alternatives to it that are technological in nature. The main character, Sam, is reconstituted by the fallen god, Yama, by means of a complex electronic machine, which gathers his *atman* from the vast magnetic cloud that encircles the planet and focuses it into an available body.

The machines of incarnation are of tremendous value to such beings as the Ratnagaris, who long ago found ways to perpetuate themselves as fields of energy. However, being from human stock, they still long for the embodied experience. One even joins Sam in joint ownership of his body until subdued by a stratagem. There is, it is rumored, a machine that will transfer an *atman* from a destroyed body to another waiting elsewhere. Yama boasted that he knew that technology, and that is the theory used to explain his disappearance at the end of the tale. Reincarnation can also be used as a form of punishment. Poor Lady Ratri, for her part in a revolution, was sentenced always to be reincarnated into the bodies of very plain, middle-aged ladies, despite her innate charm. This *atman*, or life-stuff that persists despite all, is not part of either brain or body. As Yama describes it, *atman* flows from the center of the space that is the self; it is the ultimate power that humans possess. The book summarizes, through this perspective, a philosophy of life:

> Death and Light are everywhere, always, and they begin, end, strive, attend, into and upon the Dream of the Nameless that is the world, burning words within Samsara, perhaps to create a thing of beauty.[18]

Of Realms Beyond

The idea of an entity, dual in nature and capable of existence in a disconnected state, is picturesque in itself. The very image, reminiscent of the chrysalis-to-butterfly metamorphosis, is a sufficient basis for creative elaboration. William Blake's etching *The Death of the Strong, Wicked Man*, used as an illustration for Blair's *The Grave*, captures the moment when the soul departs the body. Soul and body are pictured as twin images, one floating above the other. They are somewhat in opposition; the body faces the viewer with its head to the right; the soul floats above, moving toward the window with its back to the viewer and head toward the left. Otherwise, the same physical density pervades both. The lower body rests dejectedly while the upper soul moves swiftly and fearfully toward waiting space.

The moment of separation is particularly attractive to dramatic forms of expression. Richard Strauss's tone poem *Death and Transfiguration* is an emotionally enhanced literal enactment of this moment as it might be experienced as an interior event. The initial statement is extremely slow and gloomy, with an omnipresent drumbeat often echoing in a cavernous silence. There is little sense of forward motion conveyed by wandering scraps of melody. Harp and flute passages eventually relieve the gloom and provide a brief sense of linear progression. The key centers that frame the harmony shift about like failing sunlight.

The sudden break in this train of thought is initiated by a heavy drumbeat and a rising tide of melodic energy from the depths of the bass register. The resulting forward surge seeps through the entire range of orchestral pitch and color. Short downturning phrases move darkly within the general turmoil, underlined by the same ominous drumbeat that characterized the beginning moments. There are implications of wandering, struggle, passion, and high drama. At the climax of the accumulated sound, a broad theme with a wide tonal gap sounds forth. It is the theme of transfiguration, in which the spirit leaps free of the body.

After the graphic soul-body separation the music ripples through many key changes and into the high registers, disappearing into silence. A flute proclaims to a string accompaniment a sweet lyric melody of joyous freedom. Echoes of this theme melt again into remnants of the theme of struggle and culminate in a fanfare of triumph. The theme of joy surges upward on the inner lines in an expressive contrast to the downturning lines of the theme of struggle. The energetic web of melody lines wells from bass through treble ranges, repeating the transcendence motive as a summary.

The final section of the long tone poem is built upon a massive march tune and an underlying drumroll that melts gently into a meditative section much like the opening measures of the composition. A strong forward motion in the strings returns to the powerful march theme, which encompasses the full orchestra. It becomes a metaphor for eternal spiritual energy, a kind of tensile strength that survives the struggles of the flesh.

An equally idealistic, though somewhat more emotionally subdued version of the moment of separation is found in Larry Rubin's poem "Instructions for Dying":

When they call you from the grave, you must
Swim upward, using a winding stroke.
You must ascend swiftly through dark green
Pressures, before your eardrums burst with the force
Of what is spinning by. If you black out,
Consciousness will return, though spiral swimming
Dizzies the identity. Rise
Toward light with lungs strained to endure
The cries of drowning voices, sirens who pluck
The swimmers from the lonely vortex. Rise
Through shimmering green, past moments of forgetting
Till almost at the surface, one
Last leap toward light—then the final
Layer of foam—and burst out into air,
A child with no name, breathing above
The waters, who never learned to swim.[19]

The poetic and musical portrayals are quite similar in their sense of struggle. There are physical agonies, temptations, failures ("cries of drowning voices"), and terrors of this passage. There is the undefined ecstasy that suffuses the end of both works. The pictorial vision of Blake presents one consistent moment in the total process, using the visual metaphor of the twin figures. The poem and music move through time, giving us the process as a total lived experience.

Where are we, having emerged "breathing above the waters?" The initial answer formed in Western culture was a location called hades, which along with earth and heaven formed the three parts of all known reality. The ancient Hebrews observed the existence of a counterpart they called sheol, a murky underworld where once-living persons exist as shadow-images of their former selves. So uninviting was this prospect that Job cried out to his tormenters to leave him alone so that he might find a little comfort before he had to go to that land of gloom where light is darkness, and from which no man returns. It was a place lacking even the presence of God, according to Psalm 88, which declares through a series of rhetorical questions that the dead do not praise God or know of his presence. It is a place of forgetfulness, of half-conscious twilight where dwell the helpless and indifferent shells of life, totally removed from the ongoing life of the human species. Patroclus, appearing to Achilles in a dream, verifies this description in his incorporeal essence. Hades, he further describes, is a land beyond a river, a house with vast gates and filled with phantoms. Odysseus is able to raise the shade of Achilles by giving him the blood of a goat to drink; it is only flesh that has the power of life. Achilles' own description of his present state in hades is hardly cheering. He would, he reports, be delighted to change places with the lowliest living human rather than be the monarch of the realm of death.

The most detailed ancient account of the geography of the afterlife in Western culture is found in Book 6 of Vergil's *Aeneid*. The initial section is limbo, the successor to hades and sheol. There are gathered the ghosts of infants and those who were condemned to death on a false charge. Suicides and those who died of the sufferings of love are each gathered in appropriate zones. The last area is set aside for men famous in war, many of them still bearing the massive scars of their earthly battles and dismembering deaths. Beyond this realm the road forks in two directions, one leading to Tartarus and the other to Elysium, where punishment and reward determine the basis of existence. Christian theology transformed Vergil's limbo into a border region between heaven and hell reserved for the just persons who died before the Resurrection of Jesus. The Hebrew prophets in sheol and those who died unborn or in infancy before baptism are also included.

The next detailed account in the Western tradition of limbo is found in Dante's *Inferno*. It is circle one of that long series of descending spirals that lead inevitably to the presence of Lucifer at the center of the earth. In limbo sounds of sighing are constantly heard emanating from the countless sinless souls who died before the Incarnation. A few of Jesus' direct lineage (Abraham, Noah, Moses, David) were taken from limbo by Jesus before his Resurrection; otherwise nobody has ever escaped this circle of the unenlightened. There is within this somber place the Citadel of Human Reason, where the greatest minds outside the Christian tradition dwell illuminated only by the light of human knowledge. It is not true happiness, but it is a guide that makes their lives hopeful and reasonably content. Here Dante meets the great poets of classical Greece and Rome, legendary heroes, philosophers, mathematicians, and the foremost statesmen of that mythic past. Beyond that island of serenity lies the realm of eternal torment.

As a concept, limbo was doomed to fall into disuse by the time of the Renaissance. The image of timeless dangling between one state and another was out of tune with the doctrine of Purgatory and the perfectibility of souls. But there are even today powerful metaphors of human existence built upon the limbo theme. Pirandello's play *At the Exit* is set at the back entrance of a country cemetery. The characters who carry the action of the play are apparitions whose mortal equivalents were a fat man, a philosopher, a murdered woman, and a small boy. They encounter one another in a no-man's land between corporeal existence and some unknown destination into which they inevitably vanish. The philosopher is able to remain in this limbo indefinitely because he alone realizes that all forms are illusory—there is no "real" us. He coninues to create an appearance for himself, all the while realizing that it is artificial. The quality of lived existence is the main topic of conversation. It is not enough, the philosopher believes, for the living simply to feel; they must give expression and embodiment to these feelings. Hence graveyards are not for the dead but rather to project in visible fashion the feelings of the living. An empty church actually contains in expressed form the highest human aspirations. Ironically, the infinite dimension these embodiments represent diminishes itself in taking on such ephemeral housing. Speaking as a Platonic idealist, the philosopher believes we grow so fond of the likenesses we create of ourselves that we cannot free ourselves from them.

The fat man, already fading because he is losing his imaginative grip on the image he has of himself, is held in limbo because of regret and expectation. He regrets the time not spent in his garden, time lost in which he could have been attending to beautiful, meaningful things that spoke deeply to his spiritual hunger. He expects at any moment to see his wife, who betrayed him for another man, come through the cemetery gate. He is sure that without him to take the brunt of her erratic behavior, she will become irrational and demanding, and that her lover will kill her. And surely enough, the wife appears, laughing like something demented, in turn expecting the lover (who stabbed himself to death) to emerge through the gate. She died hoping to find at last that overwhelming warmth of emotion which had always eluded her, and the quest of which directed her entire existence. In fact, she does not vanish as the others eventually do, but runs off wildly after a living child who passes in a wagon. The small boy also maintains his visible status as long as he is propelled by desire for the pomegranate he has brought along to eat. Once satisfied, he too vanishes. Pain, joy, our very existence is a result of our illusions of ourselves and the world about us, says the philosopher. He offers the alternative of making up our minds not to live! At last the power of the illusion that holds the characters to their recognizable forms weakens and they vanish into mystery.

That mystery has proved far too significant a matter to be left to the shadows of hades or the collective history of an ethnic group. With the development of the concept of individuality came an intense interest in possible prospects. The darker prospect (hell) evolved along with its brighter counterpart (heaven) in ancient Egypt, the Vedic religion of ancient India, and at the end of the prophetic period of Judaism. Together they represented an application of the moral, axiological precepts to the human situation, and a permanent linkage of death with justice. In later Hebrew and early Christian thought the hope of an imminent messianic deliverance, an end to human history, and a cosmic resurrection assumed a prominent position in eschatological thought. As such an eventuality receded into the remote future, the immediate fate of the individual as he passed from life to death once more became the focus of attention. The expected general assize faded in popular imagination to the state of an empty form. Augustine's synthesis of these tendencies into one imaginative mythology of creation, fall, salvation, and eternal state became the normative elaboration for more than a thousand years. Its most enduring expression is found in Dante's *Inferno* and Milton's *Paradise Lost*.

Hell can be interpreted as a specific location or a general state of being. Whatever its affective ramifications, hell constituted a place in the created universe, according to both Dante and Milton. We walk daily upon the outer skin of Dante's eternal locale of anguish, for its nether regions recede like a great funnel toward the center of the earth. Its symbolic entrance, the Gate of Hell, is located directly outside the earthly city of Jerusalem in the midst of the dark wood of error. It is in this locale that Dante finds himself both physically and spiritually and—by the grace of his earthly love, Beatrice, the

Virgin Mary, and St. Lucie—is given a metaphysical revelation of the state of souls after death. Appropriately enough, the epic journey is begun on Good Friday, and, guided by Vergil, Dante emerges from this vision of death on Easter Sunday.

The whole structure of hell is based upon the law of symbolic retribution. As one has lived, and according to the choices one has made, retribution of a suitable kind is exacted after death. There is no escape from hell. Nothing suffered there achieves anything for the sufferer. Probably the abrasion of this idea with that of an eternally loving and forgiving father doomed the literal interpretation of hell for modern life. Beyond the relative peace of limbo lie three vast areas of punishment, which are, in turn, divided into circular segments. Each area is marked by specific geographical features and bordered by rivers, gates, or other defining structures.

Hell is organized according to Dante's own personal system of values, not in direct alignment with official ecclesiastical descriptions of degrees of sin. For example, Dante assigns flatterers and seducers to a lower level of hell, and therefore a higher degree of torment, than murderers or suicides. Simple bodily excesses are the lightest forms of human error, in which gluttons wallow in their own excrement, and others endure torments logically related to their form of indulgence. Both Dante and even Vergil occasionally feel sympathy for these tormented souls. Paolo and Francesca, for example, are earthly lovers who cling together as they are blown eternally about by the storms of their own passion. Their sad tale causes Dante to faint with anguish. But the depravity of mankind so increases during their downward journey as to cause Dante callously to kick one sinner in the head at the very pit of hell.

Beyond the great wall of the burning city of Dis lies the land of the violent, who boil, bake, and slowly stew in the fiery juices of their own hot blood. The minotaur and centaurs, with their human and bestial duality, stand guard over sinners screaming and cursing in lakes of boiling tar. The whole vast factory of immortal despair churns on without ceasing as Dante and Vergil tread the burning plain and come to the great waterfall that marks the end of the land of the violent.

Having descended the vast well down which the boiling river falls, the two companions enter the land of the spiritually dead, whose earthly lives were completely devoid of the quality of human sympathy. Here are the schemers who robbed and vilified their fellow men and whose cold hearts are matched by the freezing chill of this deepest area of hell. Even popes who sold church offices are numbered among the evil-doers; position and ecclesiastical connections cannot nullify acts and intentions. The sons of earth, giant embodiments of elemental forces unchecked by moral or theological law, are chained in the central pit. Antaeus, persuaded by Vergil, low-ers the travelers in his huge hand to the final floor of hell. In this frozen surface are trapped traitors, three of whom (Judas, Brutus, and Cassius) are chewed in the three mouths of Satan. Dante and Vergil crawl painfully over this shaggy hulk of pure evil and follow the river of forgetfulness, which winds upward toward the opposite surface of the planet.

Dante's version of hell holds a continuing validity because of its compelling mixture of realistic detail with metaphysical situation and symbolic references. As though the literary work were not in itself a visual triumph, an abundance of illustra-tions have been derived from its allusions. Delacroix created a memorable version of Dante and Vergil crossing the Acheron in the boat guided by Charon. The two travelers stand protec-tively together, their physical gestures eloquently expressing fear and hesitation. The powerfully muscular figure of the par-tially nude Charon is seen from the back, a sweeping mantle thrown carelessly across his laboring body. The water curls around the boat, sinking deep into the water because of the weight of the living Dante. Within the waves ghastly white bodies glint like great fish, some struggling to climb aboard the boat and threatening to tip it over. The combination of the idealistically proportioned bodies and their macabre pallor is an arresting sight. Beyond the immediate scene the walls of the great city of Dis are seen with its fires smoldering dully and reflecting into the smoky atmosphere.

The other compelling account of a literal hell is that created by John Milton in *Paradise Lost*. Its origin is traced to a revolt against God led by Satan and other defecting angels, which resulted in their being cast out of heaven and into a location described as the great deep, or chaos. Earth has not yet been created, so that hell is not in the beginning associated with that planet. There is nothing to be found at first but a burning lake, but soon the banished hordes set to work and build Pan-demonium, the great capital city with enough halls and porches to hold the entire evil population in council. The band

Fig. 33 Eugène Delacroix. ***Dante and Vergil.*** 1822. Oil on canvas, 74 × 97″. The Louvre, Paris. *Photograph courtesy of Alinari-Scala and EPA.*

determines that the best course for regaining heaven is to work deviously through mankind, whose origins are rumored. While Satan goes off to explore this possibility, another band sets out to investigate the physical world in which they find themselves. It is a place where only evil could survive, where all life dies, and where gorgons, hydras, and chimeras abound in ghastly aberration. Though this blighted land has four rivers, they too are evil. The Styx is a tide of hate; the Acheron, of sorrow; Cocytus, of lamentation; and Phlegathon, of torment. Beyond them lies a frozen continent beset with violent storms and extremes of change. The inhabitants are trapped in this dismal place behind three impenetrable gates and a hideous guardian who is susceptible to bribery and thus looses evil on our firmament. True to the intuition of God, Adam and Eve commit their transgression, inspired by Satan; his henchmen Sin and Death begin to build a wide road from hell to earth in order to dwell with men. Adam and Eve are expelled from Paradise and doomed to a life of toil and death, lightened only by knowledge of the eventual salvation to be offered mankind through the Incarnation. Their little planet turns on, connected until the end of time to the realm of darkness and chaos by a royal road and open gate.

The Medieval cathedral was incomplete without at least one rousing sculptural exposition of the state of life in hell. Typically, this theme was explored in a setting of the Last Judgment over one of the three main entrance doors. Such a project summoned every vestige of violence resident in the artistic imagination. Incomparable beasts roamed the lintels, gobbling down sinners at a single gulp. Tiny nude figures were mangled in droves by the most inventive tortures. All the resources of the sculptural repertoire were synthesized by Hieronymus Bosch in that vast tapestry of pictorial pain called *The Garden of Delights*, of which one section is devoted to the landscape of hell. As a painter, Bosch takes advantage of the potentials of color in creating moods of violence and evil. The centerpiece is a giant broken egg with the head of a man and legs of tree trunks, smiling vaguely at the mayhem covering the landscape. Behind this figure is the dark outline of a charred city lit by raging fires before which are silhouetted long lines of fleeing sinners. In a typically Dantean reversal, music, which gives such pleasure to life, is used as a means of torture in death. One body is strung upon a harp; another is being ground up by a hurdy-gurdy. One poor soul is roasting in the mouth of a burning flute, while another is being painfully tattooed with musical notation by the long, sharp tongue of a demon. Beings eaten, bitten, and mangled are set upon by creations that seemingly have no determined species. It is a world in which the vital energy of all inhabitants is bent toward some intense experience of suffering.

Hell as a vivid physical reality has very little response from the modern world, but metaphoric versions of hell as a form of existence continue to ring true. G. B. Shaw in his play *Man and Superman* establishes a satiric place called hell and populates it with Don Juan, Ana (faithful daughter of the Church), and her father in the guise of a statue. One recognizes them instantly as an elaborate charade on the theme of Don Giovanni. Don Juan explains the logic of the disposition of persons between heaven and hell. We have for bad deeds mercy without justice; for good deeds there is justice without mercy. The assignment is quite natural; one simply goes where it is most comfortable.

Fig. 34 Hieronymus Bosch. ***The Garden of Delights: Inferno*** (detail). ca. 1500. Oil on panel, 86½ × 38". Prado Gallery, Madrid. *Photograph courtesy of Scala New York/Florence and EPA.*

Hell is the home of all the virtues because on earth all the evil is done in their name. Don Juan consoles Ana about her new location by remarking that wherever ladies are is hell. And there is an advantage here in that, having no intrinsic bodies, one can appear to others under any age or condition one chooses.

Unlike Dante's and Milton's hells, Shaw's is unconfining. Ana's father was originally assigned to heaven, but wanders downward seeking good conversation. He declares that since he was a hypocrite it served him right to be placed at first in heaven; but he has determined to move because he finds that place both dull and increasingly uncomfortable. The devil, who enters soon after the father's statue, voices his observation that Don Juan is becoming less suited to hell because he lacks a capacity for enjoyment. The devil confesses to having been once a resident in the holy precincts, but having found the strain of conformity intolerable, he defected and organized hell. Far from being at eternal enmity with the heavenly realms, the devil confesses tolerantly, "It takes all sorts to make a universe." The gulf between the two realms is a matter of temperament alone, but this barrier is as impenetrable as that between the philosopher's study and the race track. Though Ana wishes to depart for heaven at once, the statue warns her that too many people are there, not because they like it, but because they believe they owe it to their social position.

In a more serious vein, Don Juan tries to persuade Ana to remain in hell because it is the home of the unreal and shelters seekers of happiness. Heaven is the state of pure reality where things are not true just because people decide they are. In heaven there is serious work instead of playing and pretending. The work there consists of contemplation and assisting the Life Force to realize itself in that blundering species called mankind. Love, beauty, passion, romance can all be had in hell without penalty, but at the price of sterility and death. To be possessed of a purpose larger than one's self and to choose a direction in which to move for the sake of this purpose is what heaven offers. Shiftless enjoyment and endless diversion without commitment is what hell offers. One can find the way easily from one frontier to the other merely by changing one's way of seeing life.

One of the most memorable modern versions of hell is Sartre's play *No Exit,* a metaphoric construction that declares forthrightly, "Hell is other people." Garcin, Inez, and Estelle are each escorted in turn to a room they will inhabit together without hope of escape for a presumably eternal period of time. Privacy is impossible, and there is no need to sleep or eat, which might break the monotony. Garcin urges the two women simply to meditate and try to forget one another. Inez replies that nothing can change the simple fact of being there, of having one's thoughts welling up in their shared psychic space.

Each has an idea of why this place has been their ultimate destiny. Garcin confesses that he treated his wife abominably for five years because she was such a good martyr that she was almost a victim by vocation. Inez cannot live without making people suffer. She tormented her cousin with whom she lived, and helped his wife kill him. Then she tormented the wife to the point that she turned on the gas one night and killed them both. Estelle had an affair, resulting in a baby which she drowned. Her lover, having witnessed the scene, became utterly distraught and shot himself to death.

The three can see vividly what is going on in their usual earthly haunts and have trouble realizing that they have nothing left there. They suffer in seeing what they believed to be memorable relationships with others forgotten in favor of someone else. Garcin and the women can give each other their bodies but not their trust. They argue and analyze endlessly, sorting through their activities when alive. From time to time they ring the bell for the valet, hoping to compel him to open the door, but he never responds. By the time Garcin forces the door open they find they cannot leave. Each is at the other's mercy. They cannot even kill themselves, because they are already dead. Perhaps worst of all, they have a deeply uneasy feeling that some malevolent intelligence knows exactly what goes on in that closed room. Sartre's vision of hell is as tragic and uncompromising as that of Dante. It has some essence of that symbolic retribution which forms the structure of the older document. It is thoroughly modern in its insistence upon a psychic rather than physical reality, though the torment is equally painful and personally felt.

And what of heaven? Is it also both a physical and a metaphoric reality? Emily Dickinson knew all about heaven:

> I never saw a Moor—
> I never saw the Sea

Yet know I how the Heather looks
And what a billow be.

I never spoke with God
Nor visited in Heaven—
Yet certain am I of the spot
As if the checks were given—[20]

Belief in a desirable immortality and in a concept of heaven rests fundamentally upon an assumption that the human species has value, and that this value is resonant in a cosmic value factor that is superior to death. God is ordinarily this superior factor, and heaven consists of a union with this divine principle. Since there is no union possible between opposites, moral goodness in a human life is necessary to achieve such a union. Hence, out of the bare assumption that humans are creatures of value evolves a whole theoretical superstructure based upon logical necessity. It is this bringing to bear of axiological ideas upon the developing concept of individual identity that led in the ancient world to a concept of desirable immortality. A thousand years before Moses the Egyptian *Book of the Dead* was basing attainment of a heavenly state upon a developed moral consciousness. Some of the earliest selections of the Vedas express a link between righteousness in this life and attainment of bliss in the next. Yet at this stage even heaven was for the few; moral equivalency was not a broadly applicable universal principle. Heaven itself, as in the myth of Valhalla, was often speculative wish fulfillment rather than a carefully worked out reciprocation between life and death.

In ancient Greece promises of a blessed afterlife were the basis for the popularity of the Eleusinian Mysteries; yet the evidence for this blessedness was more institutionally induced than theoretically based. Pythagoras's teachings drew heavily on the Orphic Mysteries and formulated a believable myth of the human soul having fallen into realms of matter and struggling to prepare for reunification with the divine life. With Plato desirable immortality became allied with perception of higher and more abstract absolutes—the perfect forms.

The Christian concept of heaven is conceived largely in the imagery of the Book of Revelation. Heaven, or New Jerusalem, is a community whose perfected individuals are engaged in a life wholly devoted to God. It is a place free of stress and conflict, without pain, sorrow, and death. Reunion with loved ones is a major part of the traditional expectation, as is an opposing belief in a major change in the very nature of bodily life. With Augustine's alliance of sin with death, heaven becomes attainable only by a direct intervention of God, who excuses our deserved punishment. But the minority opinion voiced by Irenaeus in the second century gives an equally convincing account of death as a natural fact, not a result of man's falling from some perfect state, but rather one step toward a fulfillment of his own eternal nature. Thus heaven becomes the logical next stage of action in the evolutionary process.

Visions of heaven carrying great conviction do not always wait upon theoretical justification. Vergil envisioned a heavenly section in his underworld and led his hero, Aeneas, there to be reunited with his father. It is described in the *Aeneid* as "the happy place," much like a peaceful green valley. It is a place of light and air, where sports, poetry, and dancing are the vital activities. The river Eridanus has its origin there as it rises into the world of the living. In many ways heaven is a replica of life on earth, including the shades of horses, the trappings of heroic warfare, feasting, and socializing. The population is characterized by temperaments of kindness and self-sacrifice; they live dispersed about the land without housing of any kind. There they remain until summoned to be born again.

The most complex literal account of heaven is found, as one might expect, in Dante's *Paradiso*. Following the Ptolemaic conception of the universe, heaven is located above the earth and is reached by a journey straight upward past the moon, Mercury, Venus, the sun, Mars, Jupiter, Saturn, the constellation of Gemini, the invisible vault beyond the stars, and at last to the heart of heaven. The transportation through this vast distance is simple; one merely gazes toward the light of distant heaven and rises naturally according to the logic of our destiny. It is natural for us to rise toward God, Beatrice tells Dante, as she assumes responsibility as guide from Vergil, who must return to his appointed place in limbo. The sphere of the moon reveals to Dante, who asks a scientific question about surface light, that all heavenly bodies are direct utterances of God. All souls they encounter are placed in their respective positions according to inviolate laws of love and harmony. At last, past the constellation of Gemini, Dante is told to look back to the earth, and sees it surrounded by light and love rather than physical space. At the threshold of heaven he finds the source of time and space.

The core of heaven consists of nine concentric circles representing various intelligences all revolving about a spaceless, all-embracing center that is God. Each being within these circles is a refracted image of God's love. Here all events are contemporary; there is no past or future, and questions concerning time and location do not exist. Dante sees great armies of the faithful in the spiritual bodies they will wear after the resurrection. The vast energy source of the whole heavenly cosmos is the power of love, issuing from God and shining from every being in this constellation of life.

Dante's cosmos is a visually arresting phenomenon; his descriptions give overwhelmingly visual impressions. Artists from time immemorial have attempted to portray these nether regions in such visual forms, and quite often with the same basic repertoire of references that Dante used. For example, light and order are the two most common visual cues employed to express the nature of heaven. William Blake's *Four and Twenty Elders* is typical of the genre. About a great central throne the upper bodies of classically contrived bearded figures stand symmetrically about, their visages radiating streams of light. The background colors are a subdued symphony of pale blue and gold. It is much like a mandala in complexity and orderliness.

El Greco's remarkable painting, which covers one whole wall of a chapel, deals with the *Burial of Count Orgaz*, whose body is interred within the wall beneath the picture. So pious was the count that St. Augustine and St. Jerome have appeared to lower him into his grave. Their splendid ecclesiastical trappings surround the ashen, armor-covered body of the deceased. Mourners with their identical uniforms of dark clothing and white Elizabethan collars form a fencelike background. But above this earthly throng hover the hosts of heaven. The soul of the count, a small swaddling figure held gently in the arms of an angel, is poised halfway between the two realms. Above him, in the direct center of the composition, rests the figure of Christ, seated upon the clouds and surrounded by the Virgin Mary, Peter holding the keys to the kingdom of heaven, and various other New Testament notables. The whole creation bursts into light at the ceiling, and heaven seems to open upon the viewer standing beside the tomb.

Shaw's satiric view of heaven could well have pointed as evidence to the abundance of medieval renditions of that realm. Typically sharing the lunette of a main church door with

Fig. 35 Wiliam Blake. ***The Four and Twenty Elders Casting their Crowns Before the Divine Throne.*** 1805. Watercolor, 13.75 × 11.50″. The Tate Gallery, London.

Fig. 36 El Greco. **The Burial of Count Orgaz.** 1586. Oil on canvas, 16' ×
11'10". Church of St. Thomas, Toledo. *Photograph courtesy of EPA.*

the Last Judgment and hell, heaven serves mainly as a quiet balance to the more dramatic movement that characterizes those other segments. Artists have not in all these ages originated much for people to do in heaven besides stand about looking faintly pleased and highly organized. There are, to be sure, touching scenes of reunion. There are profound feelings of utter contentment and harmony of social relationships. It is just that the ingenuity and fantasy that created the improbable beasts and irrational tortures of hell fail to respond with equal conviction to themes of peace and joy. The few modern examples of a heavenlike state such as Matisse's *Joy of Life* return to the older wish-fulfillment theme and the very earthly activities that Vergil describes in his heavenly realms. The visual cues remain the same—gentle light, symmetry of form, and slowly moving curvilinear surfaces. In the minimal art of Ad Reinhardt we encounter not heaven but oblivion, and in Picasso's abstraction not the literal content of Dante's vision but the timeless forms of Plato.

Music is an effective medium with which to conjure up visions of heavenly realms through a variety of expressive means. Though the general style of the Brahms *German Requiem* is a somewhat gloomy realism, one section is an unabashed paean to the heavenly realm. "How Lovely is Thy Dwelling Place" utters a cry from the human heart. It is Dante, breathless before the nine angelic circles. It is the vision and longing of a soul still firmly entrenched in the body, yet aspiring to the grandeur just within sight. A flood of strings begins the segment, pouring down from a height of register into a strong lyric line. The chorus begins the text with a rich chordal texture sustained over an interminable phrase of sound. The individual sections in turn take up a contrasting polyphonic interplay in which the words "how lovely" float upward at each entrance. A contrasting middle section evokes human restlessness: "My heart longs and faints for the courts of the Lord." The tempo quickens, phrases shorten, and waves of sound push forward as though struggling toward the vision of the first section. "My soul and body cry out for the living Lord," the swelling chorus continues. As though in answer, the vision returns with the same high string accompaniment as in the beginning, and the chorus closes softly under the spell of its beauty.

Near the end of the traditional requiem is that section

called the *sanctus*, which, after all the dark allusions to judgment, reveals in full glory the realms of heaven. The *sanctus*
section from the *Requiem* by Fauré gives us that vision as it
might be seen by the angel choirs. It is some of the most utterly
contemplative, decidedly fragile music in existence. It is music
in which nothing is left but a timeless apprehension of the
heart of love. Because the design is perfectly symmetrical and
nearly without dynamic inflection, the setting is quite brief.
Over a sonic foundation of harp and strings a group of men
repeat the single word "sanctus" (holy) in chantlike unison. A
group of high, ethereal children's voices echoes this musical
theme of breathless adoration. Thus each answers the other
like angel choirs from distant spaces resonating through the
vaults of heaven. The volume swells to the only abundant
sound level right in the middle of the composition, underlined
by brief support from brass instruments expressing the word
"hosannah." Harp and strings return, carrying once again the
quiet "sanctus" refrain and tapering into a deep hush.

The setting Mozart chose for the *sanctus* section of his own
Requiem is equally effective, but utterly different from each of
the foregoing. Mozart invents a brilliant dance to set the cosmos in motion—a portrayal of the splendor of God reflected, as
in Dante's vision, from the myriad of life in creation. It begins
on a mighty chord produced by full orchestra and chorus.
"Sanctus" they shout, loudly enough to stir a firmament from
slumber. Brasses ring out in brilliant punctuation as the chorus
continues the song of praise: "heaven and earth are full of They
glory; glory be to Thee, O Lord most high." Suddenly the massive bulk of this resplendent hymn resolves into a highly rhythmic fugal exposition on the text "hosannah in the highest."
Like a vast throng of joyous celebrants the chorus moves section by section into the vibrant march, culminating in a series of
rapid roulades and a few final chordial punctuations. Such
music surrounds us with the vesture of heaven, sewn perhaps
in different sytles, but equally effective in clothing the imagination with the semblance of truth.

Heaven is not only a literal concept but also a metaphoric
statement about the inner life of mankind. Heaven can be as
real as a lived experience—certainly as real as Sartre's lived
reality of hell. People who have attempted to probe the conditions and parameters of that state called heaven are called,
collectively, mystics. Their number is infinite, stretching back

to the shamans of the neolithic past. Though mystics are, by and large, practical and sensible people involved in daily life, the mystical element of their lives has fundamental links with a desirable afterlife. The object of mystical activity is to come to know the Divine Ground of all existence, to overcome the limited nature of human perceptions, and to enter into a state of being that is continuous with eternal life. Man is not a creature set over against or distinct from God; he participates in the divine life. Mystics such as Jakob Böhme and Meister Eckhart could agree that "the eye with which I see God is the same eye with which God sees me." There is an intellectual content to mystical activity, but it is nearly impossible to convey in normal time-space terms. St. Theresa of Ávila wrote that after five or six years of intense mystical activity she was unable to understand or explain it in terms conceivable in a normal mental framework.

It is not accurate to identify these "heaven seekers" exclusively with religious alliances. The nature mystics are one exception to such a classification. Others, such as Richard Jefferies, were believed during their lifetimes to be atheists. Though his mystical consciousness was highly developed, Jefferies never found in any religious system answers to those questions posed by his mystical life. His own speculations led him to a description of reality as including immortality, a kind of soul entity, a process of communication (which in religious terms is prayer), and a vast system of ideas that constitute the cosmos. Everything around us is unexplained, he believed, and everything is essentially supernatural. To the mystic this cloak of spirit thrown over every material manifestation is the ultimate enduring reality toward which we move. It can be seen and experienced in this world, and it is the nature of things after death.

Just as Dante discovered in his journey past the planets and into the vault of heaven, there is for mystics a method and a means of travel. In his allegory *The Conference of the Birds* the Sufi mystic Faird al-din Attar describes the procedure as involving successive stages of action. First is stripping away all psychic and physical encumbrances—the determination of complete devotion. Then develops the attitude of love and acceptance of the universe and one's place in it. The habit of seeing all things as manifestations of God is answered by the beginning experience of finding resonance between one's inner life and some outer spiritual force. Beyond these levels lie the experience of unity and complete absorption. Though stated in different number and terminology, these are the fundamental, universally recognized levels of mystical development. At the end of the process one is in that state which can only be described by the term *heaven*.

Pierre Teilhard de Chardin, a twentieth-century monk, explains the intricate penetration of matter by spirit:

> We imagine that in our sense-perceptions external reality humbly presents itself to us in order to serve us, to help in the building up of our integrity. But this is merely the surface of the mystery of knowledge; the deeper truth is that when the world reveals itself to us it draws us into itself: it causes us to flow outwards into something belonging to it everywhere present in it and more perfect than it.[21]

Perhaps the most popular account of mystical experience in recent literature is the episodic adventure of Carlos Casteneda who, guided by the teachings of the Yaqui shaman, Don Juan, attempts to extend himself into the unknown, which his mentor calls the *nagual*. There is a chasm that separates ordinary from nonordinary reality; twilight provides moments when the leap between the two is most easily accomplished. There is a process, and it is both tedious and arduous. The first step is to learn to quit producing an internal dialogue, that constant background of thought which keeps us in touch with the data of everyday life. Another vital step is cutting all ties with our personal histories, psychically preparing for single-minded concentration on the acquisition of proper attitude. The only wise adviser a man can trust is death, which reminds us to live completely in every moment. The great enemies of this "way of the warrior" are fear, self-delusion, temptation to misuse power, and old age, which weakens self-discipline. One who becomes accomplished in perceiving and inhabiting the *nagual* lives beyond time, free from despair and all unworthy attachments. The object of his ultimate love is the vast cosmos and the small planet in which we sail it.

And so it is that we human scraps of life dwelling on a minor planet in one of numberless galaxies comtemplate the mysteries of our being and nonbeing. As mourning survivors of the deaths of others, we create the traditions that characterize various cultures. In horror we witness the waste of life in war, the sorrow of life taken in extremities of anguish. In wonder we contemplate the alternatives of existence beyond our concepts of time and space. Loren Eiseley, with his scientist's mind and shaman's temperament, expressed the ultimate reaction of a human perspective in collision with such impenetrable mysteries in his poem "Star with a Secret":

Older than time the Jodrell Bank pulsar 1953
ticks without running down, is hanging
in constellation Cygnus, one thousand
light years away in a cold, cool timelessness,
a cave of blue having seemingly
outlasted the present universe, a survivor
of the universe before. We cannot reach it.
Jodrell Bank and the great cup at Arecibo
can only count its heartbeat and know
it is not like men or anything mortal, even stars
in the present universe. If immortality
is to outlast two universes collapsing inward,
           and their renewal,
then this creature in the constellation Cygnus
is the terrible eye of all the past, surveying
ruin undreamt of fixed on universes yet to be.
           Man, a brief flicker between two darknesses,
           has found him out in the blue
           inscrutable cavern of fire, but no one
dares ask or be answered, in human terms
how many times the play has been repeated. It is a star
with a secret unyielded, not to the finite,
           nor reveals what hand placed it,
           in the cool impenetrable cave.[22]

Notes

Chapter 1: How the Humanities Speak about Death

1. Edna St. Vincent Millay, "Lament," *Second April* (New York: Harper and Row, 1921), p. 64.
2. William Cullen Bryant, "Thanatopsis," *Poems* (Philadelphia: Carey and Hart, 1847), p. 36.
3. Louis Untermeyer, "Irony," in *Man Answers Death*, ed. Corliss Lamont (New York: Philosophical Library, 1952), p. 178.

Chapter 2: Death and the Survivor

1. Benjamin Franklin, "Epitaph," *New Colophon* 3 (1959), p. 83.
2. Paulus Silentarius, "The Epitaph—and the Reader," trans. William Cowper, in *Man Answers Death*, p. 72.
3. Thomas Gray, *Elegy Written in a Country Churchyard* (New York: George A. Leavitt, 1852) p. 5.
4. John Milton, "Lycidas," *The Complete Poetical Works of John Milton*, ed. Harris Francis Fletcher (Boston: Houghton Mifflin, 1941), p. 120.
5. Edna St. Vincent Millay, "Dirge Without Music," *The Buck in the Snow and other Poems* (New York: Harper and Row, 1928), p. 43.
6. Robert Frost, "Home Burial," *The Poetry of Robert Frost*, ed. Edward Connery Latham (New York: Holt, Rinehart and Winston, 1958), p. 69.
7. W. H. Auden, "Musée des Beaux Arts," *Collected Poems*, ed. Edward Mendelson (New York: Random House, 1975), p. 146.
8. Emily Brontë, "Remembrance," *Complete Poems of Emily Jane Brontë*, ed. C. W. Hatfield (New York: Columbia University Press, 1941), p. 223.
9. James Agee, *A Death in the Family* (New York: Grosset and Dunlap, 1967), p. 15.
10. Evelyn Waugh, *The Loved One* (New York: Dell Publishing Co., 1948), p. 101.

Chapter 3: Death and War

1. Stephen Crane, *The Red Badge of Courage* (New York: Modern Library, 1951), p. 6.

2. D. H. Lawrence, *Kangaroo* (London: Secker, 1923), p. 241.

3. Walt Whitman, "To a Certain Civilian," *The Selected Poems of Walt Whitman* (New York: Walter J. Black, 1942), p. 283.

4. Wilfred Owen, "Dulce et Decorum est pro Patria Mori," *The Collected Poems*, ed. C. Day Lewis (London: Chatto and Windus, 1963; New York; New Directions, 1964), p. 55.

5. Rudyard Kipling, "A Dead Statesman," and "Common Form," *Rudyard Kipling's Verse: Definitive Edition* (New York: Doubleday and Co., 1952), p. 388.

6. Rupert Brooke, "The Dead," *The Collected Poems of Rupert Brooke* (New York: Dodd, Mead and Co., 1915), p. 109.

7. Whitman, "When Lilacs Last in the Dooryard Bloom'd," *The Selected Poems*, p. 289.

8. Karl Shapiro, "Elegy for a Dead Soldier," *Poems: 1940–1953* (New York: Random House, 1944), p. 42.

9. W. B. Yeats, "An Irish Airman Foresees His Death," *The Variorum Edition of the Poems of W. B. Yeats*, ed. Peter Aalt and Russell Alspach (New York: Macmillan, 1957), p. 328.

10. Rhys Carpenter, *The Esthetic Basis of Greek Art* (Bloomington: Indiana University Press, 1959), p. 76.

11. Thomas Hardy, "The Man He Killed," *The Complete Poems of Thomas Hardy*, ed. James Gibson (New York: Macmillan, 1978), p. 287.

12. Owen, "Anthem for Doomed Youth," *Poems*, p. 44.

13. Owen, "Bugles Sang," p. 128.

14. Owen, "The Next War," p. 86.

15. Owen, "Parable of the Old Man and the Young," p. 42.

16. Owen, "The End," p. 89.

17. Euripides, *The Trojan Women*, in *The Plays of Euripides*, trans. Moses Hadas and John McLean (New York: The Dial Press, 1936), pp. 34, 52.

18. John Milton, "On the Late Massacre in Piedmont," *The Complete Poetical Works of John Milton*, ed. Harris Francis Fletcher (Boston: Houghton Mifflin, 1941), p. 133.

19. Whitman, "Come Up from the Fields, Father," p. 256.

20. Dylan Thomas, "Ceremony after a Fire Raid," *The Poems of Dylan Thomas* (New York: New Directions Publishing Corp., 1946), p. 144.

21. Arthur Guiterman, "The Storming of Stony Point," in *Poems of American History*, ed. Burton Egbert Stevenson (Boston: Houghton Mifflin, 1922), p. 230.

22. Stephen Spender, "Two Armies," *Collected Poems 1928–1953* (New York: Random House, 1955), p. 83.

23. Homer, *The Iliad*, trans. W. D. H. Rouse (New York: New American Library, 1938), p. 102.

24. Whitman, "Bivouac on a Mountain Side," p. 254.

25. Steven Crane, *The Red Badge of Courage*, p. 215.

26. Ibid., p. 126.

27. Ibid., p. 266.

28. Erich Maria Remarque, *All Quiet on the Western Front* (Greenwich, Conn.: Fawcett Publications, 1967), p. 119.

29. Ibid., p. 71.

30. Ibid., p. 126.

31. Norman Mailer, *The Naked and the Dead* (New York: Rinehart and Co., 1948), p. 123.

32. Ibid., pp. 371, 212.

33. Ibid., p. 719.

34. Ibid., p. 247.

35. Joseph Heller, *Catch-22* (New York: Dell Publishing Co., 1955), p. 27.

36. Ibid., p. 249.

37. Ibid., p. 267.

38. Ibid., p. 355.

Chapter 4: Voluntary Death

1. Bernard Millet, *Divine Thunder* (New York: McCall Publishing Co., 1971), p. 228–30.

2. Geoffrey Chaucer, *Chaucer's Canterbury Tales*, trans. R. M. Lumiansky (New York: Washington Square Press, 1960), p. 295.

3. Christóbal de Castillejo, "Some Day, Some Day," trans. Henry Wadsworth Longfellow, *Man Answers Death*, ed. Corliss Lamont (New York: Philosophical Library, 1952), p. 140.

4. Thomas Hardy, *Jude the Obscure* (New York: Harper and Brothers, 1923), p. 403.

5. Ibid., pp. 404–5.

6. Edwin Arlington Robinson, "Richard Cory," *Collected Poems* (New York: Macmillan, 1945), p. 82.

7. Archibald MacLeish, *J. B.* (Boston: Houghton Mifflin, 1956), p. 152.

8. Chinua Achebe, *Things Fall Apart* (Greenwich, Conn.: Fawcett Publications, 1959), p. 190.

9. Sophocles, *Oedipus Rex*, trans. Albert Cook (Boston: Houghton Mifflin, 1957), stasimon 3.

10. Vergil, *The Aeneid*, trans. C. Day Lewis (New York: Doubleday, 1953), p. 101.

11. Dante, *The Inferno*, trans. John Ciardi (New York: New American Library, 1954), p. 122.

12. William Shakespeare, *Julius Caesar*, in *The Living Shakespeare* (New York: Macmillan, 1949), p. 741.

13. Shakespeare, *Hamlet*, in *Living Shakespeare*, p. 800.

14. Shakespeare, *Romeo and Juliet*, in *Living Shakespeare*, p. 357.

15. Johann Wolfgang von Goethe, *The Sorrows of Werther*, trans. A. J. W. Morrison (Boston: Dana Estes, n. d.), p. 82.

16. Ibid., p. 89.

17. Feder Dostoevski, *The Possessed*, trans. Constance Garnett (New York: Modern Library, 1936), pp. 627–28.

18. Eugene O'Neill, *Mourning Becomes Electra*, in *Three Plays* (New York: Random House, 1959), p. 322.

19. Ibid., p. 239.

20. Jessamyn West, *The Woman Said Yes* (Greenwich, Conn.: Fawcett Publications, 1976), p. 144.

21. Ibid., p. 165.

22. Ibid., p. 221.

23. George Bernard Shaw, *Saint Joan* (Baltimore: Penguin Books, 1924 and 1952), p. 95.

Chapter 5: Immortality

1. Harriet Beecher Stowe, *Uncle Tom's Cabin* (Boston: Houghton Mifflin, 1929), pp. 290–91.

2. Archibald MacLeish, "The End of the World," in *New and Collected Poems 1917–1976* (Boston: Houghton Mifflin, 1976), p. 89.

3. John Milton, *Paradise Lost* in *The Complete Poetical Works of John Milton*, ed. Harris Francis Fletcher (Boston: Houghton Mifflin, 1941), bk. 10, 11. 289–93.

4. Bertrand Russell, "Do We Survive Death?" in *Why I am Not a Christian* (New York: Simon and Shuster, 1957).

5. D. H. Lawrence, "The Ship of Death," in *Last Poems* (New York: Viking Press, 1933), p. 308.

6. Leo Tolstoy, *The Death of Ivan Ilyich*, trans. Constance Garnett (London: William Heinemann, 1915).

7. Alan Harrington, *The Immortalist* (New York: Random House, 1969), p. 8.

8. Ibid., p. 257.

9. Robert Heinlein, *Methuselah's Children* (New York: New American Library, 1958), p. 43.

10. Ibid., p. 127.

11. John H. Hick, *Death and Eternal Life* (New York: Harper and Row, 1976).

12. Philip José Farmer, *To Your Scattered Bodies Go* (New York: Berkeley Publishing Corp., 1971), p. 141.

13. Birago Diop, "Forefathers," in *An African Treasury*, ed. Langston Hughes (New York: Crown Publishers, Inc., 1960), p. 183.

14. Larry Rubin, "The Druggist," *The World's Old Way* (Lincoln: University of Nebraska Press, 1961), p. 20.

15. Noel Coward, *Blythe Spirit* (Garden City, N.Y.: Doubleday, Doran and Co., 1942), p. 152.

16. Vergil, *The Aeneid*, trans. C. Day Lewis (New York: Doubleday, 1953), pp. 150–51.

17. W. B. Yeats, "Under Ben Bulben," in *The Variorum Edition of the Poems of W. B. Yeats*, ed. Peter Aalt and Russell Alspach (New York: Macmillan, 1957), p. 636.

18. Roger Zelazny, *Lord of Light* (New York: Avon Books, 1967), p. 319.

19. Larry Rubin, "Instructions for Dying," in *The World's Old Way*, p. 46.

20. Emily Dickinson, "I Never Saw a Moor," in *The Poems of Emily Dickinson*, ed. Thomas H. Johnson (Cambridge, Mass.: The Belknap Press of Harvard University, 1951), p. 83.

21. Teilhard de Chardin, *Hymn of the Universe* (New York: Harper and Row, 1972), p. 78.

22. Loren Eiseley, "Star with a Secret," in *Another Kind of Autumn* (New York: Charles Scribner's Sons, 1976), p. 39.

Bibliography

Achebe, Chinua. *Things Fall Apart.* Greenwich, Conn.: Fawcett Publications, 1959.

Agee, James. *A Death in the Family.* New York: Grosset and Dunlap, 1967.

Auden, W. H. *Collected Poems.* Edited by Edward Mendelson. New York: Random House, 1975.

Brontë, Emily Jane. *Complete Poems of Emily Jane Brontë.* Edited by C. W. Hatfield. New York: Columbia University Press, 1941.

Brooke, Rupert. *The Collected Poems of Rupert Brooke.* New York: Dodd, Mead and Co., 1915.

Bryant, William Cullen. *Poems.* Philadelphia: Carey and Hart, 1847.

Carpenter, Rhys. *The Esthetic Basis of Greek Art.* Bloomington: Indiana University Press, 1959.

Chardin, Teilhard de. *Hymn of the Universe.* New York: Harper and Row (Perennial Library), 1972.

Chaucer, Geoffrey. *Chaucer's Canterbury Tales.* Translated by R. M. Lumiansky. New York: Washington Square Press, 1960.

Coward, Noel. *Blythe Spirit.* Garden City, N.Y.: Doubleday, Doran and Co., 1942.

Crane, Stephen. *The Red Badge of Courage.* New York: Modern Library, 1951.

Dante. *The Inferno.* Translated by John Ciardi. New York: New American Library, 1954.

Dickinson, Emily. *The Poems of Emily Dickinson.* Edited by Thomas H. Johnson. Cambridge, Mass.: The Belknap Press of Harvard University, 1951.

231

Diop, Birago. "Forefathers." In *An African Treasury*. Edited by Langston Hughes. New York: Crown Publishers, Inc., 1960.

Dostoevski, Fedor. *The Possessed*. Translated by Constance Garnett. New York: Modern Library, 1936.

Eiseley, Loren. *Another Kind of Autumn*. New York: Charles Scribner's Sons, 1976.

Erlich, Max. *The Reincarnation of Peter Proud*. New York: Bantam Books, Inc., 1974.

Euripides. *The Trojan Women*. In *The Plays of Euripides*. Translated by Moses Hadas and John McLean. New York: The Dial Press, 1936.

Farmer, Philip José. *To Your Scattered Bodies Go*. New York: Berkeley Publishing Corp., 1971.

Franklin, Benjamin. "Epitaph." *New Colophon*. 3 (1959).

Frost, Robert. *The Poetry of Robert Frost*. Edited by Edward Connery Latham. New York: Holt, Rinehart and Winston, 1958.

Goethe, Johann Wolfgang von. *The Sorrows of Werther*. Translated by A. J. W. Morrison. Boston: Dana Estes, n.d.

Gray, Thomas. *Elegy Written in a Country Churchyard*. New York: George A. Leavitt, 1852.

Guiterman, Arthur. "The Storming of Stony Point." In *Poems of American History*. Edited by Burton Egbert Stevenson. Boston: Houghton Mifflin, 1922.

Gunn, James. *The Immortals*. New York: Simon and Shuster, 1962.

Hardy, Thomas. *The Complete Poems of Thomas Hardy*. Edited by James Gibson. New York: Macmillan, 1978.

————. *Jude the Obscure*. New York: Harper and Brothers, 1923.

Harrington, Alan. *The Immortalist*. New York: Random House, 1969.

Heinlein, Robert. *Methuselah's Children*. New York: New American Library, 1958.

Heller, Joseph. *Catch-22*. New York: Dell Publishing Co., 1955.

Hick, John H. *Death and Eternal Life*. New York: Harper and Row, 1976.

Homer. *The Iliad*. Translated by W. H. D. Rouse. New York: New American Library, 1938.

James, Henry. *The Turn of the Screw*. New York: Airmont, 1967.

Kipling, Rudyard. *Rudyard Kipling's Verse: Definitive Edition*. New York: Doubleday and Co., 1952.

Lamont, Corliss, ed. *Man Answers Death*. New York: Philosophical Library, 1952.

Lawrence, D. H. *Kangaroo.* London: Secker, 1923.

————. *Last Poems.* New York: The Viking Press, 1933.

MacLeish, Archibald. *J. B.* Boston: Houghton Mifflin, 1956.

————. *New and Collected Poems 1917–1976.* Boston: Houghton Mifflin, 1976.

Mailer, Norman. *The Naked and the Dead.* New York: Rinehart and Co., 1948.

Millay, Edna St. Vincent. *The Buck in the Snow and other Poems.* New York: Harper and Row, 1928.

————. *Second April.* New York: Harper and Row, 1921.

Millot, Bernard. *Divine Thunder.* New York: McCall Publishing Co., 1971.

Milton, John. *The Complete Poetical Works of John Milton.* Edited by Harris Francis Fletcher. New York: Houghton Mifflin, 1941.

O'Neill, Eugene. *Mourning Becomes Electra.* In *Three Plays.* New York: Random House, 1959.

Owen, Wilfred. *The Collected Poems.* Edited by C. Day Lewis. London: Chatte and Windus, 1963, and New York: New Directions, 1964.

Remarque, Erich Maria. *All Quiet on the Western Front.* Greenwich, Conn.: Fawcett Publications, 1967.

Robinson, Edwin Arlington. *Collected Poems.* New York: Macmillan, 1945.

Rubin, Larry. *The World's Old Way.* Lincoln: University of Nebraska Press, 1961.

Russell, Bertrand. *Why I Am Not a Christian.* New York: Simon and Shuster, 1957.

Sartre, Jean Paul. *No Exit.* Translated by Stuart Gilbert. New York: A. A. Knopf, 1952.

Shakespeare, William. *The Living Shakespeare.* New York: Macmillan, 1949.

Shapiro, Karl. *Poems: 1940–1953.* New York: Random House, 1944.

Shaw, George Bernard. *Man and Superman.* In *The Complete Plays of Bernard Shaw.* London: P. Hamlyn, 1965.

————. *Saint Joan.* Baltimore: Penguin Books, 1924 and 1952.

Sophocles. *Oedipus Rex.* Translated by Albert Cook. Boston: Houghton Mifflin, 1957.

Spender, Stephen. *Collected Poems 1928–1953.* New York: Random House, 1955.

Stowe, Harriet Beecher. *Uncle Tom's Cabin.* Boston: Houghton Mifflin, 1929.

Thomas, Dylan. *The Poems of Dylan Thomas*. New York: New Directions Publishing Corp., 1946.

Tolstoy, Leo. *The Death of Ivan Ilyich*. Translated by Constance Garnett. London: William Heinemann, 1915.

Vergil. *The Aeneid*. Translated by C. Day Lewis. New York: Doubleday, 1953.

Waugh, Evelyn. *The Loved One*. New York: Dell Publishing Co., 1948.

West, Jessamyn. *The Woman Said Yes*. Greenwich, Conn.: Fawcett Publications, 1976.

Whitman, Walt. *The Selected Poems of Walt Whitman*. New York: Walter J. Black, 1942.

Yeats, W. B. *The Variorum Edition of the Poems of W. B. Yeats*. Edited by Peter Aalt and Russell Alspach. New York: Macmillan, 1957.

Zelazny, Roger. *Lord of Light*. New York: Avon Books, 1967.

Index

DATE DUE

MAY 6 '86			
SEP 15 '87			

PRINTED IN U.S.A.